AF429468

The Wee Wah Beach Club in Tuxedo Park: An American Story of Social Change, published 2023 by Stuart McGregor. Printed in the United States of America. ISBN 9798218259969.

Photo credits: The photos in this book are a result of the author's family archives, the courtesy of The Tuxedo Historical Society, The Tuxedo Library, members of the Wee Wah Beach Club and as noted below.

Text: Pg 16, 17, 70, 92, 109 Courtesy of Tuxedo Historical Society; Pg 24, Post Card by George Dart; Pg 32, 41, 51, 56, 58, 59, 61, 91, 103, 208, Courtesy of the Tuxedo Library (Tuxedo Room collection); Pg 65, 101, 153, 238, 245, 258, Courtesy of former member of Wee Wah Beach Club; Pg 69, 113, 133, 152, 159, 162, 163, 166, 170, 171, 172, 178, 179, 185, 186, 188, 190 , 199, 211, 234, 274, 282, 349, 364, 371, 375, 385, 392 McGregor family archive; Pg 83, photo from "Old Buildings of New York" 1912, copyright expired; Pg 155, 164, 165 Wee Wah Beach Club Records; Pg 174, Courtesy of the Tansey family; Pg 175, Courtesy of Mihok family; Pg 231, Courtesy of the New York Times; Pg 298, 316, Courtesy of the Village of Tuxedo Park; Pg 310, "Pink Panther" The Return of the Pink Panther, United Artists, 1975; Pg 328, Courtesy of the Salierno family; Pg 354, Courtesy of Bonny Damato Takeuchi; Pg 380, Richard Kiley, 1958 Press Photo, © xJTxVintagex; pg 380, Robert Duvall, Knudsen, Ann, Los Angeles Public Library, 1984; pg 380, Howard Shore, Benjam, © New Time Cinema, 2012

Cover credits: McGregor family archive; cover designed by Leith Mcloughlin and Heather Gugger.

Stuart J. McGregor is the author of *A History of Kincraig and Family Recollections of a Time Gone By*, 2017 and *Tuxedo Park Past—Law and Disorder*, 2018.

The Wee Wah Beach Club in Tuxedo Park

An American Story of Social Change

by

Stuart J. McGregor

To my wife, Jean Connelly, who understands my love for Tuxedo and Tuxedo Park while persevering through my years of talking about this book and always supporting my dreams.

And in memory of the McGregor & Barth families that called Tuxedo Park home.

Acknowledgments

I cannot find better words to describe this book than to share those expressed by George M. Rushmore in the foreword to *his* book, *The World with a Fence Around It: Tuxedo Park: The Early Days* (Pageant Press, 1957). Said the author, "If anyone corrects me, I have an alibi, for stories change and grow in the telling. … In order to avoid a dry enumeration of the facts and people, I have, where possible, chosen the personal point of view. If any old inhabitant feels that this gives an inaccurate picture or conflicting stories have been published, I can only say that historians great and small have endured similar criticisms throughout the ages."

I would like to thank the people of Tuxedo and Tuxedo Park for their recollections and confirmations of stories passed on. A special thanks to Bonny Takeuchi for trusting me with the original Wee Wah Beach Club files and photographs. Together with many original documents passed on by my family, my files contained the original minutes, correspondence, treasurer's reports, photographs, and the like. This helped confirm the recollections of many I have communicated with over the years. Formed in 1936, the Wee Wah Beach Club was originally named the Tuxedo Community Club, and that name would change in 1978 to provide a distinction from "The Tuxedo Club." When I reference the "Beach Club," I am referring to both the Tuxedo Community Club from its inception in 1936, and to the Wee Wah Beach Club from 1978 onward.

Over the last five decades, I have met with many original members of the Wee Wah Beach Club, each of whom generously shared recollections of the early years. My wife Jean and I rented in the

Park from 1982 until we purchased our own current Tuxedo Park home in 1992. During the summers, almost nightly, I was fortunate to dine with my father and other relatives, and their friends, and perhaps most notably, given her longevity, my aunt, Marie McGregor McCarroll, who lived next door and passed away at age 96 in 2019, a mere four years before this writing. Even toward the end, my aunt's memory was extraordinary as she recounted her life in Tuxedo Park. My aunt and others confirmed the many recollections I have from my family's involvement in the Wee Wah Beach Club, including my own precious boyhood memories. I also gained wonderful insights from my uncle, James "Jim" Barth, who spent his entire life in Tuxedo Park before passing away at the age of 86 in 2010. Earlier conversations around my grandparents' dinner table, where my family was often joined by friends and neighbors, also supplied much of the background for this book. The gracious access I enjoyed to the Tuxedo Park Library Local History Room yielded a wealth of information and inspiration, as did my access to The Tuxedo Historical Society. I would be remiss not to mention my editors, Patty Smithwick, and later, South Florida author Leonard Nash, for helping me try to make readable the enormous amount of material buried in my files and my head for the past seventy-four years. Madison Spivak, a brilliant pre-med student, came on board toward the end and helped carry the ball across the goal line. And of course, I am forever grateful to my wife Jean for her support, encouragement, and dedication.

Table of Contents

Prologue

I was born August 5, 1944 in Tuxedo Hospital, built in 1931 with generous funding from George Grant Mason. I lived with my parents in a corner apartment of the Mason estate garage at Kincraig, opposite the apartment shared by my paternal grandparents, as well as my aunt and uncle both of whom were single at the time. Exploring the lives of Tuxedo Park residents George Grant Mason, Duncan McGregor, Mrs. Theodore "Lily" Frelinghuysen, and others will shed light on the social attitudes and changes that led to the Wee Wah Beach Club, and how "Tuxedo Society" evolved and continued from the nineteenth, through the twentieth, and into the twenty-first century.

I grew up and spent my early years in this secluded, private community, where Tuxedo Park's wealthy inhabitants spent much of their time engaged in sporting activities and social gatherings. Both my grandfathers were employed as estate managers and head gardeners. They were trained in their youth as horticultural gardeners, and both were well-established on other grand estates in the Northeast before coming to Tuxedo Park during the American Gilded Age at the beginning of the twentieth century. Like so many other children of estate staff, my father and mother were born and raised there as well. My parents and I left in the early 1950s for a new development in southern Bergen County, New Jersey, some thirty miles away. Tuxedo Park appeared to be dying. My grandparents and their cohorts were reaching retirement age, and my parents' generation was finding "upward mobility" with the advent of suburbia and good paying jobs for those who had completed their college educations, and thanks to the GI Bill, American men were attending college at a rate never seen before. A bustling market awaited their talents after World War II and the Korean Conflict. The move afforded my father the opportunity to purchase a home and be closer to his work as a drafting engineer. It also allowed us to return to Tuxedo Park on weekends for lunch with my father's family and dinner with my mother's family. Their homes were less than a mile apart on the west side of Tuxedo Lake. These gatherings included not only all my aunts and uncles but also friends of my grandparents who worked on other large estates.

As far back as I can recall, I was fascinated by table conversations concerning the history of Tuxedo Park and its residents. I was intrigued by the inside stories about the lives of people who seemed to represent some type of European aristocracy, like lords and ladies. To my ear, many of the families inhabiting the big houses actually spoke differently. I met many of these people and played in their homes when they were not in residence but was always reminded what my station in life was compared to theirs. We were not equals. Public television series, such as *Upstairs, Downstairs* and, more recently, *Downton Abbey* and *The Gilded Age* offer keen portrayals of how my grandparents and working families on the estates lived from the early 1900s to the early 1950s. If you are familiar with the great 1937 film *Topper,* starring Cary Grant, Constance Bennett, and, my favorite, Roland Young as Cosmo Topper, I can assure you their speech and scenarios remained a reality for many of the descendants of the original families in Tuxedo Park well into the early 1950s. Now I am later in life and married with grown children. For over thirty years, my wife and I have been fortunate to spend time in our summer home, a converted 1889 coachman's house and stable, and take our place as residents within the confines of the large imposing gatehouse signifying the very private entrance into Tuxedo Park.

Primarily, however, this is the story of a special place within Tuxedo Park: the Wee Wah Beach Club. My grandparents were instrumental in its formation. My mother, father, aunts, and uncles spent their early years and most of their lives during the summer at the Wee Wah, as did I. This tradition continued with their children and with mine. This is a story of community and of divisions, and despite much progress, some of these divisions persist even today in the 2020s. The history of Tuxedo and Tuxedo Park is a microcosm of our society over the last 135 years. As Americans, we embrace the concept that everyone has the chance to enjoy equality, and even a pathway toward wealth and high social status, no matter their origin story. While some do transcend from humble or middle-class beginnings and into great wealth and elite social status, most do not. In that spirit, we have the story of Tuxedo Park, from both sides of the gates.

For some, the Village of Tuxedo Park was, and still is, "rarified air," a place for leisure, recreation, high society gallantry, and networking between the wealthiest of America's barons of land, finance, and industry. For others, Tuxedo Park represents the center of a larger orbit, surrounded by a working-class community whose residents may no longer serve the wealthy but are employed in positions that require dinner table conversations about budgets, choices, and savings. For these folks, the community has been a safe, dependable place to live, work, and raise a family.

From any perspective, Tuxedo Park is a unique, beautiful locale, but much changed over the tumultuous course of the twentieth century, and much continues to change in this, the third decade of the twenty-first century. At every step, many Tuxedo Park residents have strived to preserve their social status, and a good many have aimed to recreate an elite social aristocracy. Concurrently, there has been much effort to blur the aristocratic lines. Throughout most of this long, wonderful, sometimes contentious history, there has been the Wee Wah Beach Club.

I can't be certain it was an original quote by my uncle, James Barth, who was a lifelong resident of Tuxedo Park, but he was the first I heard say, "No one is sure whether the gates of Tuxedo Park were built to keep people out or keep people in."

I am attempting to tell this story while avoiding confusion about the names associated with various entities within what is now known generally as the Town of Tuxedo. On December 19, 1889, the Board of Supervisors of the earlier Town of Monroe, New York approved separating the Town of Tuxedo from Monroe. The act was implemented on March 4, 1890. The new town included Tuxedo Park, as well as areas outside its gates such as Southfields and Eagle Valley.

The history can be confusing. For example, the community originally developed by Pierre Lorillard in 1885 within the massive private entrance was known as Tuxedo Park with a "hamlet" outside these gates that was now included in the newly designated Town of Tuxedo as well.

The community developed outside the gates to Tuxedo Park along the railroad north from New York City to upstate and one main road known as the Orange Turnpike was called the Hamlet or later "the village." The village was built to meet the needs of those living inside the gates. The "East Village," which contained distinct Italian and Slovak sections, also grew outside the gates, and continued across the railroad tracks and the Ramapo River to the east that ran along the main road.

The Village and these appended sections were built to service Tuxedo Park as there were no retail businesses, offices, or public buildings inside the gates of Tuxedo Park. For the next 67 years, these separate communities became more commonly known as "the Park" and "the village," with the latter typically not being capitalized, perhaps a subtle reminder of its "lesser" status.

In 1952, Tuxedo Park became a separate municipality within the State designation known officially as the Incorporated Village of Tuxedo Park in the Town of Tuxedo. The separate municipal entities continued to be referred to as "the Park" and "the village" for a few years, but to avoid confusion, those inside the gates settled on calling the community outside the gates the "Hamlet," as it was originally known in Lorillard's time. Thus, the word "Park" was now officially referenced as the Incorporated Village of Tuxedo Park and remained "the Park." The term "village" (including the East Village, the Slovak village and a number of houses on the west side of what we know as NY State Road 17) became known as the "Hamlet," and both were contained within the larger Town of Tuxedo.

Admittedly, it can be rather confusing, but in a way, that's in keeping with the story of Tuxedo Park, where life has always seemed simple at first glance, but a deeper dive into its history reveals that in many ways, this idyllic respite from the outside world could ultimately not escape the social changes happening everywhere beyond those stately gates. As a child growing up in the Park in the early 1950s, I would walk down to the "village." Today, when someone living inside the gates in Tuxedo Park wants to pay a water bill or vote for a new mayor or trustee, they go to the "Village office," located within the gates. To vote on a Tuxedo School Board issue or pay school and county taxes to the Town of Tuxedo, they go to the town offices located outside the gates in the "Hamlet." Perhaps the easiest way to describe the communities inside the gate and outside was a reference picked up by the children of the communities in the 1930s. They referred to each other as "Parkies" and "Townies."

Within the Park, Tuxedo Lake was commonly referred to as the "Big Lake." The original smaller lakes named Ponds 1 and 2 were developed in 1885 by building a dam at the north end of Tuxedo Lake. However, these small ponds dried up. This resulted in a more substantial new dam being completed further north, thus creating what is now called Pond 3, also known earlier as the "Skating Pond" or the "Little Wee Wah." Another new dam at the northern edge of Tuxedo Park then created a much larger lake always referred to as the "Wee Wah Lake."

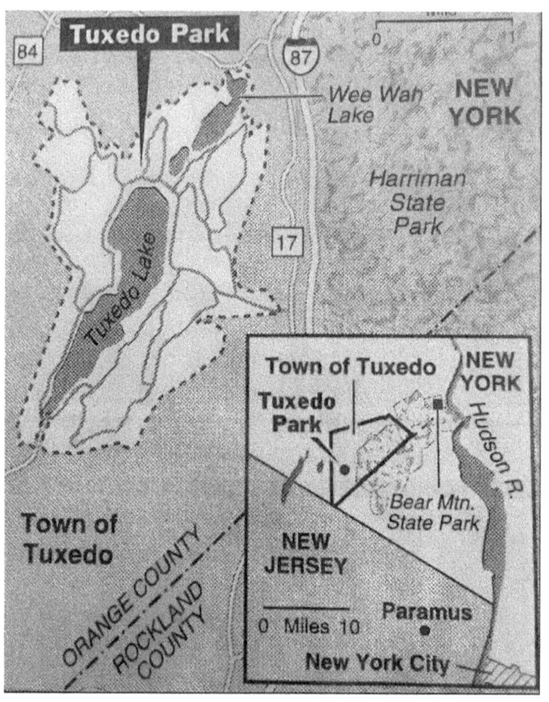

Tuxedo Park in the Town of Tuxedo, New York

Altogether, the original development of the private, fenced Tuxedo Park, the original town village, and finally, the East (Italian) and Slovak Villages outside the gates, amassed to well over 7,000 acres owned by Pierre Lorillard. He conceived the idea of a sporting club, and this led to his establishment of a land development company. Lorillard placed all the land inside Tuxedo Park, including the surrounding area outside the gates, into a holding company called the Tuxedo Park Association, or the TPA. This company owned "all" the land and all other assets built such as the roads, offices, stores, and homes outside the gates. Lorillard's plan then resulted in his forming a water company and electric company, which was later sold to Orange Utilities Company in the early 1900s. History records as many as twenty-two houses were originally built in the early years inside the gates, including the first twelve on Tower Hill Road and two on the west side of the dam on Tuxedo Lake. This infrastructure surrounding the three lakes was the first residential community to have a water and sewer system outside of the country's cities and soon incorporated the use of Thomas Edison's invention of electric lighting for the homes inside the gates.

The centerpiece of Tuxedo Park was the Tuxedo Club, located on the northern shore of Tuxedo Lake. Swimming was not allowed in Tuxedo Lake, as it was pristine and used as a reservoir to provide drinking water to the community, which it still does. Further north on a spit of land protruding out on the west side of the created Wee Wah Lake, the land was cleared, and a gun club and a beach were built for Tuxedo Club members that was referred to as Pigeon Point, as live pigeons were used for shooting. Swimming, boating, and shooting were part of the many sporting activities envisioned by Lorillard. This same location later included a field and birch tree grove for picnicking and bathing that became the Tuxedo Community Club, later renamed the Wee Wah Beach Club. Despite the official names, the area has most commonly been referred to as "the beach."

It is upon this beautiful beach where the story begins.

Chapter 1: The Beach

Summer at the beach, with a friend on the swing; Tuxedo Park, ca. 1950

My first memory of "the beach," as we called it, is from the summer of 1950, when I was six years old. Dick Tansey, the oldest son of Mabel Tansey, the Beach Club president at that time, had caught a giant fish over by the old icehouse and was heading for the beach. That was the story that made its way to us as we were playing on the swings and seesaws. I would come to view Dick, a teenager at this time, as a Huck Finn character. He always appeared to be doing something he shouldn't, such as building a raft in the cove, a prohibited area at the entry to the beach, but he was never destructive or hurtful.

We jumped off the swings and raced across the straw grass field to see what Dick had caught. He was out at the edge of the clearing, about ten yards from the abandoned Gun Club building that had been somewhat restored and now served as the bathhouse for the

Beach Club. Running through that area with bare feet was difficult, as the ground was littered with pieces of clay pigeons and shotgun shells from years of skeet shooting. We endured the pain, as we had to see this monster fish. It was a big old carp! It was enormous! It had to be fifty, no, maybe one hundred pounds! Dick was dragging it with a rope, and it looked about five feet long. Of course, I was only six years old at the time, and the fish was more than half as big as me. So, maybe the fish was only fifteen or twenty pounds and three feet long, but it was definitely the largest fish I had ever seen. Although true, it may appear we are starting with a fish story. We watched as Dick, raising his finger to his lips to signal quiet, dragged the carp to the edge of the clearing, covered it lightly with dirt and leaves, and swore us all to secrecy. We knew what was about to happen, but telling our parents or breaching secrecy would surely mean some sort of punishment for not reporting it immediately. Our lips were sealed. Two days later, the wind shifted to the southeast. The smell around the bathhouse was sickening. I remember my mother talking with her friends and assuming that a raccoon or some other animal must have gotten trapped under the bathhouse and died. Until now I have kept that smelly secret.

To reach the beach at the Wee Wah, you had to drive across a dam at the south end of the Wee Wah Lake, and with the car windows open, you could hear the water rushing down over the falls from Pond 3, the small lake above.

Tuxedo Lake is fed by springs and several brooks that flow east from Sterling Forest and the Ramapo Mountains. This lake is the main source for a design that transformed the natural terrain; the resulting dam allows the water from Tuxedo Lake to flow down through an original but now closed fish hatchery, thus creating Pond 3. Another dam at the opposite end of Pond 3 allows the water to cascade into what was a lower valley and swamp, but for a spit of land at a slightly higher elevation that appears to split the valley. Another large dam constructed at the northern end of this valley created Wee Wah Lake. From there, the water flows east into the Ramapo River. This location on top of the dam between Pond 3 and the Wee Wah offers a first look at the "beach," part of a peninsula that juts into Wee Wah Lake from the western side.

Even today, I can close my eyes and remember my heart racing at the distant sight of what are now classic cars in the parking area and people at the beachfront. In minutes, I would be jumping off the diving board into the cool, fresh water. Decades later, there has always been something so peaceful, so beautiful, and so soothing about sitting on a bench dedicated to my uncle, Randall "Buddy" McCarroll, as I gaze south across the Wee Wah toward that waterfall and the dam in the distance.

Sitting there, you can hear the rushing wind in your ears and feel the breeze on your face. On the hottest of days, when the temperature is stifling outside the private gates on Route 17 in the Hamlet, or when you can feel the sweat on your brow at home in the hills surrounding the lakes in Tuxedo Park, there is always a breeze at the beach. You not only feel the breeze, but you can see it in the ripple movements it causes on the surface of the water. It starts at the south end of Tuxedo Lake, picks up momentum passing through Turtle Point, reaches shore at the Tuxedo Club, and swoops down and through the Little Wee Wah skating pond. There it is cooled, and the breeze again falls like the water over the dam and across the Wee Wah.

The breeze comes at you, directly at that spit of land called Pigeon Point and the home of what was once called the Wee Wah Beach Club.

It is precisely at Buddy's bench where you can feel the wind's full force and recreate the historic scenes visible from this very spot. It is 1778, and on the far-left side of the lake, George Washington and his army of regulars with their oxen carts are making their way along the east shore through the swampy area on their march to West Point. Word had spread that the British were sailing up the Hudson River from New York City to divide the upper colonies from the colonies to the south.

Close your eyes and open them. It is 1886, and you can see a swampy, marshy area filling in with water flowing from the stream, and you can hear the men building another dam at the north end, expanding the Wee Wah. As the water basin rises, men shout as trees are felled and teams of horses pull plows along the shoreline to create roads. You can hear the pickaxes and shovels and the languages of Italian and Slavic workers clearing brush. You can hear the grunting and cursing as they push huge boulders, remnants from the ice age millions of years ago, to the side of the newly formed road.

Close and open your eyes again. It is 1905. Grand mansions decorate the hillsides. The graded dirt roads along the lake are filled with horse-drawn coaches, bicycles, and the sounds of "must have" European automobiles from Mercedes Benz and Rolls-Royce. Men and women walk along the roads where the foliage is resplendent with the changing leaves of fall, or in spring colors, with the rhododendron and forsythia in full bloom.

Blink again. It is 1907 and you can't see him, but you know Mark Twain is visiting, and is likely on his second or third drink while sitting on the porch of the Voss house across the lake from the beach on the hill below. Mrs. W.H.N. Voss was listed in the Social Register, a member of the American Kennel Club and a championship indoor tennis player. She was an early fan of automobile touring and racing.

W.H. Neilson Voss, a descendant of an original settler of Southampton, Long Island, whose wife was related to Grenville Kane of Tuxedo Park, built this house in 1904 upon becoming a member of the Tuxedo Club. Mark Twain rented the house in 1907, and often spent time there in his final few years. In 1945, the house was bought by Henry Cole, whose brother-in-law, Calvin Bullock, had met Otto Hapsburg, the pretender to the Austro-Hungarian throne before World War II. Hapsburg's mother, Empress Zita, was the wife of Karl I, the last emperor. The Empress was invited to stay in this house, which was later sold to her family. The property was held in the names of the Empress's children, one of whom, Elizabeth, married Heinrich, Prince of Liechtenstein. The Empress lived here until 1971, when she returned to Europe. Towering above the Voss house, the Frelinghuysen home was a large estate that was visible from the lake far above on the east side, at the very top of the hill overlooking the Wee Wah below.

Close your eyes and open them once again. It is 1925. The horse-drawn carriages have disappeared, and the road is enjoyed by Tuxedo Club members with the latest European convertible automobiles, and the finest American touring cars of the day such as the Duesenberg, Pierce Arrow, and Auburn. The mood is lively and bright as drivers and their families enjoy an escape from the city for a fall drive in the Park.

Fast forward once more to the summer of 1945. The scene is alive with the sights and sounds of fire engine sirens and gleeful people from the village who walked or drove across the dam on the south end toward the beach picnic after the Fourth of July parade in front of the Tuxedo Club. The members of the Tuxedo Club have remained there to party, swim in the pool, and enjoy tennis or boating on Tuxedo Lake. All residents and family members of the village are allowed through the gates of the Park on this one day to enjoy the holiday parade. They, along with Park residents employed and living at the mansions, outer houses, gardener cottages, garages, as well as former coach house/stables who are not members of the Tuxedo Club, used the Beach Club at the Wee Wah for their picnic festivities.

By now, the sun has passed behind the mountains to the west and it's time to return home to the hillsides or back down to the village, unless you are lucky enough to stay and use the fireplaces under the birch trees for a picnic supper. Then it's one final late swim in the Wee Wah Lake before the beach closes and darkness sets in.

Much of this nature experience, I fear, may now be lost on most who have this unique, small piece of heaven available to them every day in the warmer months. We all suffer from this kind of loss. Many people living in New York City have never been to the Statue of Liberty. Why? A typical response: "It's right there, and we can always visit it." In addition, many parents now work full-time. Air conditioning is commonplace, as are computers and other technological devices. Too often, adults and even children are more likely to spend beautiful days indoors, occupied by electronic distractions.

Margaret Chanler, an American woman raised in Rome, Italy, later in life published her 1935 memoir, *Roman Spring*.[1] In December 1886, Margaret Louisa Terry was married in Rome to Winthrop Astor

Chanler, a descendent of two prominent families, a sportsman, and a member of the Tuxedo Club. They returned to the States where she was readily accepted into high society and lived at a fashionable address on Madison Avenue in New York City. They also enjoyed a home in Newport, Rhode Island. Her husband, one of Pierre Lorillard's first members of the Tuxedo Club, was persuaded by a friend to take residence in Tuxedo Park in 1893. After four years the Chanlers ultimately moved to their Newport, Rhode Island mansion in 1897. They were members of Mrs. Astor's famous Four Hundred, and it's likely that Margaret Chanler, raised in Rome, preferred the city house and the Newport mansion to the lonely existence of year-round living in their Tuxedo Park home, which was not a mansion, but a large house referred to as one of the original "cottages" designed by Bruce Price during the early development in 1886. During her stay, Mrs. Chanler wrote she found life in Tuxedo Park to be "fundamentally distasteful. A country club community enclosed by a high fence; the entrance strictly guarded against intruders; only members and their guests were allowed to enter. I always resented the exclusion of random elements. But there was a big ugly clubhouse where parties were constantly given. And it was considered unfriendly not to attend them." However, her perspective of Tuxedo Park living was much more positive when describing the incredible beauty of the place. She continued, "The landscape of wooded hills sloping steeply down to a long lake was pleasant enough, and the air was delicious; had we been hermits we might never have found a better spot in which to withdraw from the world and meditate on the Non-Ego."

Chanler Cottage in Tuxedo Park, built by Bruce Price, ca. 1886

Chapter 2: A Perfect Site for a Beach

The high-dive platform and the diving board, along with the Frelinghuysen
and Carhart mansions atop the hill, ca. 1900

The Wee Wah Beach Club represents a story of time trying to
stand still. It is nestled inside Tuxedo Park, one of the most private and
exclusive gated communities in the United States. Although not a
municipality when formed, it even had its own police force. Tuxedo
Park was first conceived of and developed by Pierre Lorillard IV, who
later sold off parcels for the construction of a variety of mansions
(referred to as cottages at the time) featuring many architectural motifs
for the great industrialists, financiers, and socially prominent families
of the Gilded Age. Within its boundaries lies a small peninsula
stretching out into the third created lake of the community,
appropriately named Wee Wah Lake. This small segment of land was
originally known as Pigeon Point. From 1936 until the annual leases
ended in September 2021 (when the lease was not renewed by the

Village of Tuxedo Park trustees for the 2022 season), a large area of the Pigeon Point property functioned as the Tuxedo Community Club, until it was renamed the Wee Wah Beach Club in 1978. Its members represented a unique mix of today's social fabric, as opposed to those who could afford the membership of the private Tuxedo Club and who appreciated its exclusivity. Its distinctive operation remains a throwback to the Great Depression of the 1930s, the World War II years of the 1940s, and the economic boom of the 1950s. This was long before personal computers and smartphones, Early televisions were black and white, and subject to the vagaries of the horizontal hold button and mediocre antenna reception.

For more than eighty years, the "Beach Club" as it was affectionately known, was the place for family gatherings of the working class, many who lived in what are historically known as the Hamlet as well as the Slovak and East Villages directly outside the confines of the Tuxedo Park boundaries. The Beach Club, at its formation, was open for membership to people from the Hamlet, including the Italian and Slovak Villages, beyond the gates because it was these families who originally built, serviced, or worked within the gates when Tuxedo was developed. By the 1980s, on any given weekend, it was not unusual to find four generations celebrating community spirit and volunteerism, as well as a blending of social status and diverse political views. Noise levels were muted in the picnic grove, except for the occasional Scrabble argument or the broadcast of a New York Yankees game on a Sunday afternoon, amplified by the many radios tuned to the same station. The play area and waterfront reverberated with the laughter and shouting of children.

Pigeon Point was aptly named. On this spit of land, Lorillard had built a two-story building and shooting stands named the Gun Club, where pigeons were originally released for shooting contests, replicating those at the manor houses in England. It was another amenity Lorillard provided for his Tuxedo Club members and resident property owners, along with an artificial beach. These are just two of the many features that Lorillard established in keeping with his desire to create a recreational preserve for his wealthy friends. Although this area was originally private to Tuxedo Club members and their guests, by the early 1900s, the children of the hired workers from the houses in the Park found their way down to the beach through the many paths created with chiseled stone steps and bridle trails meticulously maintained by the estates. It was summer. It was hot. Late in the day, the beach used by the Tuxedo Club members was vacant, and the cool lake water beckoned. Across the lake was the home of W.H. Neilson Voss, a relative of Grenville Kane, an original lot owner and the first to occupy a home in Tuxedo Park.

Grenville Kane (July 12, 1854 – July 17, 1943)[2] was a banker and financier who served on the boards of many banks and railroads. An avid sportsman, Kane was a founder of the Tuxedo Golf Club, where the first international golf match was played. He was a competitive tennis player well respected at the Newport Casino and a yachtsman known for sailing across the Atlantic in the 1880s to take part in the Cowes Regatta on the Isle of Wright. An avid book collector, Kane curated one of the finest private libraries in the country at his home in the Park. Voss was a member of the Tuxedo Club and a descendant of one of the original settlers of Southampton, New York.

As stated earlier, in 1907, Voss rented his cottage to the legendary author Mark Twain, whose many socialite friends included

H.H. Rodgers, a Standard Oil associate of John D. Rockefeller and Tuxedo Park resident. Twain was not in the same economic or social class but was not embarrassed to enjoy their largess in return for entertaining them with his wit. Times change, but if Mark Twain could still sit on the porch of the Voss house on a late summer afternoon and look across the Wee Wah Lake today, he would not notice much of a difference in the activities taking place. A notable exception would be the social station of the people enjoying the beach. In earlier times, when the beach was used by members of the Tuxedo Club exclusively, after the end of June, most Club members had departed for their homes in Newport or Southampton or were indulging in European travels.

Mark Twain at the home of W.H. Neilson Voss, ca. 1907

By the 1920s, most Tuxedo Club members had long since deserted the Wee Wah for the activities created by the construction of a new Tuxedo Club pool. In later years, when the new beach club was formed by those in the social class working on or servicing the estates inside the gates, a few Tuxedo Club members also purchased memberships, mostly as an indication of support. They seldom, if ever, actually used the Beach Club. The Wee Wah Beach Club membership was available to residents of the Hamlet, which now included the original East and Slovak Villages. Membership was also open to all residents of the Park, without exception. However, those from "outside the gates" who met the membership criteria were subject to approval by the Tuxedo Park Association and ultimately the governors of Tuxedo Park Club.

The Beach Club had few social rules other than upholding common courtesy. For Beach Club members, the only exception would be the early rush on the Fourth of July for favorite picnic spots and tables, now secured on a first-come, first-served basis, rather than being reserved for the original members and their extended families.

The Fourth of July exception is a unique example of how tradition can change and yet remain the same. There is no longer a July Fourth parade capped by a Fireman's picnic at the beach. At the last celebration, on July 4, 2021, if Mark Twain could look down on the lake at 8:55 a.m. on the Fourth of July (although I doubt Mr. Twain would be awake at that hour), he would see cars lined up on Wee Wah Road on the west side of Wee Wah Lake. He could see "over age 65" members poised to rush around the vehicle entrance gate. The rules allowed the over-65 set to receive a five-minute head start to walk in and claim a picnic table before the beach driveway gate opened.

For the July Fourth exception in the thirty years from 1991 to 2021, the president, Bonny Takeuchi, or the lifeguard, drives up and gives the signal to the over-65 set at 8:55. At 9:00 a.m., the entrance gate opens and members drive in to claim a parking space and tables. Reminiscent of a scene from the Midwest land rush in the mid-1800s, these older runners (more like speed walkers) most of whom are descendants of the original members, seek to secure their time-honored locations for a picnic. This relatively new method of claiming a table developed after those families lost their rights to specific locations and tables that had been preserved since the beginning of the Club due to newer members coming the night before to mark their spot with beach chairs and other paraphernalia. This new practice ensured a more equal opportunity for members to secure prime locations, or whichever spot they wished, without implementing a reservation system or preference to length of family membership. After all, this was not one of those prestigious, socially exclusive private beach clubs like those found at Bailey's Beach in Newport or the Southampton Bathing Corporation, where the location of a member's locker expressed their standing and, as such, was passed down through the generations. There was, however, always an implicit understanding that members understood the areas where the original families gathered, and it was respected.

By the early 1990s, many original Beach Club members were likely represented by thirty to sixty descendants at the July Fourth gatherings. Where one family started, and where one ended, would be difficult for an outsider to tell, as most families had intermarried over the years. For example, you might see the Mottola, McCarroll, Damato, and Napolitano families welcoming each other as aunts, uncles, cousins, nephews, nieces, and in-laws. Most were inter-related.

This is the story of the Wee Wah Beach Club—its beginnings, its growth, and its end, along with the changes it faced as it continued to mirror the country's evolution where the divide in society between wealth now widens and reflects back to the Gilded Age.

Chapter 3: Tuxedo Park

The main gate entrance to Tuxedo Park, ca 1910

According to the 2018 PBS American Experience documentary *The Gilded Age*, by 1897, the richest four thousand families in the U.S. (representing less than 1% of the population) possessed about as much wealth as the other 11.6 million families combined. While today's income inequality presents a similar great divide, the top billionaires in the United States are dispersed throughout the country and enjoy easy access to a much smaller globe, thanks to their mega yachts, private jets, and worldwide real estate holdings.[3]

E. Digby Baltzell, a distinguished social historian specializing in the habits peculiar to the rich, has called Tuxedo Park "a caricature of the Victorian millionaire's mania for exclusiveness." Not just the ordinary sort of millionaire would do, however. In the beginning, the money also had to be properly aged. The highly selective standards for admission to Tuxedo Park served as a reflex response to the chaos in New York society caused by the massive invasion of nouveau riche after the Civil War. By the 1880s, the old alliance of Knickerbocker families with the post-Revolutionary mercantile rich, which had reigned supreme for nearly a century, was crumbling under the onslaught of newcomers whose unprecedented wealth and blatant opulence were socially irresistible. Tuxedo Park, like Mrs. Astor's Four Hundred, was an attempt, however ineffectual, to cope with this shattering upheaval.[4]

By the end of the nineteenth century, the super-wealthy were concentrated in the Northeast, specifically New York City, and most socialized in a tight circle that included Tuxedo Park; Newport, Rhode Island; and other summer resorts such as the Berkshires in Massachusetts; and Bar Harbor, Maine. The titans of industry, real estate, and finance were centered at Wall Street in lower Manhattan. They built new mansions in New York City as they were forced uptown by the influx of immigrants and large high-rise apartments and commercial buildings as steel became the dominant building material.

In some respects, the history of the Wee Wah Beach Club represents a microcosm of the American story. If you were to put Tuxedo Park under the microscope from its 1886 initial completion through the Roaring Twenties, it would capture the unprecedented growth taking place across the country that started after the Civil War. The development and western expansion of the railroads required workers to build them. The arrival of the telephone and household electrical devices, and the associated infrastructure, required labor to install lines and build immense electrical grids and power plants. Around the turn of the twentieth century, Rockefeller's Standard Oil, and other corporations controlling and providing natural resources, as well as food and liquor corporations, were combined into powerful monopolies called trusts. Railroads of the late nineteenth century required thousands of workers to build them and, when finished, left behind a ready and able diverse labor force. Thousands and thousands of workers were needed in Carnegie's steel mills, Armour's meat packing plants, and Henry Ford's automobile factories, which gave rise to the modern assembly line. America was changing fast. This new class of workers contributed to a focus on social issues that led to unionization, women's right to vote, and safety issues brought to America's attention through the writings of Sinclair Lewis.

Tuxedo Park was unique in that many of those responsible for the very industries that fueled the country's growth lived there and commuted to work in New York City, while still maintaining their New York City mansions. Many business decisions by these men of extraordinary wealth were made—and deals were forged—on the nonstop express train known as the "Erie Millionaire" into Wall Street or over the poker tables and recreational activities at the Tuxedo Club. These decisions then found their way to the ears of those in power in Washington and stoked economic growth through the first two decades of the 1900s.

Much has been written about the founding of Tuxedo Park established by Pierre Lorillard IV in 1886 as a retreat for sporting activities with friends and family. It was also developed as a refuge from the formalities of social life in New York, and as a spring, fall, and winter getaway, much different from the summer resorts of Newport, Rhode Island; Southampton, New York; Bar Harbor, Maine; Lenox, Massachusetts; and other destinations in the Northeast accommodating the socially prominent, wealthy families of the time.

Lorillard, a tobacco millionaire and sportsman, envisioned this project on some seven thousand acres owned by his family and used for lumbering and railroad development after the Civil War. Tucked away in a narrow valley thirty-eight miles north of New York City, surrounded by the Ramapo Mountains to the west and a mountain ridge called the Hudson Highlands separating it from the Hudson River on the east, we find the Town of Tuxedo, New York. The valley follows the Ramapo River and provides a natural route from New York City to Albany and to points west through the Catskill Mountains to the state's northern border at Niagara Falls. It served as the easiest and most direct route to West Point and forts north along the Hudson River during the Revolutionary War. It was a farming region, although the area was also rich in iron, which was mined beginning in the eighteenth century. The road in the early days of the country, if you could call it a road, was soon developed as the Orange Turnpike and later became famous as New York State Route 17. Beginning in the mid-twentieth century, this route provided access from New York City to the Catskill Mountains, home to large resorts such as the Concord, Grossinger's, and bungalow communities that mainly served as summer vacation spots popular with many in the Jewish population who had the means to escape the summer cauldron of New York City for a few weeks.

As early as the mid-1700s, the Ramapo Mountain area was rich with mines producing iron needed for the growth of the new country. During the Revolutionary War, iron from these mines was forged into the great chain used to cross the Hudson at West Point to prevent British ships from sailing up the river. Years later, in the mid-

1840s, the railroad created a spur heading directly west off the main line where the overpass at the entrance to Sloatsburg, New York exists today. That road became known as the Sterling Iron & Railroad Company, which was formed in 1865. It reached the properties of Cooper-Hewitt and the Parrott family, owners of the Parrott Iron Company, which invented and built the Parrot gun, a type of muzzle-loading rifled artillery weapon known for its long range and accuracy. The weapon was used extensively in the American Civil War.

The Village's location was fortunate, as it was served by the Erie Railroad, which ran parallel to the Ramapo River. The railroad had reached well beyond Tuxedo by 1841 along the obvious route through the valley west of the mountains overlooking the Hudson River to the east, ending with its final completion in 1851 at Dunkirk, New York on Lake Erie. This route was long used to transport iron ore and lumber southward to New York City, and to move products to the Great Lakes for shipping across the country. It became one of four ways to travel from New York City to Chicago and was the subject of a competitive war for control in the 1860s.

The Erie Railroad laid track along this route that followed the Ramapo River and had a stop that was referred to as the "woodpile." Trains at the time used wood as fuel, and the Lorillard tract supplied wood to the railroad at this stop thirty-five miles out from the line's origination in Piermont, New York on the west side of the Hudson River. Later, after the Civil War, the line was extended to Jersey City, New Jersey for more easy access to New York City and the Wall Street financial district. Peter Lorillard originally acquired the land in 1814, and it passed through the family to his son, Peter Lorillard III, who subsequently left the property to his seven children upon his death in

1867. It was at this stop, the wood pile, that Pierre Lorillard IV stepped off one day in 1885 with Bruce Price, a young architect he had hired to make his vision of a private, recreational social club a reality. Together they viewed the lush, sprawling property Lorillard envisioned as a members-only sports and hunting retreat for the prominent and very rich members of New York society. Mr. Lorillard and a great many of his friends were frequent visitors to England. They considered themselves the privileged American Aristocrats and enjoyed the invitation as well as hospitality of English titled society at their country castles and manor homes. Lorillard admired the lifestyle, luxury, and splendor of the owners of these great estates. There were few resembling it in this country, and Mr. Lorillard undertook to supply the want. Tuxedo Park was the result. "When an Englishman by sword or ledger achieves great fortune, his first impulse is to buy land."[5]

He then went about securing the property from his six brothers and sisters. In the fall of 1885, he hired the young architect, Bruce Price, and a prominent engineer from Boston, E.W. Bowditch, to build a new community of initially twelve cottages, along with stables, tennis courts, a gun club, dams, a fish hatchery, an icehouse, the entry gate, the police station, a large clubhouse, and a supporting village outside the imposing main gate entrance. Vera C. Brigham, a long-time resident of Tuxedo Park, stated in her book, *History of the Park School*, "Mr. Lorillard ordered houses the way other people might order boots."[6]

Lorillard opened an office for the newly established Tuxedo Park Association, known as the TPA, in a small house on Clubhouse Road inside the Park to manage his project. Shortly thereafter, a new office was built outside the gates along with seven cottages, two blocks of stores, and the railroad station. The Park itself was situated around a sparkling lake nestled in a glacial valley in full view of the beauty of the Ramapo Mountains. With the exception of the entrance gate, the entire Park was surrounded by an eight-foot fence topped by barbed wire. There were approximately eighteen miles of roads lit by gas lamps, three dams to create additional lakes, as well as a water and sewer system. The rather large wooden homes called "cottages" could be more than forty rooms with multiple fireplaces and servants' quarters. Describing the work of her father, Bruce Price, Emily Post, famous for her etiquette books, stated, "In beginning Tuxedo, the architect's idea was to fit buildings with the surrounding woods, and the gate-lodge and keep [a medieval tower at the entrance to a castle] were built of Graystone with as much moss and lichen as possible. The shingled cottages were stained with the color of the woods—russets and grays and dull reds—ugly to the taste of a quarter-century later, though this treatment did much to neutralize the newness of the buildings—Old World and tradition-haunted as it looks, it is new, incredibly new."[7]

A police force was formed, and individual outposts were located throughout the Park. At its inception, officers would patrol on foot, and lamplighters would make their way through the Park to light the gas lamps at dusk before the electric company was established.

Along with local craftsmen, some eighteen hundred workers imported from Italy and Slovakia completed this entire community in nine months. Tuxedo was thought to have been a name used by the native Americans to describe the area. A Tuxedo Club committee formed by William Waldorf Astor was organized to determine the origin of the name Tuxedo. The area was known by early settlers in the

1700s as a wonderful place to hunt among the cedar trees and lake, and thus they called it "Duck Cedar." However, Indian language scholars believed the name originally came from an Algonquin tribe meaning "Bear Place." The committee decided to use the settlers' name but revised it to be "Tuxedo."[8] Tuxedo Park soon attracted the leaders of American wealth and society. It also became the place where many of Mrs. Astor's New York Four Hundred came to play.

While there is some ambiguity about the origin of the name "Tuxedo," the result of Lorillard's efforts, despite the changes over nearly 140 years, remains preserved in an idyllic setting today. What started in the late 1880s, with cottage occupants centered on club life, grew into a community of magnificent estates inhabited by the social elite. A number of early members made Tuxedo Park their formal residence and commuted into New York City, although, as mentioned, most maintained large, fashionable mansions in the city continually moving up to mid-town and later to Fifth Avenue above 57th Street as the city grew and Central Park was created. Many built homes for visiting on weekends, particularly in the late spring and early summer.

Here in Tuxedo Park, they could spend weeks taking in horse, dog, and flower shows, and all visits offered the opportunity for fresh air and activities that could not be found in the cities. In late June, many left for the coastal beaches, yachting off Newport, excursions, mountain resorts, trans-Atlantic cruises to Europe and beyond, such as exotic cruises down the Nile River in Egypt, a journey extremely popular at the turn of the century. The "coaching set" with their carriages, drivers, and footmen [as there were no automobiles at this time], or should we call them the "private jet set" of their age, returned in the fall to enjoy the foliage as well as sporting activities, culminating with the Autumn Ball at the Tuxedo Club. Many came by train, accompanied by their storage trunks and hired help, but coaches were still a common means of travel, and the trip took less than a day.

A family's arrival in Tuxedo Park, ca. 1890s

The Autumn Ball included the presentation of debutantes, signaling the beginning of the winter social season in New York City. As the year came to a close, the social set again returned to Tuxedo Park for winter sports and a New Year's Ball at the Club was followed by events in the early months of the year, when the national indoor racquet, squash, and "court tennis" championships would be held at the Tennis and Racquet Club facilities. Once again, coaches, trains, and later motorcars, as well as large moving vans, would transport the families, friends, servants, and trunks out from the city for weeks of parties and winter activities.

To purchase a building lot or property in the Park, one first had to be accepted as a member of the Tuxedo Club. At the time, this was part of the selective discrimination of Lorillard's plan. Upon being denied membership to the Club, one could not purchase a lot directly from the Tuxedo Park Association. Thus, Tuxedo Park was very restricted, unlike Newport, Bar Harbor, or Southampton, where individual property could be bought and sold on the open market. Of course, anyone was free to purchase property in these resort locations. It was also possible to purchase a home from original owners in Tuxedo Park who had purchased it from Lorillard's TPA. However, unless they were acceptable to the existing members of the Tuxedo Club, were the leaders of society, or were welcomed by members of the golf, tennis, shooting, and beach clubs, there would be few social invitations, resulting in a lonely existence.

The design of the gated and fenced community was the work of some of America's greatest architects and land planners of the day. These included architects Bruce Price, designer of many of the original cottages, and John Russell Pope, along with Whitney Warren, whose firm, Warren & Wetmore, penned the blueprints for Grand Central Station. Their designs have stood the test of time as the golden period of American architecture. As to land planning, Frederick Olmstead, designer of Central Park, and E.W. Bowditch, two premier landscaping and engineering firms then located in Boston, are revered today for their beautiful work in Tuxedo Park.

Ernest W. Bowditch was born in 1850, and in his mid-thirties became the landscape architect of Tuxedo Park. He was a member of the first class to graduate from the Massachusetts Institute of Technology, and the first American landscape designer to receive a formal education in civil engineering. His work for Pierre Lorillard IV's mansion in Newport launched his public reputation when he was twenty-seven years old. Lorillard later sold the property to the Vanderbilt family, leaving the yachting community to pursue his Tuxedo Park vision. The mansion burned to the ground and Vanderbilt replaced it with what we know today as The Breakers. Today the Breakers has been fully restored, is open to the public, as a shining example of the opulence of the Gilded Age period. Within a few years, Bowditch employed sixty assistants and fifteen to twenty crews, working from Bar Harbor, Maine, to Topeka, Kansas, and from St. Paul, Minnesota, to Atlanta, Georgia, on projects ranging from gardens and parks to campuses, cemeteries, and municipal sanitation systems.

In 1885, Lorillard brought him to the land that would become Tuxedo Park to plan and construct the layout, infrastructure, and deceptively rustic amenities of the Park and its adjacent communities. The development would be centered on new dams and reconfigured bodies of water. Bowditch had previously created for himself and his friends a smaller planned summer community on an island in Maine, with improvements for the year-round population. At Tuxedo, Lorillard's expansive vision and Bowditch's expertise combined to enhance the wilderness and produce an unprecedented ideal of modern luxury. Bowditch continued a long, productive, and prosperous career, but his work at Tuxedo Park, inspired by Lorillard, represents in many ways the pinnacle of his achievement in landscape design.

Bowditch, along with Price, who also designed many of the early cottages, helped plan the community structure, which they created around three lakes comprising more than seven thousand fenced acres at the time. Many property owners used Frederick

Olmstead, the landscape creator of Central Park, to design landscapes for their great estates. Activities centered around the Tuxedo.Club, which was built on Tuxedo Lake. Skating and other winter sports took place on Tuxedo Lake. In later years, these activities moved to Pond 3, more commonly known as the "skating pond," or the Little Wee Wah. A skating cabin was built with a large stone fireplace, where one could warm up after a spirited game of ice hockey. There was a long, lighted, one-mile toboggan run that ended at the frozen lake, and one of the earliest golf clubs built in America. The third, and most northern lake, was called the Wee Wah Lake. It was created by another dam that filled a swamp. As mentioned, for Tuxedo Club members and their guests, a shooting club was built for pigeon shooting on a spit of land called Pigeon Point, which protruded from the western shore. At the tip, a beach was created for swimming activities, including platform diving and floating rafts, where one could relax out in the lake. There was a small swim tank constructed adjacent to the Clubhouse as well. No swimming was allowed in the main Tuxedo Lake, the reservoir that provided potable water to the community.

Pierre Lorillard's imaginative plan was to create a place of country estates, but on a smaller scale than the castles and manor houses of the privileged class and nobility of England. They were to be called cottages. It would not replace or compete with Newport, Bar Harbor, or Lenox, where the rich and fashionable had already settled. This would be a place of refuge from the clamor, dirt, and population explosion of New York City, where the social elite continued to migrate from their downtown mansions in favor of the fashionable Avenues on the grid with streets numbered in the Thirties, to the Forties, and, at the turn of the century, to palatial palaces on Fifth

Avenue, bordering the new Central Park.

Tuxedo Park was to be another club used by his friends to explore nature and engage in recreational pursuits. As mentioned, there was tennis, swimming, boating, hunting, fishing, as well as curling, a peculiar Scottish sport for the men played on ice in the winter. Other family winter activities included skating and tobogganing for the families. All these activities were to center around the main club. The Tuxedo Club contained all the amenities one would expect, including a stage with velvet curtains for amateur performances. A celebrity of the social elite, Cora Urquhart, married James Brown Potter, a Tuxedo Club member at the time. He was recognized as one of the original members and she was well-known in social circles for her dramatic reading and organized amateur theatrical productions at the club. Apparently, the call of the theater was too strong, and she left for England to study and to enter the professional stage. This led to a divorce from Mr. Potter, as theater people were not welcomed as members of the Tuxedo Club.

There is another very interesting description of how the thought of creating Tuxedo Park originated which is contained in the Laura Claridge book about Emily Post, the daughter of Lorillard's young architect, Bruce Price. The story was interesting to me when we think about how much women have achieved and are now recognized in today's world. History records it was Pierre Lorillard's vision that created Tuxedo Park. Claridge writes a far different description of the beginnings of Tuxedo Park.

"In 1885, Cora Brown Potter, a southern belle who thought she married money, had discovered that her husband didn't have much of a fortune left – and he wasn't very smart to boot. Through the social circles the Lorillard and the Potters shared, the redheaded beauty became, in short order, Lorillard's lover, even as she pursued her impressive talent for the stage. Several months before Bruce and Lorillard walked his land, Cora had given her restless philanderer an idea of what to do with the vast, useless (so he complained) tract of land he owned around Tuxedo Lake. Why not create a truly exclusive social club, one that played to its strength as an enclave against urban life?

Lorillard thought this a brilliant idea and immediately asked her to follow through. Cora arranged a meeting of 150 male friends and associates, where Lorillard discussed his – or Cora's vision. As a reward, Tuxedo's founder gave her a desirable plot of land to build on. Her husband, deciding he should at least appear as if he weren't being cuckolded insisted that the property be put in his name. A few years later, after Coral left him to become a professional actress, her husband and baby would inherit the Tuxedo Park house."[9]

In the summer of 1886, James Brown Potter, accompanied by his new wife Cora, travelled to London and was introduced to the Prince of Wales (Edward VII to be) at a court ball. Taken with Cora's beauty, the prince invited the Brown-Potters to Sandringham for the weekend, and they duly obliged. When James asked the prince what he should bring to wear, the Prince referred him to his tailors, recommending a short jacket, akin to what he himself preferred for informal dinners, rather than a full tailcoat. Potter followed the prince's advice.

When Potter returned home, the highlight of the fall season was the Autumn Ball, which opened the social season for the elite society and was prominent for the presentation of the debutants who would now be socially acceptable to enter passage into the adult world. It was at this Autumn Ball in 1886 at the Tuxedo Club that Potter wore his jacket instead of formal tails. This is where the formal men's suit, now known as a "tuxedo," got its name. Shortly after, the men from the Park began wearing them to Delmonico's, the most fashionable restaurant in the financial district, for dinner. Those who questioned the short coats were told "they were the Tuxedo fellows." An alternate history that has been disputed mentions Pierre Lorillard's son and his friends learning of Potter's short coat and, as a lark, cutting off their coat tails while attending the same ball.

Tuxedo Park was convenient to New York City, where winters during the late 1800s were particularly unpleasant. Thin blankets of coal soot covered buildings and streets and virtually everything one would find outdoors. The soot turned fallen snow grey in a matter of hours. The streets quickly became a mush of brown sludge from the mix of snow and dirt tracked from the carriage barns and stalls, not to mention the horse excrement from coaches traveling in every direction. Tuxedo offered a refreshing, healthy winter wonderland: crisp, clean air, virgin snow, and views on a clear day over the frozen lake that offered picture-perfect postcard scenes. It was within a day's coach or train ride from the New Jersey side of the Hudson River at Jersey City. Passengers arriving at the newly constructed Tuxedo train station designed by Bruce Price would be met by a so-called Tuxedo Club jitney, a small, one-horse coach that was painted yellow and green.[10]

Referred to as one of America's first planned communities, Tuxedo Park was a precursor to today's housing cooperatives and homeowner associations. All decisions regarding the infrastructure were made by Lorillard's holding company, the TPA. The forethoughts of Lorillard and his small group of original investors and close friends were reflected in this business model. Each Tuxedo Club member who purchased a lot was given one share of TPA stock for each $1,000 of valuation. The land, other than lots sold to those approved for Tuxedo Club membership, was sold to the TPA in return for shares of stock in the company. Lorillard retained fifty-one percent of the TPA. This included all the property outside the gates that would contain the Village. Stock in the TPA was issued, and fees for services were paid to the TPA for maintaining the community. The TPA was the management arm similar to the municipal departments of today, such as public works departments and water and sewer authorities. There was no municipality or publicly elected government. There was the Water Company and the Tuxedo Electric Company, both created by Lorillard and owned by the residents of Tuxedo Park. In fact, Tuxedo Park was one of the first communities to have its own telephone service.[11] There was no minimum wage for workers, and Social Security did not yet exist. Social class segregation was uniformly practiced. All knew their place in this very private enclave. At the turn of the century, those seeking a country place in Tuxedo Park—and allowed entry into the Tuxedo Club—expanded the originally built cottages. Many bought multiple connected lots, where they built classic mansion estates like the English country manor homes inhabited by the lords and ladies of the British aristocracy and supported by nearby villages.

One surmises that Pierre Lorillard, yachtsman, breeder of racehorses, and now developer, was not interested in the attendance at the many balls, parties, operas, and other formal traditions required of society members of the time. Rather, he was a lover of sport and particularly fond of horse racing. Lorillard then moved forward to create and develop his Tuxedo Park. His interests continued to include yachts, horseracing, and poker. As Tuxedo Park became more formal, with its parties and conformance to the rules of "society," he left Tuxedo Park in 1899 for stays in London, his New York City residence, and his extensive racehorse breeding operation at Rancocas Farm in Jobstown, New Jersey. Two years later, he fell ill in London and returned to New York City where he passed away on July 7, 1901.[12]

Chapter 4: The Hamlet and the East Village

The Hamlet on Orange Turnpike (now NY State Route 17), ca. 1900

East Village, ca. 1920

To understand Lorillard's plan and the brilliance of his concept, consider the English model of the country homes and manors outside London. To run these vast estates, little towns (or hamlets) were needed to supply and support "the help," as the workers were known at the time (and sometimes still are), necessary to run the estates. To ensure privacy and exclusiveness, and to create a sense of well-being from the crime associated with the growing population of New York City, Lorillard developed Tuxedo Park within an imposing gated fortress completely surrounded by that eight-foot fence topped with barbed-wire. There was a need for a town to house the community necessary to service the wealthy residents inside the gates. Although just over an hour by private rail car from New York City, basic needs had to be filled. The Tuxedo Park Association was responsible for the development of the community. With the advent of autos at the turn of the century, there was a car dealership, garage, and gas station. There was a private supermarket (or "stores company," as it was known then), complete with a butcher shop. A large laundry was built, along with a tailor shop and bakery.

Building continued with construction of a post office and a bank. A private home on the Orange Turnpike was purchased for a town hall, and a barbershop was added to that building. One of the original blocks of stores that originally housed single workers on the second floor burned down in 1929. After the fire, a larger building containing a drugstore with a luncheon area, as well as a hardware store with offices above for dentists, lawyers, and other service businesses was constructed. A Catholic church and Methodist church were organized. Contributions were gladly offered by members of the Park and the village, and with the help of the TPA, the churches were built. St. Mary's-in-Tuxedo Episcopal Church was also built—inside the gates—given that most Tuxedo Park owners at this time were Episcopalian. Outside the gates, a Scottish rites Masonic temple (the Lorillard Masonic Lodge) was also built, along with a small hospital. Some years later, a moving company was opened to accommodate residents moving in and out of their Fifth Avenue mansions and grand apartments built later in the 1920s on Park Avenue. A school was built, as was housing for teachers and the employees working for the stores and the various general contractors. A volunteer fire department was formed, also outside the gates in the village. All the above grew out of Lorillard's Tuxedo Park plan. The churches, school, and other community buildings were paid for through generous donations from those Tuxedo Club members living in the Park. The library designed by Bruce Price also contained showers and a bowling alley in the basement for use by the townspeople.

This approach to creating a community around a private enclave was thought to be unique in this country by the standards of the time. Lorillard maintained ownership through the TPA, which owned the land beyond the gates in what was referred to as the Tuxedo village (now commonly referred to as the Hamlet and East Village). It was related to the vast landholdings of the titled and privileged in England but on a smaller scale. In Tuxedo Park, there were several smaller estates, "Lords of the Manor" so to speak, serviced by a community outside and dependent on the estates. Houses in the Hamlet and East Village were built and rented on annual leases. Stores were constructed and leased annually as well. Business competition was closely monitored by the TPA. There would be only one hardware store, one bakery, one butcher, one cleaner, etc. A town hall containing a courtroom was constructed. If a workman and his family, a teacher, or a shop owner was creating a problem for the community or the property owners in the Park, it was a simple case of not renewing the lease and they were forced to leave Tuxedo. The one exception was the Tuxedo Stores Company that supplied food for both Tuxedo Park and the Hamlet. Certain Tuxedo Club members formed the company and contributions were required from all owners of property within the Park to ensure its success and to return profits to the owners. Club members maintained accounts and settled them periodically, while others in the village paid for their purchases at the time of sale.

Today we have State Route 17, which follows the route of the original Orange Turnpike, running parallel to the railroad and the Ramapo River. It provided the perfect setting for the creation of the Hamlet and the East Village in the Town of Tuxedo. The east side of Route 17 allowed for a thin strip of commercial development between the road and the railroad tracks. The west side had a slightly larger flat track gently sloping back to the mountains, which border the Tuxedo Park boundary line and beyond. This provided space for more commercial development, and for churches, a hospital, and school, as well as homes for shop owners, teachers, and TPA employees.

The East Village was reached by crossing both the railroad tracks behind the town hall, and then walking over a bridge across the Ramapo River. Most of us today recall our American history and the phrase of "living on the other side of the tracks." The location housed the large majority of original eighteen hundred laborers, comprised mostly of Italian and Slovak immigrants brought over specifically to develop the infrastructure and maintain the properties inside the gates of the Park. Most of the men were married and brought their families.

For a mere two dollars per month, they rented lots owned by the TPA, but their lives were difficult. They built what shelter they could out of scrap lumber and tin. There were no bathrooms, just outhouses with an open trench running along the back lot lines. The crude housing structures, such as they were, became the property of the TPA.

At first, this was a rough and squalid place, akin to the overcrowded slums of the city, but the layout allowed for separate living quarters and air flow, unlike tenement buildings. The narrow streets were named after New York City streets such as Broadway and Fifth Avenue, and the communal dining hall was known as Delmonico's. These were hard-working laborers, many with years of experience in stonecutting and masonry. It was not an easy life, and the problems of the city did not disappear in these sections of town. In 1892, the press reported that a fight had broken out between two men, which led to a much larger melee. "Then their friends joined in with knives, and finally revolvers were used. Michael Demotto was killed by a ball from a revolver and a half dozen others were cut with stilettoes and dirks. Capt. Busch of the Tuxedo police made a raid on the rioters and captured several."[13]

Occupants from outside the gate who worked in the Park were issued passes to be shown at the main gate.

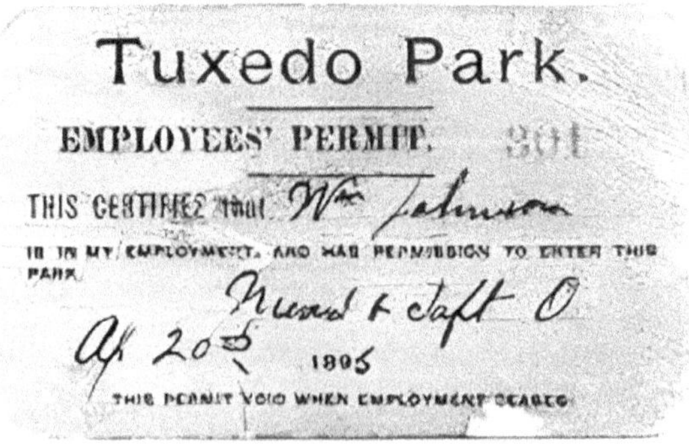

Walking was the main means of transportation, unless there was a horse and wagon to transport them to their job site. The beauty of Tuxedo Park stands as a testament to the artistry and work ethic of the stone masons and sweat effort of the laborers who built the roads, sewers, dams, and walls without the modern construction equipment available today. These East Village families grew quickly, improved their section of Tuxedo, and were determined to pursue the American Dream, including education for their families. In 1925, a gift of $500 was provided to build one of the earliest Order of the Sons of Italy, the H.H. Rodgers and Cabrini Lodge. The gift was from H.H. Rodgers, a Tuxedo Club member and resident of Tuxedo Park, who was a partner of John D. Rockefeller in the Standard Oil Trust.[14]

Many of the domestic and estate workers living within Tuxedo Park were Irish or Scottish, and resided in gardener's cottages, garages, stables, and separate small houses, plotted on the grid of the estates to stay out of view. Those who worked as staff, maids, cooks, butlers, and the like were provided rooms, usually on the upper floors, or in separate, service-oriented sections of the residences.

As for the East Village, it was a world apart from the aristocratic society across the tracks behind the gates. The eastern shore along the Hudson River Valley and the Gold Coast of Long Island were populated by wealthy families who possessed vast stretches of property and opulent mansions. These families had accumulated great wealth that had been passed along and further expanded with each generation since the founding of America. These country estates served as their country homes. Tuxedo Park, noted for its concentration of wealth and privilege, and developed as a "recreational private club," complete with its own separate village and private infrastructure, exemplified the social divisions that existed in America during the Gilded Age.

This social caste system endured for decades, reflected in the oft-quoted remarks of the late Katharine Delano Price Collier St. George, a socialite, a philanthropist, and a cousin of President Franklin Delano Roosevelt, who married George St. George who, by 1919, operated a wholesale coal brokerage on Wall Street and was a director of numerous Wall Street banking houses. George St. George was the grandson of George F. Baker, one of the richest men to live in Tuxedo Park. Mrs. St. George was a well-regarded congresswoman who lived in Tuxedo Park and represented the local Hudson Valley district for eighteen years from 1946 to 1964. Notwithstanding her social status, she tirelessly supported women's rights, including equal pay for equal work, and made herself accessible to all her constituents. She was well respected in Washington and chaired many important committees, including the House Post Office and Civil Service Committee. Instrumental in the passage of the bill establishing zip codes for the United States, it is said Congresswoman St. George was given the honor to choose the first zip code for her district that included Tuxedo Park. This zip code is 10987, as she thought it would be the easiest of the five-digit codes to remember, "ten, nine, eight, seven."

As much as Congresswoman St. George was well-liked by— and considerate of—the majority of her constituents, her society upbringing was ingrained by the different life led at home in Tuxedo Park. According to many books describing the United States social aristocracy, Congresswoman St. George began her remarks for a speech in Tuxedo at the library by first looking to one side of the room addressing the "ladies of the Park," then looking to the other side and continuing, "and women of the village," a quote that clearly illustrates the social caste system that existed in Tuxedo throughout its first sixty years of existence.[15]

In an earlier time, anticipated attendance for a speech to be given by Mark Twain in 1907 resulted in an empty room, as those in the Park believed the speech was intended for those in the Hamlet. Those in the Hamlet thought the speech was being held for the members of the Tuxedo Club residing in the Park. As a result, no one came to hear the legendary author and humorist speak!

Society life in Tuxedo Park still flourished in the early 1950s when I was a young boy, spending many hours at the St. George estate. My mother's parents lived in a gardener's cottage next door and were good friends with the McMahon family. Paddy McMahon was the stable master of the St. George estate and was also responsible for the pedigreed dogs kept in the many kennels. The dogs and horses were entered into the major shows in New York City, such as the Westminster Kennel Club and the National Horse shows at Madison Square Garden. The walls in the stables were always adorned with winning ribbons. The large, enclosed area of manicured lawn across from the main entrance drive was filled with jumps for the horse-jumping training. McMahon was also the estate's caretaker when the family was not in residence.

The St. Georges had a daughter Priscilla who married Angier Biddle Duke, a son of the famous Philadelphia banking family (Biddle) and the enormously wealthy tobacco Duke family. Theirs was one of the greatest society weddings ever held in Tuxedo Park. What seemed like the custom in those days, the wedding was followed by a gift of one million dollars, a honeymoon trip around the world, and on their return, a beautiful new custom-built home awaited them just across the cove on Tuxedo Lake. The kitchen was said to be designed for new stainless-steel appliances and a replica of what President Roosevelt had installed in the White House. The house, known as Duck Hollow, was a short walk to Priscilla's mom and dad's estate across the road.

Their child, Angier St. George Biddle Duke, known as "Pony" Duke, and later, Katherine Ryan, Priscilla's daughter following her mother's divorce and remarriage, were frequent visitors to my grandparents' gardener's cottage next door. Pony, as a young boy, was interested in hunting and trapping, and as a teenager, he was always stopping by to see if I wanted to go with him to check the traps. He spent half his time in the East and the other half at their Flying H Ranch at the head of the Shoshone River in Northwest Wyoming. Pony went on to live most of his life in the West, but always came out to Tuxedo Park to see my Uncle Jim Barth when he came to New York City for business.

Katherine, whom I knew as "Daffy," was two years older than I, and she was very comfortable at her age riding and jumping horses. Daffy would always stop by when riding. I was about seven years old at the time and eager to take my first horse ride. I will never forget one day when she asked my uncle if she could take me for a ride. He had no problem, as long as she went at a slow pace. I was lifted behind her, and we walked the horse down the road to the entrance drive to the St. George estate out of sight of my uncle. The next thing I vividly recall was her sticking in the stirrups and off we went at a full gallop with me screaming and holding tight. It took me years to get up on a horse again.

The scenes I encountered with Pony and Daffy, playing at and visiting the St. George house and estate have always reminded me of George Cukor's classic 1940 romantic comedy about a society wedding, *The Philadelphia Story*, starring Cary Grant, Katharine Hepburn, Jimmy Stewart, and, once again, Roland Young as Uncle Willie. Following around my grandfathers as they cared for the last of the big estates in the Park, I was mesmerized by the unfamiliar lifestyle, both in dress and speech, as well as the customs I observed. There was the unmistakable affected dialect in the movies of the 1930s and 1940s heard in the glamorous, large apartment scenes delivered by the likes of Katherine Hepburn or William Powell. The tweed jackets for the men and the couture dresses and jewelry worn by the women during the day were foreign to me, as were the riding clothes and the many outfits worn by those engaged in sporting activities. Horse shows, dog shows, and most events were attended in suits and dresses, while parties and events at the club required formal attire. To me at the time, these people dressed differently. Their manner of speaking varied from that of my family members, and they always seemed to be in a hurry. They lived in what was truly a very different world than that of my family and friends, who were all members of what was commonly referred to as the "working class."

Chapter 5: Pigeon Point

Pigeon Point in the upper left showing the Gun Club, with the beach in the center, ca. 1887

As Tuxedo Park developed, many amenities, including the Tennis and Racquets Club building, and the Golf Club, were added for Tuxedo Club members to enjoy. The many resident horse lovers enjoyed the bridle trails extending throughout the Park, and a large area not far from the main entrance gates (initially intended to be a polo field) became the center for horse shows, races, dog shows, and other events, including a college football game. On October 11, 1890, before a large crowd, the Princeton University "eleven" met the

Orange Athletic Club and played to a 0 - 0 tie at what is now commonly known to old timers as the "Racetrack."[16] A large grandstand was centered on the hillside, and stables were constructed at the far end of the field. Showjumping was a major event, and typically included cadets from West Point. Shooting was also a highly regarded sport among the residents, many of whom also maintained plantations and residences in South Carolina and the islands off Georgia, where hunting was the primary pastime. In addition, these Tuxedo Park residents were looking to recreate the English aristocratic living where one was invited out to the countryside home for shooting, fox hunting, and the like. In those early days of Tuxedo Park, Palm Beach, Florida had yet to become a recreational destination. Henry Flagler's East Coast Railroad did not reach that area until 1896, and "society" did not settle there until the turn of the twentieth century.

One of the first recreational facilities in Tuxedo Park was the Gun Club built on Pigeon Point. The Wee Wah Lake was the third in a progression of artificial lakes that fit perfectly into the landscape of this idyllic setting. A series of dams that created Tuxedo Lake, and the surrounding topography, supported a natural flow north from this lake down through a dam and fish hatchery to a smaller pond that later served as a winter skating rink. A dam at the south end of the skating pond created a waterfall that filled a one-time swamp and covered the Corduroy Road, which had been used by the Continental Army during the American Revolution. This engineering filled the basin, with a dam at the northern end that turned the water east and through the original Tuxedo Club golf course to the Ramapo River.

Pigeon Point was a perfect spot that caught the breezes flowing through the valley and steep hills on either side. It included a bathing facility for Tuxedo Club members and an isolated location for the Gun Club. The Gun Club itself advanced Lorillard's original plan of a rustic retreat for sporting diversions. Initially, an icehouse was built off of Pond 3. This was a thick-walled structure where ice cut into big blocks from the pond was stored for use by residents of the cottages. In later years, the growth of larger estates in the Park resulted in the construction of a much larger concrete building for this purpose at the north side of Pigeon Point on Wee Wah Lake. The ice was delivered to residences to cool iceboxes. Electric refrigerators and freezers were not common appliances, even for the ultra-wealthy, until around the turn of the century.

Pigeon Point, perfectly situated to accommodate both beach recreation and shooting activities, presented an ideal location for the construction of the Gun Club, where live pigeon shooting became popular with many Club members. It also served as the location for matches with other clubs. The release towers could be set out east toward the lake, allowing spent shot pellets to fall harmlessly into the waters of the Wee Wah. Mabel Tansey's son recalls going to the dam on the north end of the Wee Wah as a young boy and taking home injured pigeons that had floated to the dam. Pigeon shooting was a sport derived from the English aristocracy, which enjoyed bird shooting as a ritual at the country estates outside London. Wild birds, such as pheasants, turkeys, and quail were already limited in the mountainous region, and even more so as human population and construction increased. Pigeon shooting was also more convenient than trudging through the woods, a sport that required trained dogs to flush out the quarry.

Pigeon shooting turned to skeet and trap shooting after New

York State passed a law in 1894 prohibiting the use of live birds, but the shooting continued in Tuxedo Park until the end of the nineteenth century.[17] Skeet shooting in Tuxedo Park then became quite popular and attracted significant wagering during shooting contests and tournaments. Albie Winslow investigated the earlier pigeon shooting years and made some calculations in his excellent book, *Tuxedo Park*: "In its heyday when pigeons were probably sold for 10 to 15 cents apiece, the trustees of the Club, in their statements from 1885 to 1890 reported in the year ending April 30, 1887, $3,020.83 was spent on live pigeons. (In the 1950s, pigeons, which were used for training hunting dogs in marking and retrieving, were sold [and] delivered for 50 cents apiece, so an estimated cost of 10 to 15 cents apiece in 1887 would seem in line). Many of the pigeons in the early years were collected off the roofs of nearby municipalities by eager collectors anxious to make some extra income. During 1888 the Club treasurer reported $2,855.50 spent on game birds and $3,955.62 on live pigeons. During 1889 live pigeons purchased by the Club amounted to $5,902.85 and the last year the club treasurer seems to have made an item report on birds was 1890, when live pigeons bought by the Club [amounted to] $8,899.15. Just that last year it would appear a minimum of 80,000 pigeon had been shot."[18]

I find the figure of 80,000 pigeons to be astounding. I am assuming that a few escaped being shot and flew away. Perhaps the chef at the club found a popular recipe for pigeon pie, or perhaps creative accounting was used and the cost of liquor, shotgun shells, etc. found its way into the "live pigeon" expense item for the Gun Club. By 1900, the Gun Club had lost its allure, although skeet and trapshooting using "clay pigeons" continued into the early 1940s and the outbreak of World War II. The clubhouse itself was not kept up, and remained vacant for many years until it was turned over to the Tuxedo Community Club in 1947, at which time it was renovated by the volunteer work of the members for use as a bath house and social center.

Chapter 6: The Early Tuxedo Club Beach

Tuxedo Club members at the Wee Wah Beach, ca. 1900

In the last decade of the 1800s, and into the early 1900s, the Tuxedo Club was the center of activity. It fronted on Tuxedo Lake, the largest and most scenic of Tuxedo Park's lakes. It also served as the reservoir for the community; thus, there could be no swimming. However, Tuxedo Lake was used for boating (electric launches, sailboats, and canoes, but no gas-powered craft), and it was stocked for recreational fishing. In the early years, in wintertime, members would ice skate in front of the club and engage in curling matches. With the creation of the pond below the club known as the Little Wee Wah, a skating lodge was built and, because this pond froze more quickly, it became the place to skate. As we know, a designated swimming area for the members of the Tuxedo Club was soon added after completion of the Tuxedo Park off Pigeon Point, along with the Gun Club, on Wee Wah Lake.

At the south end of Pigeon Point, the Wee Wah Lake beach was an early creation by the Tuxedo Park Association for Tuxedo Club members and their guests. Lorillard's plan was succeeding on a grand scale. Over the next fifteen years from the original cottages' construction, the lot sizes provided for construction of grand mansions of every description. Surrounding the Wee Wah Lake on the hillsides, these larger homes and estates continued to be built into the early 1900s. By this time, many of the lots available for purchase had long since been sold. Tuxedo Park grew in stature from the early cottages and family focus of Pierre Lorillard and his friends. Members, no longer satisfied with the founder's "rustic" intent, began building palatial mansions and gardens overlooking this bucolic wilderness. While recovering from his many bouts of illness, Mark Twain spent extended time on the porch of W.H. Neilson Voss, which directly overlooked Pigeon Point. Large estates were built at the top of the ridges such as the ones for the Frelinghuysen family designed by Colonel Francis L.V. Hoppen in 1903, and for the Carhart family designed by Trowbridge & Livingston in 1900.

Amory Carhart estate overlooking the Wee Wah Lake ca 1920

Before setting off on vacations in Europe, Newport, or Bar Harbor, members of the Tuxedo Club traditionally gathered for bathing and swimming activities at the TPA-created beach on Pigeon Point. At this beach, all recreational activities, including fishing, boating, hunting, and so forth were restricted to members of the Tuxedo Club and their guests. The beach was not available to those who worked for the families who were members of the Tuxedo Club or who otherwise owned property in the Park. Certainly no one from outside the gates could use the beach or swim in the lake, as they needed a pass to enter the gates, and those passes were issued only for work.

In an article for *The Century Magazine* in 1911, etiquette author and authority Emily Post, daughter of Tuxedo Park architect

Bruce Price, described the early days for club members:

> "By June 1, the summer season is in full swing. The center of social life now revolves about the tennis-courts. The bathing beach also has its hour every day when children duck and splash and swim—or small ones pretend to be ducks and pretend to swim. There may be found a water chute, a raft or two, and the usual number of anxious mothers of very young children who do not want to go in or cannot be made to come out."[19]

Charlie Jones teaching a Tuxedo Club member to swim, ca. 1900

There was an approximate forty-yard area of sand cleared for entering the lake from the shore and a dock on the southwest side of the point. As with a natural beach, the sandy bottom gradually deepened, but here at the Wee Wah Lake, the swimming areas were divided by wooden structures and platforms. Log borders like telephone poles were lowered into the water as the season approached to create the boundaries, providing safety and resting points for bathers. The embankment was sanded and graded with wide stone steps leading down to the water.

Much as the social set had their private beaches in Newport, Southampton, and Bar Harbor, swimming and water sports were certainly a mainstay of Lorillard's plan for his "recreational" preserve. In Newport, the old guard initially used Easton's Beach that was an easy stroll from the Cliff Walk on the ocean side of the great mansions. In the 1890s, trolley service was extended to Easton's Beach, providing access to the public. Soon thereafter, the social set relocated beyond the trolley stop and formed an exclusive club at Bailey's Beach.[20] At Tuxedo Park, lake swimming, diving, and canoeing were all the rage. It was expected that all would take advantage of the cool, clear water of the Wee Wah that worked its way down from Tuxedo Lake where the water was pure enough to constitute the drinking water for the Park and the village. As late as the summer of 1907, the annual Tuxedo Club water sports event on July 17th at Wee Wah Lake still garnered a column in the *New York Times* describing the day's events and naming the winners.[21]

Chief of Police Gilmore O. Bush observing the annual swim day races at the
Wee Wah, 1907

These well-attended events involved bragging rights and
extensive gambling. The founder had always been active with horse
racing and yachting competitions. Mrs. Winthrop Chanler described,
"There was a great deal of big poker playing at the Club by the men."[22]
Gambling carried over to all the sporting events. The contests at Wee
Wah Beach included canoe tilting, in which Clarence Pell and Pierre
Lorillard defeated P. Kent and R. Mortimer Jr., swimming races for
girls, mixed doubles canoe racing, underwater races, egg with spoon
for men and girls (certainly no women would engage in these
competitions), sliding-down shoot (today we know it simply as a
slide), and the double canoe obstacle race. My personal favorite when
researching this was learning of the obstacle race described in the press
as down the shoot, swimming one hundred yards to a raft, putting on a
shirt, lighting a cigar, and returning the one hundred yards to the shore

with the cigar still lit. Tuxedo Park Police Chief Gilmore O. Bush acted as the sole judge for the competition. Gambling was said to be customary with many of the male Club members in Tuxedo Park. These were men who ruled Wall Street or were in the habit of competing in business all their adult lives. At the billiard room and card room in the Tuxedo Club, and at various exclusive New York City clubs, competition between members was keen. One alleged bet by the founder Pierre Lorillard IV resulted in a post in the *New York Times*. It reported that lawyer John E. Parsons had received a telegram from Pierre Lorillard IV authorizing him to deny the story that Mr. Lorillard had lost $225,000 to Allen Thorndike Rice in baccarat at the Union Club as "without any foundation." This was 1887. In today's dollars, that would be approximately $5.6 million. [23]

Tuxedo Lake itself was bordered by a long stone dam on the north side. To one side was the main club and the bachelor annex. Further down the west side was the Tennis and Racquet Club. A large swim tank was constructed across from the Tuxedo Club for those who preferred the enjoyment of a swim but did not like the pleasures of the lake swimming area at the Wee Wah on Pigeon Point. The professionally staffed Tennis and Racquet Club also provided convenient access to refreshments, lounges, and changing rooms, all of which offered a comfortable and leisurely respite after vigorous matches of grass and clay tennis, indoor squash, racquets, as well as court tennis. Played indoors, court tennis originated over eighteen hundred years ago in England. Presently, approximately a dozen court tennis facilities remain in the United States. It is said that if you can learn the rules of the game and become a member of a club that has a court, you will soon become proficient enough to win a few matches and can become nationally ranked.

The original Tuxedo Club facility, while a beautifully designed structure for its time—and in keeping with Lorillard's original rustic plan—soon proved inadequate, given the size, the increasing number of members, and the burgeoning wealth of the members, particularly those who purchased lots and built grand new mansions around the turn of the twentieth century. The signature autumn ball, which signaled the beginning of the social calendar for New York society and where the name of the new formal jacket "tuxedo" was coined, needed a more substantial structure that fit the existing spectacular setting. During World War I, not only was there no autumn ball, but the main clubhouse was closed and demolished, while the activities were transferred to the winter clubhouse that had been used in colder months, as it was smaller and fitted with steam heat. Members soon concluded that the winter clubhouse was much too small for year-round use.

In 1926, construction began on the new main clubhouse, which opened in the spring of 1928. Designed by John Russell Pope, its long lines were in striking contrast to the well-designed but obsolete square wooden building it replaced. Built in the style of English country houses, the new building featured open terraces instead of porches, and a large new pool instead of the old swimming tank. Once the new clubhouse was completed, the winter clubhouse was torn down, as Pope's new building was designed for year-round use. With the new club coming, the swimming pool was built at a level area at the foot of a gentle slope coming down from the dam, allowing water to flow into a fish hatchery at the lower Pond Three. This design tied together both the main club and the tennis and racquet club a short distance away. Club members overwhelmingly opted for the beautiful Tuxedo Club pool and its well-appointed surroundings. There they could gather to enjoy the company of their peers and have access to poolside service of food and drink as they engaged in social gossip and otherwise escaped the pressures of the outside world. With the opening of the new pool, Club members deserted the idyllic but less convenient and less comfortable beach on Pigeon Point.

Chapter 7: Swimming at the Wee Wah

A gathering of the Tripicchio, Crisci, Belnado and Lombardi families from the Village outside Tuxedo Park, near the beach at Pigeon Point, with the Pigeon tower in the background, ca. 1920s

Until around the turn of the twentieth century, Italian residents of the East Village would swim in an area called the "Lucky" section of the Ramapo River, while the Slovak residents on the north end would use the upper falls area. Neither the river nor the upper falls were particularly safe, due to rapids and rocks, nor were they ideal for family outings because of the rough terrain. Officially at the time, these workers and their families were not allowed entrance to the Park after working hours or on weekends. They could not use the beach at the Wee Wah in the Park. At that time, all who lived outside the main gate were required to have passes to enter the gates into the Park, and they were only allowed entrance by invitation or when working on the estates.

The relative abandonment of the Wee Wah Beach by Tuxedo Club members in the early 1900s, due to their increased use of the swim tank at the Tuxedo Club, resulted in the beach area becoming a source of much relaxation and enjoyment for the families of Tuxedo Park workers and "domestics" (as they were referred to at the time), although formally they were prohibited from access to Pigeon Point. The beach offered a respite from the hot summers for individuals and their families. In addition, many of the Tuxedo Club families were not in residence during late July and August. Another likely factor in permitting or "overlooking" the use of the beach by the workers and their families was the familiar phrase "a happy staff makes for a happy house."

By the 1920s, the Gun Club on Pigeon Point was typically used in the spring and fall months. Now that swimming in Wee Wah Lake had fallen out of favor with the Club members, residents of the local area outside the gates consisting of the East Village populated by the Italian families on the south end, the Slovak families to the north, and the Hamlet comprised of homes surrounding the circle by the school that was later built in 1931, and continuing north to the main gate to Tuxedo Park, were finding ways to enter Tuxedo Park and gain access to Wee Wah Beach. Another section of homes from earlier times, just north of the main gate off Route 17 across from the historic Augusta Furnace, were also included in the Hamlet. By the early 1920s the estate workers in Tuxedo Park enjoyed easy access to the bathing area after hours for years without complaint.

My aunt, Marie McGregor McCarroll, who was the daughter

of Duncan McGregor (my grandfather and the superintendent, as well as the head gardener of George Grant Mason's Kincraig estate) recalled walking down the mountain as a young girl from Kincraig with her brothers and friends. To this day, Kincraig is still located at the top of Summit Road and looks out over all three lakes. Together the children followed the well-kept stone step paths winding through the Curtis and Spencer estates to Wee Wah Road as a shortcut to the beach where they would swim.

As years passed, those living in the Hamlet and East village became well known to the gate keepers. The automobile became common and affordable with the advent of Henry Ford's Model T. The pass system was frequently overlooked as the community activity from outside the gates increased at the beach area on Pigeon Point and family groups from the Hamlet and East Village would enjoy the aquatic activities. These original residents from the creation of Tuxedo who lived outside the gates now had families and grandchildren as well. My grandparents would tell me that they had learned, through gossip by the staffs of members, that there were many opinions discussed at the Tuxedo Club as to whether Wee Wah Beach should be accessible by those who lived and worked in the Hamlet as well as the East and Slovak Village outside the Park, accessible by staff who lived in the Park, or accessible only to those who owned homes within the gates of Tuxedo Park. Of course, formal permission was never granted, and discussions never reached the level of creating a policy; instead, the matter was left to the police and the Tuxedo Park Association, as the custom continued without any problems. The two distinct social levels did not interact, nor did they encounter each other in a way that appeared to threaten the social status. Together with "some assistance" from the Tuxedo Park Association, which was comprised of workers who obviously were not members of the Tuxedo Club, the "bathing community" maintained and improved the facility.

As stated, the Tuxedo Park Association was the company Lorillard used to develop, operate, avoid liability issues, and maintain the infrastructure of Tuxedo Park. In 1924, the Lorillard family sold the company that included the land and buildings to a group of Tuxedo Park Club members who were, of course, also Tuxedo Park property owners.

Those from the Hamlet who worked in the Park could detour on their way home after work for a swim in the lake, but it was not a usual occurrence until the late 1920s and early 30s. With automobiles becoming more affordable by the 1930s, Hamlet families were driving cars and finding their way through the gates to swim at the Wee Wah, although they were not formally allowed to do so. At this time, those working at the estates and cottages used the beach after hours, but their children used it daily during the summers. Throughout the 1920s there were no formal Wee Wah Lake activities for Tuxedo Club members. With the advent of the Tuxedo Club's swimming tank, and then the construction of the present-day pool, the Wee Wah Lake beach was left to those working in the Park who were allowed to use the southern end of the Pigeon Point peninsula to enjoy a respite from the day's labors and the occasional heat as a swimming beach of their own. My father and my Aunt Marie recalled crawling onto the original boundary logs left in place by the Tuxedo Park Association at the present site with friends Betty Dimerci, my uncles George and Duncan, as well as the Barth kids (my mother, and my uncles Jim, John, Bill, and my aunt Helen).

Children of estate staff, including James McGregor, (my father), and his sister, Marie, my aunt, ca. 1927. The Voss cottage, rented in the early 1900s by Mark Twain, is barely visible in the top left.

Workers from the Park easily walked the many paths leading through the estates to reach the point, and families from both the Park and the Hamlet picnicked on the weekends. It was common to hear the shrieks and sounds of happy children enjoying summers at the beach. The fact that this beach recreation area was being used, despite its historic restriction to Tuxedo Club members, was not lost on the teenage and adult beachgoers, who understood one day the police might come and prohibit their otherwise carefree enjoyment of this TPA property. As times changed, cracks in the social stratification of this Gilded Age stronghold were emerging.

Chapter 8: The Social Set

A Day inside Tuxedo Park at the Racetrack in the 1920s

Initially, much of New York's wealthy, upper-crust society
hailed from families with roots that could be traced back to the
founding of American settlements in the 1600s. It's no secret that their
money largely derived from real estate. The Pell family, for example,
beginning with Thomas Pell, originally owned the property that
became the Bronx, along with towns in Westchester County. As the
country experienced a massive change in economic and financial
growth after the Civil War and entering the twentieth century, a level
of aristocratic society and wealth derived from the Industrial Age. In

addition to the landed gentry of Dutch and English descent who bought into Lorillard's Tuxedo Club, there were the financiers and industrialists of the day who, thanks to their wealth and influence, could marry into the successful families with historic pedigrees. There was both the society of inherited money and those with new wealth trying to enter that society. For those who may have watched the first season of Julian Fellowes's *The Gilded Age*, there could be no better example than the attempts by Bertha and George Russell to enter the circle of families receiving the social blessings of Mrs. Caroline Astor. The mix was forged in the many elite men's clubs existing in New York City at the turn of the twentieth century. The clubs served as a welcoming home for those who had no need or desire to work, and a stopping point for those leaving their offices after the workday before heading uptown to their grand homes. The resumes of the men of these aristocratic families all listed membership in numerous private clubs. As an example, Robert Goelet, an original Tuxedo Club member, was also an original stockholder of the Metropolitan Opera, a member of the Philadelphia Club, the New York Yacht Club, the Racquet Club, the American Fine Arts Society, the Up-Town Association, the Republican Club, the Players, the Southside Sportsman Club, Holland Society, the Knickerbocker Club, the Metropolitan Club, the Union Club of the City of New York, Columbia College Alumni Association, the Manuscript Club, the Tandem Club, the Philadelphia Club, the Metropolitan Club of Washington, the Royal Circle Yacht Club, the Royal Northern Yacht Club of Glasgow, and the Jekyll Island Club in coastal Georgia.[24]

In 1913, the United States Government instituted the federal income tax. This also provided opportunities for tax and trust lawyers to expand their Wall Street practices, helping ensure the wealthy could avoid as much of the new tax as legally possible. Together with President Theodore Roosevelt's trust-busting efforts in the early 1900s, and the Great War in 1917, these issues were of great importance to the members of the Tuxedo Club. Of course, many maintained residences in New York City, with additional vacation homes up and down the East Coast from Bar Harbor, Maine and Newport, Rhode Island, all the way to Palm Beach, Florida.

During the "Roaring Twenties," and despite Prohibition (1920--1933), Tuxedo Park remained a reminder that the social elite did not endure much change to their lifestyles from year to year, despite cultural and economic changes beyond the gates. There was no shortage of whiskey at the Club or in the homes where alcohol and the best wines were generously served. The houses were bigger, and the cars were unique, noticeably different from Fords or other brands marketed to the masses.

To some extent, this extravagant style of wealth diminished for many with the stock market crash of 1929 and the Great Depression that followed. Indeed, some in Tuxedo Park lost their fortunes in the crash, which caused them to lose their homes and businesses, and needless to say, several took desperate, tragic actions. Colonel Frank B. Keech, a Wall Street broker, was indicted for an intentional fire started by his chauffeur that destroyed his $200,000 mansion in Tuxedo Park in 1932. Keech later threw himself in front of a subway train rather than face trial for arson.[25]

The notorious stock market crash occurred in October 1929, but the country as a whole did not experience the most devastating results of the crash until the early 1930s. As the 1930s continued, the worst of the Depression eased, but Tuxedo Park suffered in a different way. The expense of operating a country home and finding staff became much more difficult. In-house women workers such as maids, cooks, and housekeepers left for the city to find work—and husbands. During this trying time, the men were finding jobs in factories springing up in areas outside of New York City. Some mansions were left vacant, and taxes went unpaid. Even so, Tuxedo Park still had its share of social elite who were able to continue a life of what some would call "American Royalty." Their ability to maintain their massive country estates allowed the Tuxedo Park community to escape the bread lines and devastation we associate with the Great Depression. The Park continued to employ those outside the gates and life went on. Summers meant opportunities for both communities to gather and enjoy separative activities "at the beach" or at the Tuxedo Club pool for those who were members. Automobile ownership had become increasingly common, and the Tuxedo community was changing. Men and women who served Tuxedo Park residents were now some forty years old, with a second generation fast approaching adulthood. The local staff still employed on the estates, and the service community outside the gates, took a more formal approach to the use of what they began to consider *"their"* swimming and picnicking site on Pigeon Point.

In the early 1930s, the demographics of those swimming at the beach was not the most talked about subject in the card and billiard rooms or at the dinner tables in the Tuxedo Club. Despite more government-related interference—taxes, the Depression, and regulations—there was not much of an impact on most of the members who had lived through the Gilded Age at the turn of the century. In the

1920s, extravagance and financial wealth had continued to increase by leaps and bounds. Overall, the Great Depression did not have a major effect upon most who lived in Tuxedo Park. Those who lived in the Hamlet outside the gates were not wealthy, but their work continued and they did not suffer the fate of the bread lines and loss suffered by those in the cities and across the country. Of course, there were some extremely wealthy residents of the Park who lost their fortunes as a result of the stock market crash. As the 1930s continued, the Great Depression resulted in some estates no longer being able to support the large numbers of in-house staff, or the men to work on the estates and their extensive gardens. Change was underway across America, and it was affecting both rich and poor. In the early 1930s, one issue in Tuxedo arose that emphasized the formalized social structure of the overall community and resulted in tension between the residents of Tuxedo Park and those who worked for them both in the Park and in the Hamlet.

To fully understand the history of the Wee Wah Beach Club, one must explore and understand the divisions of society in America that emerged once the country became independent after the Revolutionary War. While independence meant there was no longer a monarchy that ruled the people, the structure and daily activities of establishing order and rules remained basically unchanged in the Northeast. State and local governments were formed, creating a class of public leadership. However, this leadership class was almost totally reserved for landowners and families of wealth. The wealth derived from former land grants by the king, from the formation of companies that brought settlers to the new colonies, and from Old World businesses that expanded in the colonies.

After the American Revolution, only men could vote for representatives to serve the public but, as to those elected, the vast majority of public servants in decision-making positions were controlled by the wealthy men who lived in a class much different than the fast-growing population of the Northeastern states. Essentially, the peerage system of the British aristocracy continued to exist. In the place of appointments by the king, a limited number of male landowners had the opportunity to elect their local and state governments. As we know from the Constitution and the Bill of Rights, laws were enacted to control the power of elected officials to prevent tyranny and abuse. However, (much like today) many elected officials were beholden to those who were rich and powerful.

As the country grew in population, the reality of daily life changed radically, but class distinctions persisted. In fact, until the end of the Civil War, the separation of rich and poor could be defined in simple terms. In the South, there were plantation owners, merchants, poor whites, and slaves. In the North, there were landowners through inheritance, merchants, a fast-growing working class, and laborers. Following the Civil War, families in what became known as "society" or the "upper crust," and their children who were educated at the finest preparatory schools and universities, moved into positions of political power or chose those who would represent the populace. Laws were enacted for the general welfare and orderliness of society, but laws related to finance, business, and opportunities to become rich or remain rich, were left to those already well-entrenched. A rising tide of immigrants arrived in search of a new life in the land of opportunity and freedom, thus creating rapid changes in American society. This change would bring about a segment of the population that would later become America's "middle class."

In the early years of Tuxedo, social division was obvious to all. Allison Davis, in *Social Class Influences About Learning* (Harvard University Press, 1948), wrote, "Social classes essentially maintain barriers against intimate social participation. Those individuals, families, and social cliques which refer to each other in popular language as 'nice' or 'respectable' seldom have any intimate association, at work or in their homes, with any people from those families which are vulgarly called 'common,' 'ignorant,' or 'low.' People from the 'wrong side of the tracks' have no intimate association in any form as equals, with people 'from the right side of the tracks.'"[26]

By 1930, the so-called "melting pot," as it's often referred to in our country's history, was becoming evident in Tuxedo, as many of the children of the original families that worked and serviced Tuxedo Club members with homes in the Park began to finish high school. After graduation, many of these children went on to college or were offered jobs at Wall Street firms and banks run by Tuxedo Park residents. The beginning of what had become known as the Wee Wah Beach Club is best understood by reflecting on the social structure within Tuxedo Park during the first thirty years after its creation by Pierre Lorillard in 1886. This small community was created as a recreational diversion for the upper-most society of New York City, who, during this period, were somewhat synonymous with the incredible economic growth taking place across the country. Banking, railroads, shipping, steel, oil, and the rise of Wall Street now created great fortunes, and those that made them found acceptability in the

circles of those whose wealth was inherited from large land holdings
from the time of the creation of the republic, or from men who profited
from the beginnings of the Industrial Revolution. The separation
between this upper crust of society and the remaining populace of New
York City was evident in the growth of the city by a northern
movement of the rich and their mansions from those originally in
Washington Square in Greenwich Village, north to the streets
numbered in the thirties, to Fifth Avenue between fortieth and fiftieth
streets, and then further north toward the opulence of the mansions
bordering Central Park and Fifth Avenue above Fifty-seventh Street,
many of which still exist today. The general population was
entertained in the press daily with the comings and goings of this
society, which was comprised of many of the wealthiest families in
America.

From the late 1800s until the early 1950s, Tuxedo Park
remained a moderated "tale of two cities," with many layers of social
structure, but with a distinct division between property owners in
Tuxedo Park, who were also Tuxedo Club members, and the rest of the
community. Consider the upbringing and lives of Mrs. Elizabeth Mary
Thompson Cannon Frelinghuysen, George Grant Mason, and Duncan
McGregor, who were representatives of the main social classes present
in the Park. Mrs. Frelinghuysen, or "Lily" as she was called, was the
wife of Theodore Frelinghuysen. Her father, William G. Thompson,
was a lawyer and served as Mayor of Detroit. Throughout her life, Lily
lived a life of wealth and privilege comparable to European royalty.
The family tree of Lily's second husband, Theodore Frelinghuysen,
traces back to the 1720s when they emigrated from Germany to the
British colony of New Jersey. Theirs was "old money." After the Civil

War, a new breed of industrialists, bankers, and financiers created vast fortunes and, in many cases, married into the "old money" group. They were called capitalists. George Grant Mason, also a Tuxedo Club member, was not wealthy as a young man, but he inherited a fortune from his uncle, who was successful in Wall Street and owned an estate in Tuxedo Park until his untimely death. By the late 1800s, the push west and the new industrialization required workers. Immigration brought in a new class of people like my grandfather, Duncan McGregor, seeking to secure a better life in this new land. Duncan came from Scotland and became the head gardener and superintendent at Kincraig, Mason's Tuxedo Park estate.

As for myself, I spent my early years growing up in Tuxedo Park living in a corner garage apartment with my parents across from the apartment of my father's parents, his brothers, and sister located on Mason's estate. My mother's parents and her brothers and sister lived approximately a mile south along the west side of Tuxedo Lake in a gardener's cottage owned by the Renamor estate of George Amory. Exploring the lives of these Tuxedo Park residents sheds light on the social attitudes that led to the Wee Wah Beach Club, and how this "Tuxedo society" continued for the rest of the twentieth century and into the twenty-first century.

Chapter 9: Mrs. Theodore Frelinghuysen

Mrs. "Lily" Elizabeth Mary Thompson Cannon Frelinghuysen, (1871–1967)

From its inception, Tuxedo Park became a microcosm of the separation of classes, with the two groups living vastly different lives, yet existing nearly side by side: the wealthy, and those of humble means who worked for and served them. An example of the former can be described by the entry of Mrs. Theodore Frelinghuysen into Tuxedo Park.

Elizabeth, "Lily" Mary Thompson was an only child born in 1871 to William G. Thompson, Mayor of Detroit; and his wife, Adelaide Mary Brush, the daughter of Mr. and Mrs. Edmund A. Brush, who were prominent members of Detroit society. In her privileged early life, Lily was attended to by nannies and governesses. She attended the traditional social events in Detroit, Washington, and New York. Lily was reported to be a beautiful young woman who made her debut in Detroit.

In 1888, Lily traveled abroad for fifteen months, chaperoned by her grandmother. For those who have seen the highly praised Public Broadcasting Service (PBS) series, *Downton Abbey*, this was not unusual at the time, as many British aristocrats were seeing their fortunes decline, and American society members were seeking titles of royalty for their daughters. One may recall Cora's grandmother's performances in the PBS television series, played by Shirley McClain. Art imitates life, in this instance, as it was reported by the *Pittsburgh Post* in November 1889:

> "It is announced by cable from Berlin that Miss Elizabeth Thompson, the Detroit heiress, is to wed, in the coming spring, Count von Kleist, of the German army… Miss Thompson, who has been abroad for the past 15 months, under the chaperonage of her grandmother, Mrs. Elizabeth Brush, is rated to be worth between $2,000,000 and $3,000,000, inherited through her mother and a daughter of the late E. A. Brush of Detroit. Miss Thompson is of creole descent, in her

nineteenth year, is a petite blond and quite pretty. She is well known in Washington society circles."[27]

Apparently, the Count and Lily, or perhaps her grandmother and family, found the flame did not burn that brightly and Lily, unwed, returned to America to live with her grandmother, who purchased a home on Fifth Avenue in New York City. Here there were relatives, well-known in fashion and New York Society, who could make the proper introductions for her granddaughter. As a result of her beauty and pedigree, Lily soon became prominent in the New York social scene. She attended coming out parties for other young women of similar means and families, such as the Havemeyer sisters, who were the daughters of H.O. Havemeyer, who controlled the sugar industry by creating the American Sugar Refining Company (the Sugar Trust). Havemeyer was a Tuxedo Club member who owned a large estate in Tuxedo Park.

These parties were attended by the wealthiest young men and women in the city. These were mostly held at New York City family residences, which could easily accommodate from 200 to 400 guests for dinner and ballroom dancing. It was also not unusual for there to be smaller dinner parties prior to the coming out parties. Before the coming out party for the Havemeyer girls, Mrs. Brush gave a dinner party at her residence in New York. Of the 10 young people at the table, there was a very handsome young man, Henry LeGrand Cannon.[28] Cannon's family was from Burlington, Vermont and owned the Lake Champlain Transportation Company.

A mere four months later, Mrs. Brush gave another more formal dinner party for Lily, as the reason was much more significant. On Saturday evening, May 26, this twenty-course dinner, with an orchestra and dancing, celebrated the bridal party of Lily Thompson and Henry LeGrand Cannon. Lily's father was absent, as he was giving a large dinner party at the Manhattan Club to gentlemen from Detroit, who were to be guests at the wedding.

Shortly thereafter, on Sunday, June 9, 1891, Miss Elizabeth Mary Thompson walked down the aisle on the arm of her father at St. Thomas Church in New York City to become the bride of Mr. Henry LeGrand Cannon.

The crowds outside the Church were kept back by a large contingent of police. Fifth Avenue traffic was halted as the carriages formed a procession after the ceremony to the Cutting mansion at 101 Fifth Avenue for the reception of 250, where an English breakfast was served. In the late afternoon the couple went aboard a steam yacht for a sail up the Hudson River. Later in the month they travelled to the Cannon estate in Burlington, Vermont.

The *Detroit Free Press* had called their June 9, 1891 wedding "one of the important events of the kind that Summer." The newspaper said that Cannon was "well known as an artist, and especially so as a clubman."[29]

The recent television production, *The Gilded Age,* well captures the recorded history from this period in American history. As an example, The *Boston Globe* reported how the honeymoon would be spent at Mr. Legrand B. Cannon's beautiful place near Burlington, Vermont, noting that preparations had been made for their arrival and that a dinner would be given to the working people "after the manner of wedding festivities for the tenantry on great English estates."[30]

After returning to New York City, the couple sailed for Europe on June 25, 1891. There they took a four-month coaching tour through

England, and then toured the Continent, before returning home to reside with Henry's father, Col. LeGrand Cannon at 311 Fifth Avenue.

When Henry and Lily returned to New York City, another interesting change took place. Prior to his marriage, Henry LeGrand Cannon was a handsome young man who was sought after by the younger set. He attracted the attention and acceptance of Mrs. Astor, who directed her social gatekeeper, Ward McAllister, to welcome Henry into her group of 400. In late 1891, Henry apparently attempted a coup to replace McAllister as the leader of society. In the past, Henry was given the important social role of the leader of the cotillion to arrange the dancing at various balls attended by society. In December of 1891, "Ward McAllister proved that in spite of all efforts to remove him from his throne, he still wielded the scepter. Using Henry's recent marriage as an excuse, McAllister replaced him, and he was now just another face in the background."[31]

They returned to New York City after their honeymoon, only to discover that lower Fifth Avenue in New York City had changed. Newer mansions of the Gilded Age were being built further up the Avenue and commerce was closing in above Washington Square. Yet on June 15, 1890, the *New York Times* reported "The property at 60 Fifth Avenue, having a frontage of two full lots, was sold for $160,000. This price would have been considered very low a few years ago, but since Fifth Avenue below Fourteenth Street is now well out of the line of travel, it is quite as good a price as could be expected."[32]

Mintern Mansion, ca. 1900

The family had purchased the house in 1890 for the soon-to-become newlyweds. The pair would have two children, a girl and a boy. Life appeared to be good for the couple, despite their significant age difference. When their first child, Elizabeth Adelaide Cannon, was born in New York on April 28, 1892, her father, Henry Legrand Cannon, was thirty-five years old, and her mother, Elizabeth Mary Thompson, was twenty-one.

On January 13, 1893, 225 guests filled the drawing rooms at the home as Harry Le Grand Cannon hosted a "private salon concert" by the entire Boston Symphony Orchestra. It was the second of a series of such events in the house. "The large drawing rooms and adjacent halls of the mansion … proved admirably adapted to the large orchestra," said the *New York Times* the following day. The guest list included the most elite names in New York and Tuxedo Park society, including Fish, Havemeyer, Iselin, Kernochan, Sloane, Schuyler, Townsend, Vanderbilt, Whitney, Oelrichs, Burden, Alexander, Clews, and Mrs. John Minturn.[33]

The handsome couple stood atop New York Society, and given her young age, one can understand how Lily carried herself as we see her unforeseen future unfold—overlooking Tuxedo Park from her mansion on the hill. While Lily would go on to live a long life, her seemingly wonderful society marriage ended tragically just five years later. After a short illness, Henry passed away at home from what was referred to as an abscess of the brain. On May 6, 1895, Lily was left a widow with two young children, Elizabeth Adelaide and Le Grand B. Cannon.[34]

New York mourned, as Henry LeGrand Cannon was well-known for more than his wealth and position; he had been an active vestryman at the Church of the Ascension and was active in the East Side Mission and other charity work. He was thirty-eight years old. Elizabeth Mary Thompson Cannon now found herself, at twenty-four years of age, to be an heiress but also a widow and mother traveling in a society scene comprised of the oldest families of New York City, Newport, Tuxedo Park, and other vacation enclaves of the rich.

Theodore Frelinghuysen was born in 1865 to one of the most prominent families in America, and the singularly most prominent family in New Jersey. The Frelinghuysen roots date back to pre-revolutionary times. The Frelinghuysen family earned a number six spot on the *Washington Post*'s "America's Top Dynasty" behind the John Adams family (two former Presidents) at number five, and the Prescott Bush family, which would later include two presidents and a Florida governor in its family tree, at number seven. Reverend

Theodorus Frelinghuysen came to America from Holland in 1720 and settled in Raritan, the British colony of New Jersey. His grandson Frederick born in 1753, became a lawyer and was a member of the Continental Congress. President George Washington appointed him Brigadier General in the United States Army for the 1790 campaign against the western Indians. He was elected to the United States Senate and served from March 4, 1793, to November 12, 1796. He died in 1804, leaving three sons who had been born in quick succession: John (1776), Theodore (1777), and Frederick T. (1788).

The family quickly branched out into politics and business. John followed in his father's footsteps and became a Brigadier General in the War of 1812. Frederick T. died at 32, leaving a young son, also named Frederick Theodore, who was adopted by his Uncle Theodore. This Theodore had no children and was a lawyer appointed the Attorney General of New Jersey. He was elected to the US Senate in 1829 and later married Matilda Griswold in 1842. Together they had three daughters and three sons, Frederick, George Griswold, and Theodore. He returned as Mayor of the newly incorporated City of Newark and later was chosen as the Chancellor of the University of New York. In 1844 he was nominated as the Vice President of the Whig party to run with Henry Clay, and after losing, his uncle once again returned to New Jersey and accepted the position of President of Rutgers College, the State University of New Jersey.

Frederick Theodore followed in the footsteps of his uncle, Theodore, who had adopted and raised him. Frederick Theodore graduated from Rutgers College and studied law under his uncle. He entered public service, becoming City Attorney for Newark, and was elected to a seat on the City Council. He would later be appointed

Attorney General of New Jersey, as had his adopted father before him, and served this position during the Civil War, only to resign to fill a seat in the US Senate. Reelected from 1871–1877, he was later appointed Secretary of State when Chester A. Arthur became President upon James Garfield's assassination in 1881.

As this political and social dynasty continued to grow, Theodore was born in 1865. His brothers Frederick and George entered the business world. As the new twentieth century began, Frederick became an attorney and was soon a counselor to a number of financial institutions, including the Mutual Benefit Life Insurance Company. George Griswold Frelinghuysen received his law degree from Columbia University and became a patent lawyer, eventually working for and becoming President of P. Ballantine & Sons, one of the largest brewing companies in the Northeast. No doubt his rise in some measure resulted from his marriage to Sara L. Ballantine in 1881. His cousin Joseph (1869–1948) carried on the political tradition. He too served in the US Senate, from 1917 to 1923, and was a close friend, golfing partner, and confidante of his Senate colleague and future United States President, Warren G. Harding. Theodore and his cousin Joseph remained close, as both maintained winter homes in Palm Beach.

Theodore entered the coal business in Pennsylvania, and then became involved with the Coats Thread business, soon to become one of the largest thread manufacturers in the world. Theodore joined the Spool Cotton Company of New York and quickly assumed the role of treasurer after his marriage to James Coats's daughter in 1885. Reported as a very handsome and socially adept young man just out of his teen years, he was a member of all the right private clubs. He made the acquaintance of Alice Coats, four years his senior. Alice Dudley Coats was the daughter of Sir James Coats, 1st Baronet of Auchendrane, and Sarah Ann Auchincloss. Her mother was an Auchincloss, a family firmly entrenched in New England society. After a suitable period of engagement, Alice married Theodore Frelinghuysen, son of Hon. Frederick Frelinghuysen, on Tuesday, August 25, 1885, a ceremony attended by former President Chester A. Arthur. Theodore's father, Frederick T Frelinghuysen, died in May and was Arthur's Secretary of State. As a result, the families had not wanted to stage an elaborate wedding; however, the *Burlington Free Press* (Burlington, Vermont) on page one headlined, "A Brilliant Social Event" in its August 27th edition, calling the wedding the leading event of the Newport, Rhode Island season. Theodore's best man was his brother Frederick. The wedding gifts included diamonds from Mr. and Mrs. Coats and a large check from her father as well. "In the afternoon the couple left for Boston and then to New York, whence they will sail on Saturday on the Etruria for Scotland, and pass the honeymoon at her grandfather's, Sir Peter Coats, estate in Scotland." [35]

Tragedy struck this young couple as it had Lily and Henry Le Grand Cannon. After four years of marriage, Alice died on March 2, 1889.

Through his inheritance after Alice's death, and his own family wealth, Theodore was a very rich young man now working in New York, a member of all the clubs, and much sought after for parties, cotillions, and society events. Theodore remained a partner of the J. & P. Coats New York agency. J. & P. Coats grew into the largest textile company and third largest manufacturing company in Britain by 1905, and the largest textile company in the world by 1912. Theodore, now a widower, was one of the most eligible men in New York society circles.

After an appropriate period of mourning of Harry's death in 1895 by Lily Cannon, the stars seemed aligned for Lily and Theodore. A handsome widower and a beautiful widow traveling in the same social circles resulted in a relationship that led to marriage in 1898. Elizabeth and Theodore married in Grace Church where "about 100 people, many of them prominent in New York society," gathered "to witness one of the most fashionable and at the same time one of the most unostentatious church weddings of the year. … The guests adjourned to the bride's home, at 60 Fifth Avenue, where Mr. and Mrs. Frelinghuysen will probably live, and a wedding reception took place there," said The *New York Times*.[36] The June wedding was well attended by the society of the day, including many who were residents of Tuxedo Park and, as required, members of the Tuxedo Club.

Having secured the company's position in the U.S., Theodore remained treasurer of the Spool Cotton Company until 1911, but his marriage and social events began to occupy more of his time. Now married to Theodore, Elizabeth was determined to establish her place in the upper circle at the top of the matriarchal society structure originally controlled by Mrs. Astor and Mrs. Vanderbilt. This was "old money," as they say, and during the mid-1880s, upper-class society considered New York City to be "home," with the summer seasons, as previously mentioned, focused on Bar Harbor, Maine; Newport, Rhode Island; Lenox, Massachusetts; and Southampton on the southeastern tip of Long Island. Tuxedo Park, thanks in part to its easy accessibility, had also become a locale for fall and winter recreation, as well as parties and gaiety. Parties were held on a continual basis, and many invited guests would ultimately purchase their own properties in the wonderful Tuxedo Club community. The men would commute to their offices on Wall Street.

However, a change took place after the first ten years in Tuxedo Park. In the late 1890s, old money, like that of the Goelet family, was joining with the new money of those referred to as "capitalists." This occurred because of the capitalist's incredible wealth created by population increase, expansion of the country, and the development of great new industries after the Civil War. Carnegie revolutionized steel. Rockefeller, Rodgers, and Pratt created Standard Oil. J.P. Morgan and numerous others were dynamically changing the banking and investment business centered around Wall Street. "New names" with incredible wealth were now being recognized. Society opened its doors to this new wealth and the resulting marriages that followed. At the turn of the century in Tuxedo Park, large tracts of land were available for purchase, and stately mansions of unique architectural design were built more toward the style of Newport than the style of the original cottages. Despite their size and the immense costs associated with building and maintenance, these homes would be used sparingly. There was a French chateau, an Italian villa, English Tudor manor houses, and a Scottish castle built of rough-hewed stone, to name just a few.

Tuxedo Park had become very fashionable. The Frelinghuysens were frequent guests of social friends and blood relations such as the Griswold's, who were original residents of Tuxedo Park. Pierre Lorillard's mother was a Griswold, a mercantile family with an immense fortune with interests in the importation of rum, sugar, and tea. The Frelinghuysen family had also married into the

Griswold family, and thus were also related to the Lorillards. Lily wanted to be in Tuxedo Park, and not just in a small cottage. Elizabeth Mary "Lily" Frelinghuysen was quite a demanding woman and sought to reach a place at the very pinnacle of the society of the time. Shortly after the marriage, Lily began making plans for their "country cottage," which was to be a mansion more suited to the large new estates being built in Tuxedo Park. Her husband was one of the early members of the Tuxedo Club. Theodore was a dedicated clubman (as a member of all the right clubs), related to and friendly with George Griswold, an original member of the Lorillard family group. For his and Lily's intended estate, Frelinghuysen purchased a six-acre lot on the east hilltop overlooking Wee Wah Lake.

Theodore Frelinghuysen (left) and his brother Fred at a horse show in Tuxedo Park, ca. 1920s

Their Tuxedo Park home would not be like one of the earlier Bruce Price cottages, but instead, a mansion like those in Newport, and like one Lily later built in the then-new community of Palm Beach. The Frelinghuysens were familiar with the work of Colonel Francis L.V. Hoppin, who designed nearby Tuxedo Park estates such as the Charles W. Cooper house built in 1900. Francis Hoppin apprenticed with McKim, Mead and White, the most prominent architectural firm in New York and very active in designing estates in Tuxedo Park. The mansion, built in 1903, offered extensive views across the lake-filled valley, and the sunsets to the west directly over Wee Wah Lake. This was the residence of Theodore and Elizabeth Frelinghuysen.

The Frelinghuysen Estate, ca. 1904

The views to the west from the back of the residence, set on a precipice of rock overlooking Wee Wah Lake, were spectacular. The peacefulness of these commanding views of nature would take your breath away. Below, on Pigeon Point jutting out into the Wee Wah was the original setting of the Tuxedo Club beach. By the 1920s, the beach was becoming used mainly by the children of staff who lived in the Park, but only late on the day after Club members had returned to their homes. Following construction of the new Tuxedo Club and pool in 1928, the beach simply was no longer used by Tuxedo Club members. "After the working day" it became common beginning in 1928, and continuing into the 1930s, for employees and staff working on the estates to use the beach to escape the rigors of the day and the summer heat at day's end before heading home. After all, life in Tuxedo Park revolved around spring and fall, with a brief winter period for the Tuxedo Club members. After the turn of the century, Club members primarily spent the early months of the year in the newly developed resort of Palm Beach, and spent their summers in Newport, Bar Harbor, or Southampton, and sailing abroad. There were those like Theodore Frelinghuysen, who worked in the city, but even with their home in New York City, they preferred the New Jersey locations of Long Branch and inland country estates in the summers. After all, the Frelinghuysen family was a New Jersey dynasty.

From the beginning, and up to the turn of the century, most of the cottages inhabited by the early members of the Tuxedo Club had kitchens that were supplied with ice for their refrigeration from the TPA icehouse. Other than grand parties, most dining occurred at the Club.

As many of the large newer houses were built in the early 1900s, as stated previously, these properties were more properly called "mansions," and featured elaborate kitchens that required a staff. The need for ice increased, and so a much larger facility was constructed at Pigeon Point on the northwest side of Wee Wah Lake. This also served as a maintenance area for the Tuxedo Park Association but could not be seen by the mansions above on the east side of the lake. Without getting into a modern-day argument over global warming, suffice it to say that the community could always depend on the winter months to freeze the lakes to a depth where large blocks of ice could be cut and stored for use during the rest of the year. Of course, America was now developing new inventions that reduced dependence on Mother Nature. Tuxedo Park was one of the first communities to have electricity and telephones. As electricity became more common, refrigerators replaced the need for iceboxes. Some Park residents remained wedded to the past, creating a substantial period where automobiles and horse-drawn carriages shared the roads, but those building their mansions in the new century were anxious to meld the new modern conveniences into their lives and into their homes. The owners could afford them and, just as today, one could boast of their latest acquisitions. These changing times are reflected in the correspondences of Theodore Frelinghuysen. No expense was spared for Lily's country home, as indicated by Theodore's letter reflecting on the installation of the new refrigeration systems of the day. On September 12, 1907, he wrote to the Brunswick Refrigerating Company from his office at the Spool Cotton Company at 80-82 White Street in New York City:

Henry Flagler was a former executive with H.H. Rodgers and Henry Tilford (both Tuxedo Club members and residents) in John D. Rockefeller's Standard Oil. Flagler left the company when President Theodore Roosevelt succeeded in breaking up the Standard Oil Trust. Always fascinated with railroads, Flagler created a railroad from the Northeast into Florida at Jacksonville. He then extended this line to St Augustine, where he built a grand hotel. Next came Palm Beach, as he developed a resort hotel and sold property to his wealthy friends. Once the house in Tuxedo Park was completed, Lily set her sights on Palm Beach as well. They moved on to Palm Beach for winters after the customary New Year's parties in Tuxedo Park. Now that she and her husband were already a part of the Fifth Avenue-Tuxedo Park social set, Mrs. Frelinghuysen again retained Colonel Francis L.V. Hoppin as the architect to build a Palm Beach estate she named, Southways, the family's winter home—and by far the most prominent residence in Palm Beach at the time.

President Warren G. Harding visited the island of Palm Beach in 1923 on the Presidential yacht and was reportedly entertained at Southways. As a result, the cottage colony began calling the house "The Winter White House," a moniker that endures today used by another mansion owned by a more recent resident of Palm Beach. The widower and the widow became bold-faced names on the Social Register's timetable of dog shows, horse shows, and dinner parties.

Theodore Frelinghuysen died in 1928, but his wife kept both the home in Tuxedo Park and Southways for another forty years, until her death in 1967. The *New York Times* referred to her as a "grande dame of a bygone era."[38] A widow once again, Lily spent her time enjoying summers in Tuxedo Park and her winters in Palm Beach, always maintaining her position at the top of the social ladder. Mrs. Frelinghuysen was certainly one of the more important women in high society and a mainstay of the party circuit well into the 1930s. Known for her formality, she believed in carrying on the traditions and customs of top society dating back to the turn of the century. My grandmother and Aunt Marie both recalled the stories told at card games and social events with staff from the other houses in the Park in the early days. A favorite was that Mrs. Frelinghuysen avoided the use of toilet paper and required linen instead for her toilette.

If it was a horse show, all the judges would dine at the Frelinghuysen mansion. It is said that as automobiles became more common in Tuxedo Park as the twentieth century began, she would crack her whip at them as they drove past her in her small carriage. I am sure that in Lily's opinion, motorcars were noisy, disturbed the serenity of the Park, and certainly were not suitable for women. One can only imagine her opinion of women, many of whom had been invitees to her own parties in the early years, as they took to the roads driving coaches, now fashionable as a sport. As described in the April 19, 1903, edition of the *New York Times*, in the Teacup Tattle column on the social gossip page: "One of the sensations of the week has been the taking of the coach Pioneer by the Ladies' Driving Club. This club owes its existence to the coaching fad two years ago. Among the most enthusiastic members are Mrs. Thomas Hastings, Mrs. Roche, the Misses Gerry, Mrs. Harry Paine Whitney, Mrs. Lee Tailer, Mrs. Jules Vatable, and others of the Tuxedo and Saratoga racing sets. ..."[39] Such was the pedigree and lifestyle of society's upper tier.

Lily spent early summers in her Tuxedo Park home arranging and giving parties, coordinating the June horse and dog show activities, and relaxing on the porch for afternoon tea and visits from friends. Mrs. Astor's 400 were long gone, but Lily Frelinghuysen continued to live in the style to which she had been accustomed her entire privileged life. The early 1920s saw a change in the lifestyle of Tuxedo Park. The Wall Street crash of 1929 was yet to occur. However, the result of income taxes and the trust busting of Teddy Roosevelt was having an effect. These events did change Tuxedo Park but not the lifestyle of Mrs. Frelinghuysen. Large house parties continued, as did ostentatious consumption, and the maintenance of the estates went along uninterrupted. However, the original staff and those that had built, serviced, and maintained Tuxedo Park were now raising their own families, with these children now reaching their teenage years and early adulthood. Times were changing, but not so for Lily Frelinghuysen, whose social set remained tied to the customs and fashion of an earlier time.

Chapter 10: The Rumor Leads to North Beach

Note on photo reflects Bessie, Francie, & Mabel Jones (Mabel would marry
Joe Tansey and later become a longtime president of the Wee Wah Beach
Club), Dick & Violet Dodd, and Eileen at the "new beach," ca. early 1930s

As previously noted, with the completion of the new Tuxedo
Club pool, members had deserted the beach at the Wee Wah, so during
the summer months, those outside the gates who worked in or served
the Park, as well as outside "help" living on the estates, along with

their families, largely had the beach to themselves. Apparently, this did not sit well with Mrs. Frelinghuysen, who, it's safe to say, believed that she should not have to enjoy tea on her porch looking at and listening to "those people" (assuming the noise could be heard at the top of the mountain) frolicking down below at the beach. As she looked out over the Wee Wah and Pond 3 back toward the Tuxedo Club, as well as across at the mansions on the top of the mountain further south, she felt something should be done to eliminate this distraction.

Late spring and early summers in Tuxedo Park at the turn of the century, and into the late 1920s, was a period of what one might call "fun and games." It was an idyllic place where one could escape the problems of the fast-growing metropolis only an hour away. Movement in New York City had continued north from Downtown, with longtime city residents eager to escape the crowded streets now filled with immigrants. The wealthy built extravagant mansions on Fifth Avenue and bordering Central Park, helping them avoid the area below Fifty-ninth Street, now teeming with horse-drawn carriages, streetcars, and automobiles. That portion of New York had become a mess of factories, noise, and bad air. Immigrants were flowing out of the Lower East Side and filling the West Side and East Side beyond Forty-second Street.

Tuxedo Park offered fresh air, scenic beauty, casual attire (ironic, considering how the community's name has become synonymous with formal menswear), and a more relaxed attitude than found in Newport, which, of course, still had its season. Life centered on the Club, where boundless activities for the men included golf, tennis, boating, horse and dog shows, shooting, fishing, hiking, swimming, along with indoor sports such as squash, racquets, and court tennis. Women, especially younger women, were finding it much more acceptable to join in these activities. In addition, lunch could be enjoyed at the Club while the children took their swimming lessons under the watchful eyes of nannies and governesses. For the men, the convenience of the private cars of E. H. Harriman"s Erie Railroad provided quick, easy commute to the city and the opportunity to discuss the issues of the day. Many of these discussions led to ideas and proposals that affected business interests vital to the country as a whole. Banks and Trust companies were proliferating, the stock exchange was increasing with new companies seeking capital investment, and deals were made. Needless to say, during its first forty years, Tuxedo Park remained a center for life of the Gilded Age. Those at the top could be found enjoying the wealth in Tuxedo Park, and on the train, the barons of finance and industry formed interlocking directorates. If one were to research the banks and companies, one would find the same names appearing on numerous Boards of Directors, many of whom had estates and homes in Tuxedo Park and were Tuxedo Club members.

During these times, Mrs. Frelinghuysen could look out her window or sit on her veranda and see other stately homes such as those belonging to the Lorillards, the Carhart, the Curtis, and the Spedden of the same social set. Parties were arranged and guest lists prepared, all under her supervision, as staff with responsibility for carrying it out constantly approached her for approvals. It was a close-knit family on the Frelinghuysen side, powerful and political. Lily's upbringing at the very top of old society represented a different class of wealth, and she carried herself in a way that one would not forget it.

Times were changing. New money was flowing into Tuxedo Park. Self-made men who had achieved great success in business, or who had married into such wealth, were now welcomed. Prominent landowning families, most of whom could be traced back to the American Revolution and Colonial times were now joined by this new class of wealth. The country had endured the Great War, since dubbed World War I. American men returning home found jobs to be plentiful, the fast-growing economy was boosted by the expansion of the railroads, and in 1920, women achieved the right to vote. In Tuxedo Park, the stables and coach houses, less needed with the advent of the automobile, were now being rented by the children of the original staff who now had families of their own. The population needed for support of the estate owners of Tuxedo Park and members of the Tuxedo Club was growing fast in the leadup to the 1929 stock market crash.

By the late 1920s, the Club's beach was now being used almost exclusively by the children and their parents who were not members of the Tuxedo Club but worked on the estates or in the Hamlet supplying the infrastructure needed by those who lived in the Park. This early picture shows the summer life at the beach.

"The Gang" at the early beach before the relocation, ca.1920s

Despite the onset of the Great Depression, life remained mostly the same for the residents outside the gates living in the Hamlet, East, Slavic Villages and the staff workers on the estates in the Park. Their jobs were hard and their pay, in many instances, depended on the largess of the families of the estates. For the working class, swimming at Wee Wah Beach went on as usual, but trouble was brewing. It came to pass that apparently the noise of these children and families who were of this "lower social class" at times would reach the ears of the widow Frelinghuysen and interfere with the atmosphere of her setting. This was not a distance of hundreds of yards, but the crest of the hilltop was significantly removed from the beach below. However, you could see the goings on, and, at times, the sounds would carry. Albert Foster Winslow described her in his book, *Tuxedo Park, A Journal of Recollections* on page 55:

> "Mrs. Theodore Frelinghuysen was one of the great ladies of Tuxedo and was an important hostess during the first quarter of the twentieth century. She was formal and severe and dealt little with the ridiculous or the amusing."[40]

As a youngster, I overheard references to this matter many times from my grandparents and their friends, all of whom considered these impressions of Mrs. Frelinghuysen to be factual. Apparently, this distraction had caused Mrs. Frelinghuysen to complain to the board of governors at the Tuxedo Club that something should be done to alleviate this unpleasant view of workers cavorting within her eyesight, along with the faint noises that apparently reached her ears at times.

The timing of this rumored complaint proved suspicious, because the following summer the TPA informed those using the beach that it was now off limits. However, the TPA was advised to create a new beach on the far north side of Pigeon Point by the unused icehouse, and they would build two bath changing houses, all of which would be hidden from the view of Mrs. Frelinghuysen. Thus, a relatively safe and beautiful beachfront, originally created to meet the demanding standards of Tuxedo Club members, would no longer be available. The problem was apparently easily solved. The TPA cleared a new area for bathing and "the help" were allowed to continue using the lake in the summer months. The news was announced and spread quickly through the small community of the Hamlet. Staff in the Park were advised by their employers. The new area was now referred to as North Beach.

North Beach, ca. 1930

The TPA had been given the task of creating this new swimming area. A dock and raft were built, along with the two new bathing houses, one for men and one for women, that could be used for changing. What appeared to be a suitable solution for Mrs. Frelinghuysen's complaints was also tacitly seen as acceptance that Tuxedo Park residents had now formalized that those who were not members of the Tuxedo Club could indeed use the Wee Wah for recreation.

Problem solved, or so Mrs. Frelinghuysen must have thought when she returned from Palm Beach for the next summer season. What she had not considered when looking out from the veranda at the lakes below was the future of the original T. Suffern Taylor estate, which had been bought by James Smith in 1901 (more about Smith later). This estate, which Smith had named Kincraig, sat on the opposite side of the lakes. Smith had died at a young age and Kincraig, along with a substantial fortune, was now inherited by Smith's nephew, George Grant Mason. Mason epitomized the change regarding who was now acceptable in high society. He was from the Midwest, and after his uncle paid for his education at Yale, he started at the bottom on the railroads, where he grew to understand the life of a working man. Taking residence in Kincraig, Mason also hired an estate supervisor and head gardener who had developed an excellent reputation in the Park. His name was Duncan McGregor, my paternal grandfather.

Looking back at the new location for the beach at the Wee Wah, there was one major problem. Where the new beach was located, rather than a gradual and wide descent out into the lake with a sandy bottom, there was a short walk out in shallow water, followed by a steep and unexpected descent into deep water.

Prior to this time, there had only been two drownings reported in Tuxedo. In 1903, a butler perished when his canoe tipped over at what is now named Mountain Lake—a murky pond containing unusually dark water which, at that time, was commonly called something else, a name that included a repulsive racist epithet. The day of the drowning, the family of William Pierson Hamilton, one of whom's ancestors was Alexander Hamilton, was hosting a picnic for their employees who invited their friends. They lived outside Tuxedo Park on an estate of several hundred acres just south of the Park border, now called Eagle Valley in the Town of Tuxedo. Reported the *New York Times*, "The day was passed in gaiety, and all were about to return when Owen went out in a canoe. As he was not accustomed to rowing, he accidently upset the boat and at once sank to the bottom."[41]

The second documented Tuxedo drowning occurred in Wee Wah Lake itself, twenty-four years later, when Club member and well-known banker, Major Garrard Comly, was seized with a cramp some distance from shore. Before help could reach him, he went under. His body was soon recovered, and the drowning was reported the next day in the June 28, 1927 edition of the *New York Times*.[42]

Not long after the beach had been moved to the new location, Tuxedo Park apparently suffered another drowning when a bather who could not yet swim wandered too far out. Although there were no public records, a second drowning is said to have soon followed in this new beach area. It was passed on to me that a bather was a guest of a family from outside the gates who should not have been allowed into the Park. It would not be unusual for Tuxedo Park at that time to suppress a report that did not involve families of "importance," but these drownings were apparently mentioned in a statement made years later by Mabel Tansey to the mayor and trustees at a meeting concerning the Wee Wah Beach Club. The story was overheard many times being told by others when I was growing up. Supposedly the body was recovered, and the "guest" family immediately left the Park with the deceased concealed and with any subsequent report or paperwork left to that family. Such paperwork would ostensibly suggest that the drowning had occurred elsewhere. Had this alleged drowning been reported at the time and location in which it actually occurred, use of the Wee Wah for swimming would undoubtedly have been discontinued. Over the years, I heard this story from others of the original members of what was first known as the Tuxedo Community Club, as well as from family members discussing the history of the Wee Wah Beach Club. I could not find any documents to support this rumor, and to the extent that there were changes to the location of the beach, history suggests there were others who supported this story true or otherwise in order to effect a change back to the original beach location. Matters such as this were typically handled by officers and board members at the Tuxedo Club, and directions were given to the manager of the TPA.

It was not unusual that stories that could create questions or reflect poorly about goings on in Tuxedo Park would "stay inside the Park" or be "cleaned up," as they say. Weekend parties were frequent at the estates, and socially acceptable young men often entertained young women from New York City. In April of 1915, the well-dressed body of a young woman was found floating on the surface of one of the brooks flowing into Tuxedo Lake. Reports claimed the body had been in the water for almost two months and "could not be identified." Word of the discovery leaked out, but the case was quickly closed by

"Officer Smith of the Tuxedo Park Police," a coroner called, and it was determined to be a case of suicide.[43]

I was not allowed access to Tuxedo Club records for the purpose of researching this book. Then again, perhaps the drownings were just rumors used to prevent young children and other unskilled bathers from swimming off the dock at the new north beach, where there was no lifeguard.

Either way, the new area was unacceptable as a swimming beach. This was expressed to certain members of the Tuxedo Club who were open to such discussions with their staff about the problem. Duncan McGregor, now with four children, spoke with George Grant Mason about the change of location, as did others who had close relationships with their respective estate owners. While no policy was publicly expressed, change did occur.

Over several years, bathers gradually returned to the old beach, which had a wide sandy bottom. The slope was suitable for children and families, as there was a gradual descent with a good distance of shallow water. Those who preferred to swim could simply venture further out. The adjacent area was also cleared for picnicking, and open areas were created for sporting activities. For whatever reason, the TPA did not interfere with this move back to the original beach. In fact, in the early 1930s, wooden beach structures in the water that had fallen into disrepair were removed by the TPA, except for the wooden dock that protruded out from the shoreline on a stone boulder foundation.

By 1935, bathers from the estate staffs in Tuxedo Park, and those who worked in the Park but lived outside the gates, were using the beach without any attempts to prevent them by the TPA. I am not aware of any further objections from Mrs. Frelinghuysen. If she did complain, her concerns were apparently dismissed. In time, those using the beach became more organized and actively communicated with the TPA, as many of the employees of the Association were also using the beach. The Association had a stone wall constructed at the top of the rise, and they restored the stone steps leading down to the water. This formerly abandoned swimming beach was now active again, and more formal summer activity areas were developed. The two new bathhouses constructed by the Tuxedo Park Association were moved back from the north side to an unused area at the very tip of land below the children's play area and out of view of the beachfront. While there is no record of further complaints from Mrs. Frelinghuysen, community members using the beach were undoubtedly ready to demonstrate their desire to enjoy the beach.

Therein lies the origination of what would become the much beloved Wee Wah Beach Club. How did this happen? We shall see in the next chapters.

Chapter 11: George Grant Mason

George Grant Mason (1868–1954)

Most early Tuxedo Park residents and Tuxedo Club members were relatives and friends of Pierre Lorillard IV. With few exceptions, these wealthy families descended from "old money," families who had accumulated their wealth through real estate at the beginning of the Republic. Others were "new money" industrialists or "capitalists," as they were described at the time, who had made fortunes during and after the Civil War. By 1900, Tuxedo Park had become quite fashionable. Rather than constructing additional Bruce Price-designed shingled cottages, they purchased the larger estate mansions that had recently been built, or they designed and built their own grand homes. Many of these men had not been born into families of high social standing or great wealth. Some had married into wealth after achieving their own fortunes. A few climbed the economic ladder from humble beginnings as youths, working side by side with the workers of the day. Among those Tuxedo Club members who had worked their way up from humble economic beginnings, we have George Grant Mason and George F. Baker. In Mason's case, he was not part of the Northeastern social hierarchy, but had been bequeathed the money by his uncle. Mason and Baker soon became the most charitable with their donations to the community of Tuxedo.

Baker, the son of a shoe store owner, made his fortune in banking and became a founder of the First National Bank of New York (today's Citibank). He became Chairman of its Board of Directors in 1909. The local high school in Tuxedo named after him was just one result of his willingness to support those living outside the gates. Perhaps due to his humble beginnings, Baker had no qualms mixing with staff and other locals.

George Grant Mason started working on a railroad in the Midwest. He was also a major contributor to Tuxedo. In the Hamlet, the elementary school today bears his name. He also made a significant contribution to the construction of the new Tuxedo Club and the Tuxedo Memorial Hospital.

Although families living in the Park, including the Frelinghuysen family, were generous over time with contributions to various causes and institutions, the Frelinghuysens came from a background where the distinction between their status and those outside or below was a line that was not easily crossed when it came to socializing.

You can see the difference in philosophy between Mason and Theodore Frelinghuysen by their correspondence. With reference to building a "new and enlarged" Tuxedo Club, Frelinghuysen preferred improving the existing Tuxedo Club and a management that recognized "young men … who know the class and age of men who join clubs."[44]

Dear Mr. Stevens:

I regret not to comply with the wishes of a Committee the members of which I esteem so highly as I do yours, but as I do not feel that the best interests of, either the Club, or the property owners would be served by the proposition you offer I must decline to subscribe.

To saddle the Club with a house costing $450.000. [sic] largely paid for by a very few of the members, and those members who use the Club little and are not familiar with its needs, or what is required to draw members to a country club, or how a club should be run, would be fatal to any club, besides placing the other members in a most unpleasant position.

The present condition of Tuxedo Club has been brought about by the Governors assuming the guarantee, and so placing the management in the absolute control of a few who are not in touch with club matters here or elsewhere, and the proposed plan would make this arrangement permanent.

With $100.000, the present house could be made better than the plan submitted, and could be run more cheaply, and leave a way open for a reorganization of the management, so that we could have it managed by young men in touch with those who use country clubs, and who know the class and age of men who join clubs.

Sincerely yours,

Theodore Frelinghuysen

Mason simply signed a pledge card for $25,000 (over $600,000) today for a new Tuxedo Club.

No. 10 WALL STREET
NEW YORK

Jan. 23, 1917.

Joseph E. Stevens, Esq.,
17 Battery Place,
New York City.

Dear Joe:-

I have your letter of yesterday, and I herewith enclose the card duly signed, showing my subscription toward a new club house at Tuxedo Park for $25,000. I should like very much to talk over this matter with you further, and for that purpose will you not lunch with me at the Midday Club on Thursday next at any hour that suits your convenience.

Sincerely yours,

(encl)

Mason was comfortable communicating with his staff and those who served the residents of the Park. His concern for the workers and their families inside and adjacent to Tuxedo Park is crucial to the Wee Wah Beach Club story.

By 1930, George Grant Mason had long owned the estate and mansion now called Kincraig. Perched on one of the highest bluffs, with a central view of all of Tuxedo Park, was the estate originally built for T. Suffern Tailer and his wife Maude, the youngest daughter of Pierre Lorillard. Thomas Suffern "Tony" Tailer was a lawyer and member of the New York Stock Exchange. An active sportsman and one of the principal members of the Tuxedo Club, he encouraged construction of the Racquet and Tennis Club, which included a few guest apartments. He was recognized as one of the best "whips" in the country, racing coaches in what was then a popular society sport. When in Europe, he was frequently involved in the coach races from Paris to Versailles. The Lorillards were not thrilled with their daughter's choice, but his family was socially acceptable, so the Tailers were married on April 14, 1893, with a reception at the Lorillard residence serving as one of the top social events of the year.

As was customary, the honeymoon consisted of a trip around the world before the couple returned to their new Tuxedo Park mansion built by her father. The property stretched along what was called Summit Road and included vast vegetable gardens, orchards, greenhouses, formal Italian gardens, and ponds. At the base of the long winding driveway was a three-story, L-shaped stable containing staff quarters, stables for horses, and large storage areas for the coaches. There were gardeners' cottages, a large stone water tank, root cellars, a potting shed for the gardens, and meticulously manicured grounds.

Soon after Maude Tailor divorced Tony Tailor in 1902, James Henry "Silent" Smith, a Wall Street investor, quickly purchased the estate, named it Kincraig, and continued to insert himself into the upper echelon of society. He became President of the Tuxedo Racquet Club built by Tailor. Smith paid to have the silver trophy made and presented it with a monetary prize to the champion racquet player of America.

Kincraig was left to Mason by "Silent" Smith who happened to be his uncle. Tuxedo Park had changed little with the times. This was still a bastion of privileged society, with all its rules and proper manners. While Mrs. Frelinghuysen was a fixture at the top of society, her interaction with the Tailers in the early years reflected their station of old money and membership in the Tuxedo Club. While the Tailers were acceptable because Maude was a daughter of the founder, Mr. Smith inherited a fortune, and in August of 1906 married Annie Stewart, the divorced Mrs. William Rhinelander Stewart. Stewart was both a banker and a member of the early real estate scions of New York, a man who enjoyed his position at the top of society at the time. At the turn of the century, money, marriage, and the proper introductions could elevate one into elite society.

The ancestry and upbringing of Elizabeth Frelinghuysen and George Grant Mason could not have been more different than a rare French chateau-grown wine and a home-brewed beer.

George Grant Mason was born in Millburn, Illinois, on September 15, 1868, into a working-class family. Mason's trajectory truly begins in 1882, when his uncle James Henry Smith came west to meet with his relatives two years after Smith's uncle, George "Chicago" Smith, returned to London from Chicago. This is when

James Smith met his nephews George and William Mason for the first time.

Chicago Smith remained single his entire life and died in a West End club in London, leaving a substantial fortune he had accumulated owning railroads in the Midwest. James Smith's uncle, George, had treated him with an education in London and set him up to manage the fortune in New York City, where James became known as "Silent Smith." James now did the same and took both George Grant Mason and William under his wing by providing the funds and access to Yale. They ventured east, and both attended the Sheffield Institute of Technology at Yale, Class of 1888. They then attended Stevens Institute of Technology for another year of studies. Following the advice of their uncle, they returned to the Midwest and entered the employ of the Chicago, Milwaukee & St. Paul Railway to learn the business from the bottom up. The railroad had been owned by their great-uncle, Chicago Smith, and now the stock was held by their uncle, James. Both started in the mechanical department as shop employees in the Milwaukee office in 1889, where they remained for five years. While William remained in Milwaukee, George moved on to Green Bay, Wisconsin, as a foreman of the roundhouse. In Green Bay, he met Marion Peake, the daughter of Mrs. A. C. Neville, who was very active in Green Bay circles and throughout all of Wisconsin. George and Marion married and later returned to Milwaukee, where he was given the position of chief draughtsman. Meanwhile, William left the railroad and entered the banking industry in Evanston, Illinois. Shortly thereafter, George was appointed trainmaster in Mason City, Iowa. In 1905, he became a division superintendent, settling in Aberdeen, South Dakota, with Marion and their eight-year-old daughter, Margaret, and a newborn boy, George Grant Mason Jr. It was a comfortable life with good neighbors and friends. Marion became active with the Consumers' League, whose mission was to provide better conditions for working women. They were comfortable, but not rich by any means, and certainly not at the top of the social world.

In 1907, George Grant Mason was called to New York after the family was notified that his uncle James Henry "Silent" Smith had died in Japan on his honeymoon.[45] While James had not been personally in touch with his relatives, he was always generous financially and concerned about their welfare. He was believed to be in good health and active.

The Mason brothers were present when the will was read on May 7, 1907. When all was said and done, his nephew, George Grant Mason, and his brother, William H. Mason, were the principal beneficiaries, with George receiving two thirds and William one third. William had left the railroad business for a successful career in banking. For George, the amount was $12 million to $15 million (over $500 million today), and William received more than $6 million. As one of the five executors, George Grant Mason carried out the provisions of the will, with many distributions to family, servants, and gifts such as $100,000 each to St. Luke's Hospital and Orthopedic Hospital of New York, on whose boards Smith had served. William had no desire to stay in New York, but George decided to leave the railroad and carry on the business career of his uncle. George took possession of the Whitney mansion on Fifth Avenue that Smith had purchased, and the estate known as Kincraig in Tuxedo Park. He also took title to the exceptionally large property on the west side of Central Park, where Smith had intended to build stables.[46]

An interesting aside is how James Smith came into his wealth. It is the story of how George Smith, who never married, left a fortune to his nephew, "Silent Smith," who then died childless and left an even greater fortune to his nephews, George and William Mason.

George Smith left Scotland for New York and traveled to Chicago by wagon train in 1834, with merely a few dollars in his pocket. It was not the story of American blue blood ancestry that typically inhabited Tuxedo Park when it was developed by Pierre Lorillard IV in the late 1800s. Smith bought and sold real estate, both in Chicago and in Wisconsin. A few years later he returned to Scotland and raised money for investment in America. Returning to the states with his friend from Scotland, Alexander Mitchell, and after the great fire in Chicago, he bought up large tracts of land containing destroyed buildings. In 1837, he sold off some of his holdings and formed the Wisconsin Marine and Fire Insurance Company in Milwaukee. This corporate vehicle allowed Smith to open and operate banks. Soon after, he became a leader in the banking business and "Smith's Bank" became the richest in the West. Smith stretched his banking operations across the West and South. Notes issued by his institutions, known popularly as "George Smith's money," had a high reputation in those days of "wildcat" currency. Until the creation of the Federal Reserve in 1913, banks could issue their own notes backed by state bonds or mortgages. These notes could then be used as currency backed by the bank. Many of these notes were, in fact, worthless, but Smith's reputation was excellent for paying off the notes when presented for redemption. Wildcat banks issued their own currency until the National Bank Act of 1863 forbade this practice. After a time, Mitchell retired and, with his wife, returned to Scotland with $20 million. George

Smith remained in Chicago.

George Smith, who acquired the nickname "Chicago Smith," also invested heavily in railroad properties. His largest holding was in the Chicago, Minneapolis & St. Paul Railway. He returned to London in 1880, leaving all his financial interests under the direction of Geddes and Smith, financial advisors in New York. The Smith in the name was his nephew, James Henry Smith.

James Smith and his sister, May, were born in Evanston, Illinois and were favored by their uncle George at an early age. Both were sent to London by their Uncle George, where May could find a suitable husband and James could be educated at King's College. He returned to the States at age twenty-one. He studied at Columbia Law School and was admitted to the New York Bar. Due to the relationship with his uncle, James quickly joined Peter Geddes, who managed the affairs of London-based George Smith in New York. Peter Geddes had been sent to New York to manage George's financial affairs, and now, joined by James Smith, they formed the Geddes & Smith brokerage firm at No. 10, Wall Street with the sole purpose of managing George's money—and following his investment instructions. Smith's companies, worth some $50 million, were based in London and thus paid no taxes in the United States. At the firm and around town, James was known as "Silent Smith" and "the silent man of Wall Street," amassing a few million dollars in his own right.

George Smith returned to London and never visited America again. He settled into a very private, frugal life. He lived as a recluse, renting an upstairs bedroom at the Reform Club of London in the West End. As previously stated, nineteen years later, on October 7, 1899, George Smith died at 91years of age in his London club. "Chicago

Smith" never became an American citizen. As a result, his estate was taxed by the Exchequer of England in the amount of £900,000 for death duties, which was slightly less than 50 percent of all English inheritance taxes received by the Exchequer in 1899.

Informed of his uncle's death, James departed for London. He was introduced as a prominent figure in a social campaign arranged by Alice, the wife of George Keppel, a close friend of Prince Albert Edward, the Prince of Wales, and the son of Queen Victoria. Alice Keppel was a favorite of Albert, who was soon to become King Edward VII. Uncle George had left the bulk of his estate to Sir George Cooper, a good friend who had married James's sister May, now known as Lady Cooper. George had left much of the remainder of his $65 million estate to his nephew, James, whose share was worth approximately $1.5 billion in early twenty-first century dollars. Much smaller bequests were left to relatives in the Midwest, including $100,000 each to great-nephews George Grant Mason, George's brother William Smith Mason, and their sister Lucy.

A remarkable transformation took place shortly after Silent Smith's return from London. He grew to welcome the attention stirred up by his newfound wealth and abandoned his custom of spending long hours in the office and returning to his residence or club for the evening. Back in New York after settling his uncle's final arrangements, he was now well up among the richest multi-millionaires in the United States. James was a quiet man, as his nickname suggests. Although established in all the proper clubs, few members spent time in his company. He was a member of the Union, University, Racquet, Wool, Seawanhaka Corinthian Yacht, and Downtown clubs, but an infrequent visitor with few friends. He maintained two apartments at No. 1 West Thirtieth Street and on Fifth Avenue. Smith, always impeccably dressed, spent most of his time at the office working, in a window seat at a club reading, or at home. He was not one to arrange parties nor did he accept invitations.

James Henry Smith becomes "Silent" no more. The visits to his clubs to read in solitude were replaced with expensive "coaching parties," which had become very fashionable. A coaching party involved hiring a group of well-outfitted coaches for afternoon runs from the city to places in the "country," such as Inwood or to the Morris Park horse races for afternoon teas and dinners at great expense.

With the new year of 1901, society's expectations were high as to who would gain Mr. Smith's favor. All the doors were open. He had now also been welcomed as a member of the top clubs, including the New York Yacht Club. On Thursday, February 14, 1901, the New York Times reported Smith gave an extravagant dinner dance that reported his debut as a member of the inner 400. He was taken in by Mrs. Hamilton Fish, Mrs. Ogden Mills, and Mrs. Cornelius Vanderbilt. Seated at his table, among others, were T. Suffern Tailor and Stanley Mortimer, original settlers of Tuxedo Park.[47]

Now actively involved in the upper reaches of society, James surrounded himself with the trappings of great wealth. He purchased the home, art, and furnishings of William H. Whitney at 871 Fifth Avenue and 68th Street in 1902 and continued to acquire art of the masters. In addition, he donated many purchases such as Peter Paul Rubens's "The Holy Family" to the Metropolitan Museum of Art.

He also purchased an estate from T. Suffern Tailer in Tuxedo Park, naming it "Kincraig," after a beautiful village at the heart of the highlands in Scotland, to insure his new marital status and position at the top of the social circuit. Through the clubs and coaching circuit, Smith and Tailer became acquainted and, due to Tailer's marital problems, the Tuxedo estate became available.

James began to spend much less time on business and lived handsomely off the income while the principal continued to grow. Every summer, he returned to Scotland for relaxation and shooting. He became a prominent member of the Coaching Club in New York City and spent $500,000 buying up lots on West 55th Street and 56th Street to construct private stables and a building for the enjoyment of his friends on the west side of Central Park. He donated $500,000 to St. Luke's Hospital in Chicago for an annex in memory of his uncle George "Chicago" Smith.

Although a most sought-after bachelor, Mr. Smith found comfort in the company of one family in particular. Most society reports indicated Mr. Smith would attend parties, travel widely, and entertain Mr. and Mrs. William Rhinclander Stewart. The couple and Mr. Smith became inseparable companions on long yachting trips. The Stewarts were reportedly seen regularly in Mr. Smith's box at the opera. The Rhinelander Stewart name had great prominence in society. William's wife, Annie M. Armstrong of Baltimore, was related to the Drexel banking family in Philadelphia that dates back to the American Revolution. The Stewarts had a son and a daughter. Smith was very fond of the daughter, Anita. In Smith's Whitney house on Fifth Avenue, a ball was given in honor of Anita. Mrs. Stewart was a frequent visitor to the mansion.

In June of 1905, William's wife, Annie, departed for Sioux Falls, South Dakota (the "Las Vegas" of the time in terms of expedited marriage dissolutions), seeking a divorce from William on the grounds of desertion. There was no contest, and the divorce was granted in August of 1906. No alimony was reported, and Mrs. Stewart retained custody of her daughter. Her son remained in the custody of his father.[48]

In the summer of 1906, Mr. Smith took his usual journey back to Scotland. After the divorce, Annie and her daughter returned to New York by the fastest train and immediately set sail for Scotland. However, it was not Anita that everyone thought was the interest of James Smith. One month later, on September 13, 1906, James Henry Smith married the former Mrs. Rhinelander Stewart in the parish church at Alvie, Inverness-shire. It was reported that Smith settled an amount of $15 million for his stepdaughter, Anita, in his will prepared the day of the marriage. Once included in the top level of society, and with the money necessary to sustain the lifestyle, social indiscretions did not result in ostracism, as evidenced by the Tailer divorce earlier.

After the wedding and a short sojourn at one of Mr. Smith's estates in Scotland, the couple set off on a tour of the world aboard the Drexel family yacht, *Marguerita*. They were joined by Annie's daughter, Anita, and included the wedding party and the Duke and Duchess of Manchester. It was a leisurely cruise with many stops, such as Naples in Italy, and then through the Suez Canal to India.

They continued on through the Indian Ocean and arrived in Hong Kong, China, before proceeding to Japan. Complaining of a toothache, Mr. Smith was taken off the yacht when it arrived in Kyoto, Japan. James Henry Smith died on March 27, 1907, at a hotel in Kyoto. He was 53 years old. The Duke of Manchester announced Smith had "died of acute Bright's disease, ending in pneumonia.

Everything known to science was tried to check the complaint without avail. His body will be transported to his home in America by earliest steamer."[49] The social world was anxiously awaiting the details of the will as it was already widespread knowledge that his stepdaughter, Anita, had been specifically bequeathed $15 million on his wedding day, making her now one of the richest young women in the world. Rumors were rampant that the value of Smith's estate exceeded $75 million.

In truth, the value of the estate was somewhat overestimated and closer to $25 million, according to Herman S. LeRoy, A Tuxedo Club member and one of the five executors.

At the time of his uncle's death, George Grant Mason was thirty-eight years old. He was accustomed to working long hours and getting his hands dirty. He and Marion were now raising their two children in Aberdeen, and their Midwest life was quite comfortable due to his position with the railroad. Mason was a down-to-earth young man, and on arriving in New York, his wife reportedly responded to all questions by stating, "We are just plain people." Mason declined interviews while staying with his wife in two rooms at the Netherlands Hotel. When asked for his plans regarding taking over or disposing of the Whitney Mansion on Fifth Avenue, which the will indicated should be sold, Mason was quoted as saying, "Oh, I'll just rent." The *New York Times* quoted one of the executors as saying, "He is even 'silenter' than Silent Smith."[50]

Mason's new fortune was a shock to the family, which had been very happy in Aberdeen. George Mason stated he expected it would take at least a year to put everything in perspective and learn more about his uncle James' business. In actuality, this process continued for the rest of his life.

In January of 1910, Mason sold the "famous Whitney mansion" at 871 Fifth Avenue, which he had inherited, back to Harry Payne Whitney.[51] The Mason family made Tuxedo Park their home as a welcome respite from the considerable hustle and activity in New York City. They often traveled back to the Midwest to visit friends, family, and especially Marion's mother, Mrs. Neville, in Green Bay.

Back East, they enjoyed the seasons and social living at Kincraig in Tuxedo Park while also keeping a place in the city. The children were growing quickly. The family enjoyed summers in Maine, and no matter the season, George enjoyed time with the family, as well as busying himself with his growing portfolio of financial involvements. He was thought to be quiet, thoughtful, and highly intelligent, with a good sense for business at the Tuxedo Club, to which he was readily admitted. On the daily train between Tuxedo and Wall Street surrounded by others of great wealth and business interests, he was well respected for his views. He became a director of many banks and railroads.

The Erie Railroad was the line that took the Tuxedo Club members in and out of the city. In the early days, there were individual private cars, but by the 1920s these were replaced with a "banker's train," which was exclusively nonstop for residents of Tuxedo Park, their guests, and others living in great estates nearby to Tuxedo. This nonstop train between Tuxedo and New York City was appropriately called "The Millionaire."

Think of the major industrial, financial, and railroad businesses in those days as a game of Monopoly. In fact, George Mason looked very much the part of the neatly dressed man with the mustache found in the popular board game. Railroads were bought, sold, traded, and reorganized with one ultimate goal: once you had control of certain lines and the support systems for delivering goods across the country, you could control prices. Just as players sit around a Monopoly game board, these real-life men sat around tables on the train out of Tuxedo freely deciding what prices should be; buying, selling, and trading properties; cutting financing deals; and discussing all manner of investments. But unlike in Monopoly, there were no losers.

Consider the change in the holdings of the primary Smith investment in the Chicago, Milwaukee & St. Paul Railway in 1902. The Armour meatpacking family held 20 percent of the stock, William Rockefeller owned 20 percent, and Donald G. Geddes owned the 20 percent controlled by Smith. The Armour family sold their interest to none other than E. H. Harriman—with the understanding that all work from South Dakota to the Pacific Coast would be dropped. Not surprisingly, some four years later, the Union Pacific, which was controlled by Harriman and the Southern Pacific, merged into one line. Thus, the transcontinental line was fully completed. These deals were all financed on Wall Street. One can only imagine the men sitting around a hypothetical Monopoly board as the "bankers train" headed for Wall Street with E. H. Harriman in one seat and Silent Smith sitting across from him. Once Mason was accepted and became comfortable with the rules and ways of these financiers, he slipped into the seat previously occupied by his late uncle, James Smith.

At the turn of the twentieth century, Tuxedo was becoming a microcosm of the United States, which was entering a period of social change. The small number of individuals who controlled industry, banking, and financial markets, along with many elected government positions, were dwarfed by the increase in the general population. America was prospering and expanding west. Industrialization created new jobs with the advent of the assembly line. Reconstruction and the false "separate but equal" doctrine allowed the South to have influence in government and slowly rebuild their economy with investment from Northern industrialists and financiers. America had survived World War I, and these social changes were rapidly underway.

Times had changed, and the needs of Tuxedo Park owners, and residents (on both sides of the gates), continued to increase. By now, many of the working families had lived there for more than thirty years, and their children were now raising families of their own. Something had to be done, especially for those who lived outside the gates, and many inside Tuxedo Park were attempting to solve these community issues. Few, however, came close to the generosity and foresight of George F. Baker and George Grant Mason. They had experienced growing up and working beside the common laborer. Unlike many of their Tuxedo Park neighbors, these privileged men were not born with the proverbial "silver spoon in their mouth." Pierre Lorillard had created the Tuxedo Park Association to manage Tuxedo Park and the village outside the gates, akin to how today's local governments govern communities across the country.

Whenever social, educational, and medical needs went unmet in the community, Baker and Mason were always approached for help. In most instances, they wrote checks and required no further discussion. In the late 1920s the most pressing needs were a top-rated hospital and a new school for the children outside the gates and for those whose parents worked on the estates in the Park. Sure enough, Baker and Mason put up the money. Once they signed on as what is now commonly known as "grand benefactors," others followed their lead, giving lesser amounts. Baker, Mason, and the other donors attached no requirements other than that the new facilities should be well-designed, modern, and capable of providing the services needed. For example, the auditorium of the new school would be used for assemblies, recitals, plays, and the arts. Thus, the TPA oversaw construction and hired architects who created a design for the auditorium and stage that would replicate the great theaters of New York.

From the outset, after inheriting his uncle's assets, George Grant Mason was a generous philanthropist. In early 1911, George and his brother, William, gave a combined gift of $250,000 (about $6 million today) for an experimental mechanical laboratory to the Sheffield Engineering School at Yale University. Named in their honor, the Mason Laboratory continues its mission to this day. It was the second largest gift the school had ever received at that time. In 1927, George and Marion donated $50,000 for the construction and furnishing of the Neville Public Museum in Green Bay in honor of Marion's mother. During the late 1920s, Mason continued to increase his wealth and enjoyed many of the fruits of this great fortune. He spent summers in Bar Harbor, Maine, and traveled to Yeaman's Hall Club, a former plantation and private enclave he developed with friends for relaxation and golf outside of Charleston, South Carolina.[52]

Mason, an avid golfer, frequently played at the Tuxedo Golf Club. While he adhered to most Tuxedo Club and Tuxedo Park rules and regulations, Mason wanted others to enjoy the benefits. When he was politely approached, he was more than willing to help estate employees enjoy golf too, even though they were technically not allowed on the course. Many were Scotsmen, such as my grandfather, Duncan McGregor, who shared Mason's great love for the game. Mason and a select group of members made it possible for my grandfather and others to play the course during certain hours, much like many private clubs in our time have "caddy day," when their course is closed for maintenance and the caddies can play.

Mason's greatest interest was time spent with his family, in keeping with his Midwest upbringing, rather than fulfilling the social requirements of proper high society. The Masons were not interested in the party circuit or the society pages, as was Mrs. Frelinghuysen. Unfortunately, Mrs. Mason became ill in the mid-1920s, and, after a few years of poor health, she died on August 2, 1929. A private service for family was held at Kincraig on Tuesday, August 6, and she was buried at St. Mary's-in-Tuxedo Episcopal Church.[53] The long illness had a sobering effect on Mason, who nonetheless continued his work and travels. He also increased his interest in sharing his wealth. He was especially close to those in his employ. Mason's concerns involved not just the Tuxedo Club social activities, but as previously mentioned, he had great concern for the Tuxedo community as a whole. He seemed to approach each day with a commitment to making life better for others. He was always available for advice and open to my grandfather's opinions on many matters, as Duncan McGregor was his superintendent, and his responsibilities and interests did not just involve the operation of the estate.

At Kincraig, the large coach house had earlier become a garage. And what a garage it was! The size of a football field, the cobblestone floor housed not only several autos, but also trucks that could move furniture and household needs to Mason's homes in Bar

Harbor; to Yeaman's Hall, the golf course and private club developed by Mason outside of Charleston, South Carolina; and to his apartment at 740 Park Avenue in Manhattan. One section of the huge garage contained a wood floor that was finished in a highly polished black enamel paint that would reflect the car sitting on it. This heated area was reserved for the main limousine whenever Mason was at Kincraig. The garage at Kincraig also contained several apartments within the building for chauffeurs (at one time, Mason employed three) and other staff. The largest corner apartment, which consisted of nine rooms and two baths, housed my grandfather. When I was born, my father and mother moved into an apartment in another upstairs corner of the garage. As a young boy, I sometimes threw tennis balls against the wall adjacent to the highly polished section of the garage floor as if it were a handball court. More than a few times I was reprimanded because of the spots I created on the floor. Eventually I accepted that this was strictly a "do not walk or play" area.

Mason, as well as his wife, Marion, in the early years before her illness, were very approachable. They demonstrated a keen interest in those who lived and worked in Tuxedo, and they were supportive of their hard-working staff. Operating and maintaining Kincraig was no simple operation. My grandfather, the superintendent and head gardener, was greatly respected by the Masons. Inside the main house the staff numbered in the dozens. Outside help including chauffeurs, yardmen, and gardeners could also number over twenty when the vegetable gardens and fruit orchards were producing. There were greenhouses, where tropical plants and large palms were grown to stock the main house that contained a glass conservatory that overlooked the lakes and the Tuxedo Club below. In addition, plants, flowers, and vegetables were driven into the city daily when Mason was at his New York apartment. The staff tended meadows, ponds, and a formal Italian garden with columns, fountains, benches, and plants suitable to the climate of northern Italy. One could sit in the formal garden and believe they were at a villa on Lake Como. I would watch through the bushes when the limousine came down from the main house taking Mr. Mason to the train station. I would then see my uncle and other workers raking the main winding white gravel drive that stretched almost a quarter mile to even out the tire tracks. On the sides of the road, gardeners tended to seasonal plants and flowers. I don't know to what extent Mr. Mason insisted on such meticulous maintenance, such as raking the drive, but that is how many of the estates were managed at the time.

After his wife's death, Mason spent much less time in Tuxedo Park. Instead, he retreated to his New York City apartment. The building, known for its Art Deco design at 740 Park Avenue, contained some of the most expensive apartments in the world and continues to do so today.

Following the stock market crash of 1929, which led to the Great Depression, the Hamlet continued to grow. Outside the main gate, ground was broken for the new school. A hospital with all the modern requirements of the time was built on the hill above Our Lady of Mount Carmel (the local Catholic church), and the Lorillard Masonic Lodge. Scottish Rite Masons were an integral part of the growth of Tuxedo Park.

On January 7, 1932, the large cornerstone, inscribed 1931, for the new $400,000 George F. Baker High School, was laid by the officers of the Grand Lodge of Masons of the State of New York. Just to the right of the main entrance, the cornerstone was left unfinished during the building's construction and was now removed. A metal box was placed into the cavity "containing, among other things, names of the Board of Education members, names and portraits of the donors, names of the building committee members, a history of the school, a pencil sketch of the old building, and a list of the first graduating class in the new school." The stone was replaced and secured. What followed was the masonic consecration ceremony performed jointly by state and local masons in attendance. As reported on page 8 in the *Middletown Times Record* on Thursday, January 7, 1932:

"The formalities included a test of the stone squareness by the Grand Master, a test for levelness by W.R. Betts of Tuxedo, acting Senior Grand Warren, and a test for plumbness by John M. Gaynor of Middletown, Junior Grand Warren. The rite of consecration was accomplished by showering of kernels of corn over the newly laid cornerstone as a symbol of plenty by Paul B. Murphy of Nyack, District Deputy Grand Master, the pouring of wine by Mr. Betts as a symbol of refreshment and gladness, and oil by Mr. Gaynor as indicative of peace and joy."[54]

Neither Mason nor Baker attended, as was their custom with such giving. Mason was represented by his daughter, Margaret Sloan Colt, herself a donor to the school.

One other honored guest from Tuxedo Park can be seen standing in the newspaper photograph at the ceremony. He was Duncan McGregor, who arranged the event. In addition to being George Grant Mason's superintendent and head gardener at Kincraig, my grandfather was master of the Lorillard Lodge at Tuxedo and acting steward for the ceremonies.

Chapter 12: Duncan McGregor

Duncan McGregor (1883–1959), the author's paternal grandfather, ca. 1950

Duncan McGregor well-represents the stratification of social life so prevalent in the American populace during the early 1900s. The Gilded Age of the Astors and Vanderbilts was ending. There was old money such as Mrs. Frelinghuysen, new money such as Mason, and the working class. We now come to this third individual who, together with Mrs. Frelinghuysen and George Grant Mason, was instrumental in creating the Wee Wah Beach Club. Mrs. Frelinghuysen and other grand dames of social aristocracy would keep high society on the newspaper pages well into the 1940s and 1950s. The so-named Industrial Age that resulted from the efforts of Rockefeller, Carnegie, Harriman, Havemeyer, and Mason (through his uncle James Smith), and so many others had created unimaginable wealth that was not tied to an aristocratic and formal style, which tended to copy English royalty. One statistic cited by the *Gilded Age,* a television documentary, is that by the time of that 1897 ball, the richest 4,000 families in the U.S. (representing less than 1% of the population) had about as much wealth as the other 11.6 million families all together."[55] By the late 1920s, America's distinctive middle class was taking shape. High society in New York City had completed their last move of creating opulent mansions above Fifty-seventh Street on Fifth Avenue. The population growth and development of commerce forced the rich to build larger and larger residences starting after the Civil War at the beginning of Fifth Avenue at Washington Square, later moving to the Grammercy Park area, then the Murray Hill section above 34th Street, then north toward city streets in the 40th and 50th blocks on Fifth Avenue. With its creation in the 1850s, Central Park became a definitive east-west delineation for commercial and residential buildings.

Duncan McGregor, my paternal grandfather (whom I will refer to as "Duncan" in this section), was not born into wealth. Born in 1893, he was the son of Duncan and Jessie McGregor, a farming family outside Elgin, Scotland. My grandfather was one of nine children, including one brother, James, who was killed in World War I, and seven sisters. He trained in horticulture at Brodie Castle, built in 1567 and located in Forres in Morayshire, west of Elgin on the road to Inverness. The "blasted heath," where Shakespeare's Macbeth is said to have met the three witches, is located on the lands of Brodie Castle. In his late teens, Duncan moved to the world-renowned Glasgow Botanical Gardens to continue his training.

Continuing his pursuit of a better life, in 1910, Duncan came to the United States and lived with his sisters, who had immigrated earlier to Kearney, New Jersey.

Scotland had become the largest producer in the world of a new floor covering called linoleum and was exporting to the United States. The American Nairn Linoleum Company (now the Congoleum Corporation) was established in Kearney, New Jersey in 1887. Immigrants from Scotland flocked to Kearney to work in the new linoleum factories and the area became known as "little Scotland."

As a trained horticulturalist, Duncan found work in the gardens on Duke Farms located not far from Kearney in Somerset County, New Jersey. This was an undertaking for James Buchanan Duke from North Carolina, founder of the American Tobacco Company and Duke Power.

In 1893, James Buchanan Duke, known as Buck, built his fortune from tobacco. He established the American Tobacco Company in New Jersey, which offered the most favorable terms for incorporation at the time. That same year, he purchased a 357-acre farm on a picturesque stretch of the Raritan River. He soon acquired forty adjacent farms, expanding Duke Farms to 2,200 acres. Over the years, through careful planning and a $10 million investment, the property developed into one of the most magnificent estates in the world. Between 1899 and 1905, massive numbers of trees were planted, including sixty thousand of different species in one order from Europe, and twenty thousand blue spruces in another. Duke recorded every purchase and claimed to have planted more than two million trees. In 1905, he completed a reservoir, five lakes, and a series of carriage drives with well houses, pergolas, spectacular fountains, and stone walls.

Although the property was maintained by hundreds of workers, Duke never completed the main house and relocated back to North Carolina. The abandoned foundation remains visible today. Designed by Lord & Burnham Company and patterned after Kew Gardens, it was planned to be a massive estate of over 1,000 acres. My grandfather found work in the conservatories propagating plants, but prospects for his future looked bleak. Despite creating beautiful gardens, Duke lost interest in the estate and ceased construction on the house after the foundation was built. At over 2.700 beautiful acres, Duke Farms remains open to the public today thanks to a trust created by Duke's daughter, Doris Duke, in 1958.

Through contacts, and as a result of his hard-earned reputation for success with propagation on Duke Farms, Duncan found work in Tuxedo Park, where he was first employed at the Wanamaker Estate. John Wanamaker was a successful merchant with stores in New York City, Philadelphia, London, and Paris. He was appointed Postmaster

General under President Benjamin Harrison. He also owned homes in Philadelphia; Cape May, New Jersey; Bay Head, New Jersey; New York City; Florida; and overseas in London, Paris, and Biarritz. Bronze busts honoring Wanamaker and seven other industry magnates stand between the Chicago River and the Merchandise Mart in Chicago. Sometimes dubbed the originator of modern advertising, upon his death in 1922, Wannamaker left behind an estate that would now be worth roughly $1.5 billion.

At this time in Tuxedo Park, William "Billy" Stuart (and his wife, affectionately known as Granny Stuart), lived on Kincraig, where he had first worked for Mason's uncle, James Henry "Silent" Smith. Billy was originally a footman for Smith and later a chauffeur for Mason. He was jovial, outspoken, and as the chauffeur had the ear of George Grant Mason. Through this connection with the Stuarts, who also had immigrated, Duncan McGregor met his future wife, Marie Stuart, who was Billy's niece.

Marie Stuart was also born in Scotland and worked as a governess and nanny in several castles. She once oversaw a playdate between one of her young charges and a little girl who would later become known to the world as the Queen Mother, the mother of Queen Elizabeth II. In approximately 1906, Marie sought better work through a London agency. As a result, she came to work for the Scottish American industrialist Andrew Carnegie.

When Andrew Carnegie's only daughter, Margaret, was born in 1897, he bought a Highlands estate in Scotland, which he called Skibo Castle. It had a view of the sea, a private harbor for his yacht, a waterfall, a trout stream, and room for a golf course. Carnegie soon acquired adjacent properties, doubling the size of the sprawling estate.

A pipe organ was installed to be played every morning at breakfast, and a piper called everyone to dinner in the evening. Guests included many Rockefellers, Helen Keller, Rudyard Kipling, and King Edward VII, who was enamored with the bathroom plumbing and returned to Buckingham Palace to copy it.

In 1907, ten-year-old Margaret was no longer in need of a nanny. Andrew Carnegie, one of the richest men in the world, and his wife, Louise, were looking for a governess to oversee Margaret during the summer at Skibo Castle. Louise had contacted the London agency around the same time that my grandmother had submitted her resume. Louise was given Marie's name and a letter of recommendation from Marie's then-employer, the Countess of Southesk.

Marie Stuart began work at Skibo Castle in 1907 as Margaret Carnegie's governess, and she worked for the family until 1912. During this time, Andrew Carnegie, who had sold his steel business in 1901 to U.S. Steel for more than $200 million, was busy giving away his fortune. He spent summers with his wife and daughter at Skibo Castle, and the family maintained their primary residence in New York City at 2 East 91st Street at Fifth Avenue, overlooking Central Park. The Carnegie family maintained a staff of thirty at Skibo Castle and twenty in New York. As Margaret's governess, Marie traveled with the family, making eleven Atlantic crossings during her five-year employment.

Marie recalled Margaret roller-skating down the hallways at the New York mansion, now the Cooper-Hewitt National Design Museum. Marie would often take her charge for walks around the reservoir in Central Park, accompanied close behind by a private detective to protect Margaret from would-be kidnappers. When she had time to herself, Marie would venture to Tuxedo Park to visit her Uncle Billy. There she was introduced to Duncan. In 1912, Marie gave notice to the Carnegies, moved to Tuxedo Park, and married Duncan.

With the death of James Henry "Silent" Smith, Kincraig's head gardener left for a position at another estate, Blairhame, in Tuxedo Park. Billy then spoke to Smith's heir, Mason, and Duncan was offered the position of head gardener. He accepted and left the Wannamaker estate. Mason soon promoted Duncan to superintendent of Kincraig, and this is where my grandfather remained until the mid-1950s, when the estate was divided and sold at auction after George Grant Mason's death.

During the first half of the twentieth century, horticulture was as popular as horse and dog shows. Garden club and estate displays in Tuxedo Park and county-wide, in the Hudson Valley of New York State, as well as at the Waldorf Astoria and other locations in New York City, attracted many enthusiasts. There was much competition for head gardener and superintendent positions, as horticulture was a source of much competition among Tuxedo Club members who owned the larger estates. Duncan was highly respected for his management and horticultural skills by everyone within Tuxedo Park and outside the gates as well. He was also recognized and appreciated for his congeniality and community spirit. He served as treasurer of the Tuxedo Horticultural Society, served on the Tuxedo Park Volunteer Fire Department, and was accepted into the Order of the Masons.

Being a head gardener on a large estate was not just a matter of managing the landscaping and tending to flower and vegetable gardens. Horticulturists in Tuxedo Park developed new breeds of flowers, fruits, and vegetables. These men were highly respected and valued staff members of their various estates. There was heavy competition when it came to who would decorate the Tuxedo Club for events, such as the Autumn Ball and Christmas. The election was a source of pride not only for those chosen but for the estate owners whose head gardeners were tapped for these highly visible responsibilities.

The *New York Times,* in its "Society" section, covered the Tuxedo Park flower shows that preceded the national and internationally recognized shows in the fall at the Museum of Natural History and the Grand Central Plaza in New York City. Competition was fierce between the head gardeners of the estates that included both my grandfathers. In September of 1934, it was Duncan who brought home many awards for George Grant Mason, as reported in the *New York Times*.[56]

Five years later, a September 15, 1939, article headlined "Flower Display Opens in Tuxedo Park" reported that Renamor estate owner George Armory received thirteen awards on the show's first day. No doubt his head gardener and superintendent, Emil Barth (my maternal grandfather), was also suitably rewarded.[57]

On November 13, 1939, the Thirty-second Annual Autumn Exhibition of the Horticultural Society of New York attracted a record crowd. All told, 27,419 people filled the halls and corridors of the American Museum of Natural History. My grandfather brought home many silver bowls and cups awarded as prizes to the winners. I am sure he was suitably compensated for his efforts by Mr. Mason as well.[58]

The Mason family was very considerate to my grandfather and grandmother and their four children. When my grandmother gave birth to her fourth child, my aunt Marie, Mrs. Mason went so far as to hire a maid for my grandmother so her life maintaining the apartment in a corner of the estate garage and raising the children would be easier. One of the estate chauffeurs drove the children to and from the school in the Hamlet. Like other superintendents who worked for estate owners who did not embrace the rigidity of old social customs, Duncan had the ear of both Mr. and Mrs. Mason. Times were changing. Mason and a few other Club members even arranged for their help to play golf (as previously mentioned), skate at the skating pond, and otherwise enjoy benefits that were reserved for Club members but, of course, not at times when Tuxedo Club members and their guests were using the facilities.

In the early 1930s, due to the rumor of Mrs. Frelinghuysen raising her concern over Tuxedo Park staff and their families using the beach at Pigeon Point, Duncan approached Mr. Mason with an idea that he had discussed with other respected leaders of the service community both inside and outside the gates to the Park. The ensuing conversations led to the potential for a swimming beach to be used for those who worked or were otherwise "in house" within the Park, as well as those outside the gates in the Hamlet who originally built, serviced or worked inside the Park.

Chapter 13: The Tuxedo Community Club Is Born

A Day Back at the Old Beach, ca. 1930

The rumored drowning in the late 1920s at the newly formed beach to the north caused great concern among everyone, especially when there continued to be a beautiful, unused beach location that had originally been developed for the Tuxedo Park members. Here, largely abandoned because of Mrs. Frelinghuysen's complaint, there was a perfectly good beach that staff and their families living inside and outside the Park had been safely using and enjoying for years. In the early 1930s, more than eighty children of Tuxedo Park estates' staff attended school in the Hamlet. There was much discussion among these families, and others on both sides of the gates, about the issue of beach recreation. They decided to approach the Tuxedo Club Board of Governors and the TPA. The leadership group included representatives from the various social classes both inside and outside the Park.

What makes Tuxedo Park and the Hamlet such an interesting

historical study is the successful attempt by Pierre Lorillard and Tuxedo Club members to recreate a British aristocracy in this small enclave of the United States at a time when the Industrial Revolution was breaking down social barriers. In Tuxedo, at the top were Tuxedo Park property owners, who also had to be members of the Tuxedo Club in order to buy a home or own property and build in the Park. This social caste was followed by the outside estate staff, who lived inside the gates. They included house staff, estate managers, chauffeurs, butlers, head gardeners, and their families. The rigidity of earlier times was relaxed in the early 1900s, when "single" staff members working inside the great houses were allowed to marry.

This social stratum was followed by the "Stores" group, better identified as those in the Hamlet who serviced the residents and members of Tuxedo Park, as well as the rest of the community. They were the shop owners, the teachers, and the business community. Last on the spectrum were the Italian and Slovak families, among others, who built the homes and infrastructure of Tuxedo Park and were employed both on the estates to work in the gardens, as well as for businesses in the Hamlet.

In a letter to his children dated August 27, 2005, Charles Frost explained his early life in Tuxedo. He was born and raised in a small house "with running water and an inside bathroom— (a luxury in Tuxedo in 1920) on Circle Drive [in the Hamlet]" and graduated from George F. Baker High School in 1938. As did many of the boys at that time, through connections he secured a job as a copy boy at a Wall Street brokerage firm. He went on to further his education and enjoyed an illustrious career into his eighties as a noted arbitrator in major labor industry disputes. In 1988, he was invited back to give the commencement speech to the graduating class of the high school that included these words:

"Tuxedo was a community of 'the ultimate caste system,' in the British way. There were the high and mighty: the members of The Park who lived in big, fancy houses, some of which had as many as fifty servants (butlers, cooks, maids, gardeners, chauffeurs, etc.). Life there was a good illustration of the success of American capitalism. Most Park members lived there only in the spring and fall. They were about 150 ultra-wealthy people, including the Lorillard, Tilford, Baker, Morgan, and Blair families, among others. The community was founded by Pierre Lorillard in 1885. He sought a place in the country where he could also be close to New York City. Tuxedo Park brought work and relative wealth to that poor south end of Orange County. The caste system was apparent when entering town. While not officially structured in accordance with the British system, it was much like it. There were the 'ladies and gentlemen of the Park,' and the 'men and women of the [Hamlet] village.' However, in building Tuxedo Park, Lorillard created a community that provided secure employment for hundreds of people. Given my penchant for numbers, I recall that jobs in the surrounding communities paid far less than comparable jobs in Tuxedo. One did not go very far from the caste into which they were born. First, there were the Park members. Then there was the 'management class, which lived in a village called 'The Grove.' The rest, like my parents, also lived in the [Hamlet] village, or on the estates within the Park. They were the workers."

By 1936, when many like Frost and my parents were finishing high school, these strict social divisions began to break down, except for the main social wall between Tuxedo Club members and property owners inside the Park gates, and the "others" outside the gates. Over time, the claim our country was founded upon, "All men are created equal," became more apparent. Intermarriage between the different ethnic groups in the Hamlet and the East Village, as well as those working outside on the estates inside the Park, were becoming common. Today, hereditary pedigree or religious belief is no longer a barrier, and there are now members of the Tuxedo Club whose grandparents were not allowed in Tuxedo Park without a pass. Yet, some divisions from the old social structure continued to exist, including those focused around the Wee Wah Beach Club. There is still a sense of social difference by some inside and outside the gates based on where one resides.

After the summer of 1932, staff within the Park who held significant and respected positions on the larger estates were keenly aware of those Tuxedo Club members who were voicing concerns about how the Wee Wah Beach was being used. There were also those members who supported the needs and interests of the larger community. Many Tuxedo Club members sided with views in line with those expressed by Mrs. Frelinghuysen. The estate staffs and Hamlet population feared that access to the original Wee Wah Beach would again be denied. Duncan McGregor was among the group of community leaders who had a good relationship with Tuxedo Club members and the TPA officers.

In the summer of 1933, the idea for a "beach club" originated, and an informal arrangement developed that allowed use of the beach to resume. Although the land was owned by the TPA and thus controlled by many of the Tuxedo Club members who were Park residents and shareholders of the TPA, there was a tacit understanding that the staff employed in the Park, as well as residents of the Hamlet, could access the beach area. However, the service community who used the beach, not the TPA, was responsible for improvements and maintenance of the beachfront, the picnic area, the bathhouses, and the lifeguards. My paternal and maternal grandfathers, Duncan McGregor and Emil Barth, with nine children between their families (together with others from both the Park and leaders of the Hamlet) developed a plan to create this "beach club" that would offer memberships and collect dues to pay for the beach operations. By the fall of 1935, after two years of planning and implementation, these community leaders were looking for a more formal agreement about their rights to use the beach area. They were improving the property, despite having no assurance that Mrs. Frelinghuysen, or another Tuxedo Club member, would not once again convince the TPA to shut down their beach access whenever they felt the use of the beach infringed on their privacy and security, as well as the quiet enjoyment of their nearby residences.

Duncan created a committee of the more senior estate employees, Hamlet managers, and workers, as well as leading residents of the East Village, to prepare a plan that would formally allow use of the premises and create memberships so dues could be charged to improve and maintain the facilities, hire lifeguards, and manage the use of the beach.

Their plan was to form a club, but first, they had to approach the TPA, along with a select group of Tuxedo Club members who were known to be supportive of the concept. Duncan started with George Grant Mason, his boss. As estate manager, Duncan met regularly with Mr. Mason and knew Mason had started as a working man himself, getting his hands dirty performing actual labor. He had not grown up as a member of the privileged class. Indeed, he was now spectacularly rich, but when it came to Tuxedo and the Hamlet, he was generous with his money. Mr. and Mrs. Mason were not particularly concerned with exploiting their social status.

Mr. Mason had three chauffeurs at the time. The two main chauffeurs, James C. Murphy and Charles Rudd, were involved in the plan to form a beach club. They had Mason's ear to promote the plan while driving him in and out of the city. When Mason's wife died in 1929, their interaction with their boss increased as Mason made more frequent trips to his apartment in the city at 790 Park Avenue.

My grandfather also encouraged others, such as head gardeners like Emil Barth, my maternal grandfather, to speak with their employers about the matter. As I have noted, Emil Barth was the superintendent and head gardener for George Amory, who was the vice president, director, and treasurer of Seatrain Lines, one of the largest shipping companies of the time. In 1924, Amory married Rene Carhart, who had grown up at Villa Blanca next to the Frelinghuysen estate overlooking the Wee Wah Lake. The Amory estate, Renamor, consisted of twenty-five acres designed by George's brother-in-law, Edward H. Hubbard from 1928 to 1929.

Emil Barth was married and had five children who became close friends with the McGregor children. Amory provided the Barth family with a rent-free and beautiful gardener's cottage in Tuxedo Park on the west side of Tuxedo Lake. Like the McGregor apartment in the garage at Mason's Kincraig, Barth's cottage was spacious and had four bedrooms upstairs, including two master bedrooms, each containing a fireplace. The main floor had a large living room and formal dining room, with a butler's pantry connecting to the kitchen. A call box by the kitchen signaled a ring from any of the bedrooms. It was a beautiful home and not what one would imagine as a gardener's cottage. The grounds contained a vegetable garden, a pond, a large garage, and attached dog kennels for Amory's hunting dogs. I recall my grandfather coming home for lunch and to feed the dogs. For every type of hunt there was a dog, such as the big black Labrador, the pointer, the golden retriever, and the Irish setter. The family often lamented that the hamburger meat fed to the dogs was higher quality than the meat they could afford for themselves. The property also had a tennis court, a chicken coop, and a barn.

Not only would Emil Barth often speak to Mr. Amory, but he also maintained the hunting dogs and accompanied his boss on most occasions whenever Mr. Amory went shooting. What better time to lobby for the beach plan than when you are sitting in a duck blind, sharing whiskey on a cold fall day.

Those men (and women) from the Park and the Hamlet who had close relationships with Tuxedo Club members were part of the plan to get something in writing to formally allow them to use Wee Wah Beach during the summer. Many had children the same ages as my future father and mother, and all had enjoyed the Wee Wah Beach for many years. A letter would soon be forthcoming.

Other Tuxedo Park workers also sought and received support from their employers. William Muir was the head gardener for the Julliard family, known for funding the Julliard School of Music at Lincoln Center in New York City. Mrs. Koenig's husband worked for the Julliard family as well. The gardeners had the ears of the wives as they brought flowers to the houses daily and arranged them. Although most lived in the Park, Ralph Fioretti was a well-respected head gardener who lived outside the gates in the East Village.

Inside the houses, Eugene Mitchell worked for the Blairs, and John Moder worked for Mrs. Adelle Colgate, heir to the Colgate toothpaste fortune. A great help was Tilford's cook, a favorite in the household, and Fred Curtiss was a butler for Mr. Frederic O. Spedden. Frederic Spedden was very generous and always thinking of the Tuxedo Park help. His estate bordered the Wee Wah Lake, and he was one of very few who had a boathouse on this lake. Spedden and one of his good friends, a frequent visitor to Tuxedo Park, would buy tickets for all the Tuxedo High School boys and girls basketball teams and covered the expenses of sending them to Madison Square Garden in New York City to see college teams play. Much of Spedden's generosity and concern for children might have been inspired by the loss of his only son, Douglas, who was struck by a car at camp in Maine and died at the age of ten. Three years prior, the boy and his parents had survived the sinking of the *Titanic* on that fateful evening of April 15, 1912.[59] When not in Bar Harbor for the summer or wintering at various resorts around the world, Spedden spent a great deal of time at his Tuxedo Park estate, Wee Wah Lodge, with his wife, Margaretta Corning Stone, known to all as "Daisy."

Robert Sadd was a valet and houseman who later lived in the Hamlet on Augusta Place. Whenever opportunities arose, Village residents working in support positions on the estates promoted the community beach plan to their employers who were members of the Tuxedo Club. Irving Snyder worked at the post office with Fred Bentley. Charles Gebauer lived in the Hamlet on Patterson Hill and worked in the Tuxedo garage. H. Hinxman worked for the telephone company. William H. (Bill) Dickenson worked in the Tuxedo Community Bank. Joseph Mosher worked in the hardware store. Arthur Toker was the sexton of St Mary's Church. These highly regarded men in the community were able to get a word in with those Club members who were known to be supportive of their cause.

By early 1936, the community group's lobbying was enjoying positive feedback and ready for the next step. Duncan again spoke with Mr. Mason about how to approach the Tuxedo Club Board of Governors. George Grant Mason had already spoken with other supportive Tuxedo Club members and suggested to Duncan that it was time to take a more formal approach. Mr. Mason directed Duncan to talk with Vincent Macaluso (the TPA's vice president and general manager, who reported to the Board of Governors) and provide him with a written request. Macaluso would then present that to the Tuxedo Club Board of Governors. Mason and others would support it. The letter should set forth the community group's plan to create memberships and collect dues to improve and maintain the facilities, hire lifeguards, and operate a beach club.

In May of 1936, a letter was prepared and delivered to the TPA. It was signed by the group's leaders, and also by J.M. Winters of the TPA, and Henry Chisholm, a Tuxedo Club member who also owned the dry goods store in the Hamlet. The odds were improving. The agreement to form the club and admit members was subject to approval by the TPA, which was basically controlled by certain Park residents who at the time were also members of the Tuxedo Club.

It appeared the Tuxedo Club Board of Governors, along with Tuxedo Park Associates, approved the plan for the Tuxedo Community Club for the summer of 1936, although the beach property was owned by the TPA, which traditionally meant it was intended for the exclusive use of Tuxedo Club members. The discussions centered on the need for a recreational facility for the workers and service families who supported residents of Tuxedo Park and their families. The Board of Governors of the Tuxedo Club left the implementation of this agreement to the TPA, which reported to them. The agreement would clearly benefit those living in the Hamlet and working for or supporting Tuxedo Park residents.

The acceptance of the letter by the TPA and approved by the members of the Tuxedo Club now memorialized the return to the original beach area we know today and marked the official creation of the Tuxedo Community Club in 1936, which later became the Wee Wah Beach Club in 1978.

Tuxedo Park,New York.
May 18th,1936

The Tuxedo Park Association,
Tuxedo Park,
New York.

<u>Attention, Mr. Macaluso, General Manager.</u>

Dear Sir:

For the past several years we have had permission from the Park members and the Association to use the Wee Wah during the summer months for swimming purposes.

We presume that this privilege will be given us this year as it has in the past.

In order to maintain the floats and grounds and to keep a life guard in attendance during certain months we would like to form a swimming club so that we can obtain enough funds to defray the expenses of maintenance.

The amount charged per season to be $2.00 for each adult, $1.00 for junior members over 15 years of age and free to children.

Unless you have any objection to this plan we will issue season tickets to members and restrict this portion of the beach to them only.

Very truly yours,

Joseph Crisaione
Fred. Curtis
C. O. Bostwic.
Ralph A. Fiorette
Robert Badd

Mrs. C. B. Dickinson
William H. Dickinson
R. D. Cooley
Joseph Mosher
Hans Hansen
G. Martens
Eugene J. Mitchell
Mrs. Chas Getauer
Mrs. André Fuchs
Mrs. E. Koenig Sr.

152

Chapter 14: The Tuxedo Community Club Takes Shape

Children of early members from the Hamlet at the soon to be Tuxedo
Community Club, ca. 1930s

Now that the use of the beach had been approved, the group sat down to draft Articles of Incorporation and Bylaws to support and formalize the Tuxedo Community Club. They needed to define the geographical territory that would determine whether one could become a member, as well as the rules and regulations for the operation of this new organization. These were not uneducated men, although most had not attended college. These were hardworking, knowledgeable, practical men who were experts at their respective positions in the community. They were also helped by their children, many of whom had graduated from high school and, with financial help from their family's employers, were now attending college. Once they were given the approval, it did not take long to prepare the final documents. They adopted a constitution, selected officers, and established rules and regulations. Memberships were made available to all Tuxedo Park employees and service supporters who lived within a geographic boundary that included the Hamlet and the East Village.

With the final approval of the Tuxedo Club Board of Governors and under the direction of the TPA, the community leaders who drafted and signed the documents went to work. The Tuxedo Community Club now had use of the property, but managing a beach required organization. The summer of 1936 was a happy time for those who had formed the Tuxedo Community Club, but much work was left to formalize the organization. Meetings had to be scheduled to appoint Officers and a Board of Directors for the upcoming 1937–1938 season. The first president was Luis Euvrard, the high school principal who was highly respected in the community. Emil Barth, my paternal grandfather, was elected vice president, and his daughter, Margaret Barth (my mother, who later married James McGregor, my father and the son of Duncan), was elected treasurer. Eleanor Bentley was elected secretary. Patrick Cassidy, who lived close by in an area called Wildcat by the North Gate, was selected as lifeguard, and William Hamm was also chosen, as his parents resided within the Park. The meeting did not include an election as we know it today. Rather, there were suggestions, followed by a willingness to serve, and that was that. The Articles of Incorporation were ratified.

THE CONSTITUTION OF TUXEDO COMMUNITY CLUB

Article 1 - Section I

    A. Name

        1. This Club shall be called the Tuxedo Community Club

Article 1 - Section II

    A. Purpose

        1. To promote the social relations between the fellow members of this community.

        2. To improve the community beach through an organized effort by the people of the community.

Article I - Section III

    A. Who Shall Be Members

        1. All local residents living in the village of Tuxedo who have been voted on and passed by the people at a regular meeting.

        2. Non residents

            (a) Must be passed upon by an entrance board.
            (b) Voted upon by the Board of Directors.

Article I - Section IV

    A. Government of the Club

        1. Board of Directors

            (a) Body of 10 or 12 men
                (1) Shall be elected by people at the annual meeting.
                (2) Serve for a term of one (1) year

            (b) Powers of the Board
                (1) Pass upon non-residents applying for admission
                (2) Highest Authority

        2. President

            (a) Shall be elected for term of 1 year by the people at the annual meeting.

            (b) Conduct all meetings

(continued)

155

(c) May call all special meetings whenever
he deems it necessary.

(d) May elect members to serve on committees

3. Secretary

(a) Elected by people at the annual meeting
for a term of one year.

(b) Gives an accurate account of each meeting.

(c) Sends out notices & transact all secretar-
ial work.

4. Treasurer

(a) Elected for term of one year by people
at the annual meeting.

(b) Handles all bills & other financial matters.

(c) Gives a complete financial statement at
each regular meeting of the resources
of the club.

Article I - Section V

A. Meetings

1. Annual Meeting

(a) Shall be held the second Wednesday
in June of each year.
(1) election of officers
(2) renewal of dues

2. Regular Meetings

(a) Shall be held the second Wednesday
of each month

3. Special Meetings

(a) Shall be posted & called wherever necessary

4. Quorum

(a) Annual Meeting
(1) Quorum shall consist of at least
15 members
(b) Regular Meeting
(1) Quorum shall consist of at least
10 members.

(continued)

Article I - Section VI

    A. Dues

        1. Families

            (a) Dues shall consist of $2 per year &
                shall include Parents and all children
                under the age of 21 and unemployed.

        2. Junior Members

            (a) All persons who have reached the
                age of 21 years and are employed
                steadily, shall be charged $1 a year.

--- 0 ---

[Handwritten notes:]

Officers 1937-38

  President - Mrs L. Everard — Frank Cassidy   1

  Vice Pres. - Mr. E Barth

  Treasurer - Margaret Barth — Mrs Alex. Henderson   2

  Secretary - Eleanor Buntley — Arthur Takser   3

1941

Board of Directors:

  Rev. Father Tahy   Life Guard — Newton Harris

(1) Mr. U. Macaluso

(2) Mr. R. Husted ✓

(3) Mr. L. Everard ✓ Tax 40 ✓

(4) Mr. R. Fioretti ✓

(5) Mr. D. McGregor ✓

  ~~Mr. H. Hinfman~~

(6) Mr. C. Mottola ✓

  ~~Mr. A. Gulden~~

(7) Mr. N. Chisholm ✓

(8) Mr. J. H. Winters ✓   Al - Tax 269

(9) [illegible]

(10) Mr. F. W. Murray   Irving Snyder

Dues were set at $2 per family for the entire season. To ensure an avenue of communication, and the ability for the TPA to monitor activities, Vincent Macaluso, the TPA's vice president and general manager, and Tuxedo Club member H. Chisholm, were appointed to the Board. Henry L. Chisholm was a financier who made Tuxedo Park his home. He was a director of the Tuxedo Stores Company, and also owned a dry goods store in the Hamlet where he donated all profits to the Tuxedo Memorial Hospital.

The Board and the TPA agreed to a residence boundary outside the Park for the Hamlet and East Village memberships. The beach area was cleaned, and a picnic area outlined. A small parking area was planned to avoid intruding on the Gun Club, which was off limits to the Tuxedo Community Club and continued to be active with shooting in the fall and winter months, along with skating and the toboggan run, well into the 1930s. Gun club members were not about to allow their facility to be used by anyone other than Tuxedo Club members, families, and guests. Large boulders were placed along the entrance to Pigeon Point, except for an opening that led to the Gun Club portico that now served as entrance to the Beach Club. This checkpoint ensured that only members were allowed access. The "checker," a member of the new Beach Club, sat next to the covered portico, and a rope was drawn across the entrance attached to the Gun Club building. The job of the checker was to oversee who was coming through. Members were issued passes. Those from the Hamlet would also have to show their passes to enter the main gate into the Park. The checker recorded the member's name and lowered the rope allowing access to the parking area and beach. Those who did not arrive by car walked to the beach, but all passed through the same gate. The checker was responsible for making sure nobody accessed the beach without a club card. While there were no fences, most followed the rules because everyone knew this privilege could easily be revoked by the TPA. Of course, teenagers of the time would, on occasion, enter the beach from every conceivable entry point. In those days, one could be sure that if caught there would be a stern lecture—or worse—from their parents.

Chapter 15: The Early Years

Front: Charles Gegoun (sp), Albert Gineri (sp), Mabel Tansey, Fred Bentley
Second: Marie McGregor, Evelyn Moles, Majorie Ellings, Violet Martin
Third: Charles Bower, Bill Bowns, Pat Cassidy, James McGregor, ca. 1936

After the initial season in 1936, Luis Euvrard stepped down and Pat Cassidy, the lifeguard for that season, was elected president. Pat's appointment made perfect sense as he had spent so much time at the beach and understood how it could be improved. He lived in

Wildcat, just outside the North Gate within the boundaries approved by the TPA at that time. Members made many suggestions for improvements, but the main issues involved creating the areas for child play, picnicking, and clearing the beachfront. The sweat and hard work paid off once Beach Club members could finally jump into the lake to cool off and enjoy the wonderful views from the point. The picnic area faced the lake to the south within a beautiful, shade-providing strand of white birch trees. The old wooden retaining logs and platforms of the Tuxedo Club beach had been removed by the TPA. They left the original retaining wall and the stone foundation of the dock reaching out from the sandy beachfront. The TPA was supportive and helpful, as indicated by my mother's letter of August 13, 1937, and the reply from Vincent Macaluso, general manager of the TPA, on August 14, 1937.

Tuxedo Park, N.Y.
August 13, 1937

Dear Sir:

The Tuxedo Community Club wish to express their appreciation and thanks for the interest which you have shown in helping it to organize and develop.

You have our deep gratitude for the many things which you, and the Tuxedo Association have done for us.

Very truly yours,
Tuxedo Community Club
Margaret Barth
Treasurer

Mr. Vincent Macaluso
Tuxedo Park
New York.

August 14,1937

Miss Margaret Barth, Treasurer,
Tuxedo Community Club,
Tuxedo Park,
New York.

My dear Miss Barth:

          This will acknowledge receipt of your
check of $112.07 as payment to The Tuxedo Park
Association from The Tuxedo Community Club for all
work done to date at the swimming beach.

          The Tuxedo Park Association is very
glad indeed to cooperate fully with the Club and
will try as soon as possible to move the bath houses
to a better location so as to be more convenient
for its members. We are indeed very pleased to know
that you are satisfied with our efforts in behalf
of the Club for what we have tried to do.

                              Very truly yours,

                              General Manager.

In May of 1940, Pat Cassidy's letter to members announced the opening of the new season.

TUXEDO COMMUNITY CLUB

Tuxedo, New York

May 31, 1940

Dear Friends:

Another year in our beach season has passed and a new one begun.

Enclosed is a yearly report of the financial standing of the club.

As you can see, the balance is very low and therefore in order to maintain our beach as formerly and keep a guard in charge it is necessary that all dues, which are two dollars a family for the entire season, must be paid by the thirtieth of June. Dues may be paid to any of the officers or to Margaret Barth, Treasurer.

You will be notified as to the date of the annual meeting, at which time new officers will be elected and the work to be done at the beach this year discussed.

Sincerely,

TUXEDO COMMUNITY CLUB

Patrick Cassidy
President

The treasurer's report by Margaret Barth from the 1939 summer season showed 119 members and $2.20 cash on hand as of June 1, 1940.

TUXEDO COMMUNITY CLUB

May 31, 1940

Treasurer's Report

June 1, 1939   June 1, 1940

Present Bank Balance $44.46

119 Members @ $2.00	$238.00	Bal. in Bank	$133.66
Bank Balance last year	133.66	July 3 yearly dues	106.00
	$371.66	July 10 yearly dues	66.00
		Nov. 8 cash deposits	16.37
		Cash expenditures	47.43
Total Receipts for year 1939		Cash on hand	2.20
			$371.66

		Expenditures	
Receipts	$371.66	Cash	$ 47.43
Expenditures	327.20	Checks	279.77
Balance	$ 44.46		$327.20

Cash on hand June 1, 1939
$ 52.00

Cash Expenditures

Gas for grass cutter	.50
100 1g postal cards	1.00
Medals for picnic	6.31
Spreading sand	8.00
Lumber	4.32
Rake, chain, padlock	2.50
Relief life guard 2 days	4.00
Medicine for first aid kit	.59
Picnic supplies, 20 qts. ice cream, etc.	13.98
Home Service, paint, nails, broom, etc.	7.23
	$47.43
Cash deposited in bank	2.37
	$49.80

Cash on hand June 1, 1940 $ 49.80
                            2.20

The members constructed horseshoe pits, erected a swing set, and volunteers created a sand play area. A standard size rowboat was purchased for use by the lifeguard. Carl Spiers was paid $6 per week for maintenance work and for cutting the grass during the season. Lifeguards were paid $10 per week for the season that opened on June 24 and closed on September 9. There was a concern among all the members who were responsible for balancing the expenses with the revenues. Besides ongoing maintenance, there was the constant need for future improvements. As with any facility, the Beach Club would grapple with these same issues for years to come.

The first secretary was Eleanor Bentley, followed by Arthur Tocher a few years later. As the Great Depression dragged on, this new beach club offered a welcome respite from the difficult realities for many in the Hamlet outside the Tuxedo Park gates.

Chapter 16: The 1940s

Tuxedo Community Club members, with the pigeon release stand in the background, ca. 1940

Throughout the 1940s and into the 1950s, the Tuxedo Community Club continued to grow. Many residents of the Hamlet, and staff living and working in the Park, became members in greater numbers. The original residents of the early Tuxedo community were seeing their children, now grown men and women, having children of their own. Both inside and outside the Park, college and work took these young families to places far from the solitude, seclusion, and class distinctions of the Tuxedo Club and Tuxedo Park. For many original Tuxedo Park residents, the lifestyle of the Gilded Age had long since passed. The Great Depression, income taxes, the war, and new job growth afterward had taken a toll, creating an inability to hire help to maintain large estates. Many original Gilded Age owners were now deceased, and their children no longer wanted to maintain such incredible but highly demanding properties. The owners of the largest estates could no longer find staff or justify the expense of maintaining part-time occupancy. Prior to this period, many Tuxedo Club members had maintained four or five residences up the East Coast, from Maine or Rhode Island, and down to Florida. Now many were opting to maintain just three residential properties, such as a winter home in Palm Beach, a full-time address in New York City, and a home in Tuxedo Park. If there was staff, it might be a butler, cook, housekeepers, groundskeeper, and chauffeur. Cleveland Amory, author of several successful books on Aristocracy in America, wrote in *The Last Resorts,* published in 1948, that Edith Wetmore left Chateau Sur Mer, Newport's first large mansion built for her grandfather 100 years ago, to the Society of New England Antiquities. Miss Whetmore remarked "We're at the end of an era, if you please." The large properties that were built around the turn of the twentieth century were now an albatross for the sons and daughters who either had no interest in owning the properties, or perhaps were fond of the properties, but could no longer afford to maintain them.[60]

Some Tuxedo Park estates, including Mason's Kincraig and Amory's Renamor, continued to thrive into the 1950s, thus providing work for both of my grandfathers and other longtime dedicated staff members and their families. However, society culture was not dead. The Tuxedo Club membership and its activities, as well as the occupancy of the many cottages, did not change. Customs remained basically the same, and one always understood their place in this community. Children growing up continued using the phrases "Parkies" and "Townies" to denote where one resided.

The country had changed rapidly from the Depression years,

thanks in part to social plans to create work such as the Works Project Administration (WPA). The regal social settings established in the Gilded Age had long since passed. Those outside the gates were finding jobs in industry. The sons and daughters of the original village residents were continuing on to college and entering professions once reserved for those with Ivy League degrees and family connections. However, the difference in how those living in Tuxedo Park continued an affluent lifestyle with respect to those who lived outside the gates and were not members of the Tuxedo Club was clearly on display. An example would be the Fourth of July, or Independence Day. It was still celebrated in a unique way. In the early years, this was the only day that all people who lived outside the gates were allowed in the Park without a pass for a parade inside the Park ending at the Tuxedo Club. After the parade there were races and contests for prizes, and lunch was spread out around the Tuxedo Club. Now, since the formation of the Tuxedo Community Club (later the Wee Wah Beach Club), the activities have moved to the beach for those who were not Tuxedo Club members. This situation proved more "convenient" for everyone, as those from the Hamlet had no need to have access to the Tuxedo Club grounds, nor was there the annual "discomfort," as some would have delicately described it, brought about by the temporary mix of the different social statuses.

Activities had slowed during the World War II years, as many men and women in town and the Park volunteered their services to our country. Once again, it was easy to see the distinction between those serving from the Park and those serving from the Hamlet. All were eager to serve the country, but the majority of those whose families worked and lived in the Park or resided outside the gates were enlisted, while those members of the Tuxedo Club from the Park received commissions as officers. One can only marvel that even well into the 1940s, life at some Tuxedo Park estates still resembled a style of life as portrayed in the hit PBS series *Downton Abbey*. Certainly, the social status survived. Several estates and large houses were still operating, and the Tuxedo Club remained a bastion of privacy, comprised of members with a familial connection to old society and/or substantial wealth.

However, July Fourth was a day for everyone, no matter what their social class. In the 1940s, the parade would start at the north end of Pond 3 and come up the road to the main club. There it would make a right turn down by the Tennis and Racquet Club and up the hill where it would round the triangle on West Lake Road and return to finish at the main entrance to the Club.

The parade procession passing the Tuxedo Club—and then returning after passing the Club pool, July 4, 1948

From its inception, the parade was led by the Volunteer Fire Department, but by the mid-1940s, it was led by a marching band brought in by the Tuxedo Club. The parade included the Women's Auxiliary, the Tuxedo Park Police Department, Boy Scouts, Girl Scouts, and other community groups. At the end of the parade, the children, whether from the Hamlet or the more privileged sons and daughters of Tuxedo Club members, could jump on the fire trucks for a wild ride around Pond 3 with sirens wailing.

The author appears in the first photo, fourth from the right at the rear of the truck, July 4, 1948

Tuxedo Club members would then retire to the Club, and the local community would follow the fire engines and the band to Wee Wah Beach. At the Beach, races and other events were held and prizes were awarded. Sports were a big part of the activities and there were always spirited games of horseshoes and bocce. I am confident that money changed hands, as wagering was common.

The fire department set out tables where everyone would line up for free sandwiches of ham salad or cheese, a soft drink, and a paper cup of ice cream with a small flat wooden spoon. The cup of ice crème was a favorite because when you pulled the lid off, there was always a picture of a movie star on the inside cover. Needless to say, you would never find an ice crème top on the ground at the picnic as they were highly prized collectible items and the subject of many trades by the children as the day wore on. Of course, there were soft drinks, but this was a firemen's picnic. The line that never ended was the one for adults leading toward the beer kegs. Fortunately, my uncle, George McGregor, a longtime volunteer fireman, never recalled any fires on the Fourth of July. I suppose few residents wanted to be on the road when the beer kegs were empty and the fire engines departed at the end of the day, with their sirens blaring and with their volunteer members hanging off the sides.

During these early years, the beach opening followed by the July Fourth picnic were the main events at the start of the season. Other well-attended activities were the annual picnic, usually in August, when the children of members would participate in events such as land and water races, followed by an abundance of food and drink.

The beach community grew, and the Tuxedo Community Club enjoyed great success, due in large measure to the steady, dedicated leadership of Mabel Tansey, elected President in 1945. Mabel Jones Tansey was the daughter of Charlie Jones.

Mabel Tansey (1911–2000), President of The Tuxedo Community Club from 1945 to 1979

Mabel was born in a small house across the road from Pigeon Point. Her grandfather, Luke Jones, resided in Jones Point, an isolated community now known as part of Bear Mountain State Park. Luke Jones was a woodsman who cut wood for the railroad in the winter. He was known as something of a mountain man. The Jones family had lived in the area for as long as anyone could remember, having moved to Tuxedo with the early development by Pierre Lorillard. Mabel's father, Charlie, took after his father. Charlie Jones was responsible for maintaining the Gun Club, alternatively called the Pigeon Grounds, and was lifeguard for the Tuxedo Club members at the beach in the early years of the Park. He taught swimming as well. Charlie was an avid hunter, trapper, and fisherman. Stories abound about Charlie Jones, but the favorite story of the locals involves him chasing down a deer. It was reported that Charlie was hunting with his two dogs when they spotted a deer and the chase began. Soon Charlie had caught up with his dogs, gathered one under each arm, and continued the chase till he closed in and brought down the deer.

Mabel was raised in Tuxedo Park and attended school in the Hamlet. She attended the State University of New York at Cortland, taking courses in physical education. Each year she took a summer job as a lifeguard at the Tuxedo Club pool, where she had the opportunity to teach swimming to many notable youngsters including the actor, Fred Gwynne, famous for his role on the TV series, *The Munsters*. She could recall President Harry Truman and his daughter, Margaret, at the pool. Most days, the children at the Tuxedo Club pool were accompanied by Scottish nannies and French nurses.

Mabel Tansey at the Tuxedo Club Pool, ca. 1926

For a time, Mabel returned to Tuxedo and taught gym and coached, but after a slip and fall injury on the school stairs left her unable to continue teaching gym, she attended Columbia University and earned a bachelor of science and a master's degree. She then returned to Tuxedo High School as a guidance counselor and, informally, served as what we would call a "dean of students" today. Mabel was a favorite of all the students for many years.

Mabel married Joe Tansey, an expert horticulturalist, naturalist, and gardener for the Tilford estate on June 30, 1934. Joe studied and worked at the Botanical Gardens with my uncle, George McGregor. Not only did they finish near the top of their class, but they also were important members of the Botanical Gardens baseball team, which played semi-pro teams throughout the five boroughs of New York City. George returned to the Park to work with my grandfather at Kincraig, George Grant Mason's estate, and was the first to teach me how to play baseball. I still have an autographed baseball my uncle gave me from the great New York Yankee legend, Babe Ruth, who frequently visited the Tuxedo Golf Club as well as many of the bars and nightclubs in nearby Greenwood Lake.

During summers at the Beach Club, Mabel also taught swimming to generations of members and, when not working at the Tuxedo Club, she was at the beach morning, noon, and night during the season. Mabel was personable, always had a smile, and was full of energy. However, she was not afraid to speak her mind, and there were no discipline problems in her classes or at the beach. When she blew the whistle, you stopped. She was elected president in 1945. Her oldest son Dick, daughter Barbara (better known as Boz), and young Joe (better known as JoJo) also served as lifeguards as they grew up. Boz took over the swimming lessons and taught me how to swim. Speaking of lifeguard traditions, records reveal that Beach Club family members have served in this important position for generations, as we will see.

In the mid-1940s, Mabel ran a local recreation program for all the children of the Town of Tuxedo. In the 1950s, the State of New York under Governor Nelson Rockefeller began a program that would provide $1,000 to any town that would also contribute $1,000 to set up and run a local recreation program. Mabel jumped at this chance to enroll in this program for the youth of Tuxedo. A recreation program was created, and the youth of the community enjoyed mornings of games and crafts at George F. Baker High School, followed by a bus ride to the Beach Club for an afternoon of swimming lessons and water sports. Mabel expanded the program to include outings like hiking trips, fishing trips to Mountain Lake, roller skating at the covered open-air roller rink on the shore of Lake Kanawauke in Bear Mountain State Park, and many other fun activities. As stated, the person in charge and leader of all activities was Mabel Tansey. The end of recreation each season was celebrated by a picnic at the beach with both land and water races for all the children. Recreation days at the beach continued well into the twenty-first century, and believe it or not, the same races were run in the same place, and with the same start and finish lines.

A joyous season-ending recreation day, ca. early 1940s

The author, second from the left, 1949

The author's youngest son, Michael, third from the right, 1993

In the 1940s, the Tuxedo Community Club served as the center of summer activities, firmly establishing its place in the history of Tuxedo Park. During this time work began in earnest to upgrade the facilities, and much of what one sees today was constructed at that time. The picnic area was cleared, as was the land where a basketball court and volleyball pit exist today. The remnants of broken clay pigeons and shotgun shells were removed.

The 1946 season began with the reelection of officers. Member volunteers cleared many trees felled by a bad storm in early spring, repaired the docks and the diving board, removed poison ivy (an annual problem), and discussed the possibility of constructing a fountain for drinking water. Other decisions included the "election" by popular vote of lifeguards from those applying for a salary of $20 a week, and they voted to continue the "no dogs allowed" policy. Lifeguards worked 12:00 to 6:00 p.m. daily, with the beach closing at 9:00 p.m. Dues for the full summer season were raised from the usual

$2 to $5 per family.

That season, Tillie Henderson (who worked as the lady's maid for Mrs. Amory at the Renamor estate) together with John Modder, organized a raffle on July 14 for a case of assorted liquors and wines, with the funds to be used for installation of a drinking fountain. Along with Tillie, my grandfather Emil Barth (superintendent of the Amory Estate), and Tillie's husband Alec (George Amory's houseman) mentioned the project to Mrs. Amory, who donated $10 and one quart of liquor. She then mentioned it to other Tuxedo Club members. Mrs. H. P. Rodgers gave $20. Mrs. Bonnet supplied a picnic table and benches for the Beach Club. These women, whose husbands were well-respected members of the Tuxedo Club, were very supportive of the new Beach Club. Other members of the Beach Club from the Hamlet also each donated a quart of liquor. The raffle raised almost $175, and the minutes reflect that a "John Winslow" was the winner. There were additional raffle prizes mentioned in the minutes as well, with "Mrs. McMahon's own cake" earning the Beach Club another $15. Her husband, Paddy McMahon, was responsible for maintaining the prize-winning National Horse Show jumpers, as well as the Westminster Dog Show prize setter and pointer dogs kept in the kennels and stables at the George St. George estate on West Lake Road. If you lived in Tuxedo, you knew that a cake baked by Mrs. McMahon and desserts made by Alice Rigby (a cook for H. P. Rogers), were highly prized.

After the July Fourth picnic in 1946, a meeting was called to discuss the large number of picnickers and swimmers who had gained entrance to the Park as guests of known Beach Club members. One must remember that the Beach Club operated under a lease from the

Tuxedo Park Association, which was responsible for the overall administration of the Park on behalf of Tuxedo Club members. Although rent was paid to the TPA, use of the Wee Wah by its members—both Park and Hamlet residents—was considered by Tuxedo Club members to be a privilege and not a right. At this meeting, it was decided that a limitation on guests was needed. Starting the following season, "two guests per day" would be allowed for each family membership, and guests had to be accompanied by known Beach Club members. The "guest passes" would continue to be a source of friction for years to come.

In 1947, the abandoned Gun Club was turned over to the Beach Club to be used for additional bath houses and a post for the "checker." The interior became available for changing rooms and areas for community activities. As had always been the case, volunteers stepped forward. One of the sad decisions that had to be made regarding the Gun Club resulted from the nature of young boys, and sometimes girls, who felt that windows were better used as targets for rock throwing than to provide views of the outside. The Gun Club was surrounded by windows on both floors. By the time the Beach Club was given permission to use the structure, all the windows were broken. The decision was made to board up the openings as replacing the windows would just encourage the children to continue practicing the art of rock throwing. This also served to provide more privacy for the areas that were now converted into changing rooms.

A major change took place in May 1947. From the beginning of the Lorillard development in 1885, residents of the Hamlet outside the gates were tenants of properties owned by the TPA. The TPA reportedly decided to divest most property outside the Park, and village residents were given the chance to buy their homes. *"Many of the tenants are employed by the association in the maintenance of public facilities and service department by the Tuxedo Club and by residents and businessmen."* Thus, many original employees of the large estates, and many of their grown children who were renting small one, two, and four-family homes now had the opportunity to become property owners. Building lots were also made available.[61]

The original TPA was owned by Lorillard and a few others. Prior to this time, all property in the Hamlet was owned by this group and continued the TPA policy of renting all property in the Hamlet. This allowed for control over the quantity and type of businesses, and it allowed for control over the population outside the gate. However, in order to raise funds to pay off the original shareholders, in 1947 the TPA offered those renting the houses in the Hamlet and East Village an opportunity to purchase them. Many had a connection to Tuxedo Park as a result of their parents originally working in the park or servicing Park residents. These renters were given forty-five days to decide, and they were offered discounts based on their years of service to residents of Tuxedo Park.

The same was true for many young fathers and mothers who had grown up in the Park and were raising their families in many of the old carriage houses, garage apartments, and small staff cottages remaining from the great estates. Most of these properties were owned by a company called Tuxedo Homes, owned by a resident member of the Tuxedo Club who had purchased the Tuxedo Park properties from the TPA. Many of the original stables and coach houses that serviced smaller estates were located along roads with names such as Clubhouse, Upper Clubhouse, East Stable, and Stable. These properties, now being rented as homes, were originally built on TPA property because several of the earliest Tuxedo Park cottages and residences had no room for their own stables. Privately owned cottages and separate staff quarters on the larger estates had been sold off and were also now inhabited and rented by the next generation of original employees of the large estates.

Closing the beach at the end of the season in these times required towing the dock around the bend to the "old" north beach where Mr. Sahler, a local contractor, used his truck to haul it ashore. Volunteers would then drag in the ropes and turn off the water to the Gun Club and the grounds.

In 1947, my uncle Jim Barth replaced my maternal grandfather, Emil or "Barth" as he was affectionately known, on the Executive Committee. Barth was among the original group to create the Tuxedo Community Club (or Beach Club) and had served since the beginning. Jim Barth's brother's wife, my aunt Sis Barth, also was selected for the Committee. As with the other members, my grandfather was an active participant in the growth of the Beach Club in these early years. He also contributed much time and labor, as evidenced by the large communal stone fireplace he built in the small picnic area that was a centerpiece for many years.

As mentioned earlier, it was during this year that Mabel Tansey approached the TPA and requested that the Tuxedo Community Club be allowed to use the Gun Club, which was falling into disrepair from lack of use. The TPA agreed, as long as the Beach Club would give it proper care; however, there was some discussion about selling that piece of property at a later date. The TPA agreed that if the property should be sold, the Beach Club would be reimbursed $1 for every hour of volunteer work involved in the building's restoration and maintenance. The TPA also agreed to install toilet fixtures, turn on the water, and have a mason rebuild the fireplaces. Lastly, the TPA agreed that the Beach Club could operate a refreshment concession in the building. In July 1947, the Beach Club held a card party and $25 raffle each Sunday during the Beach Club season, with tickets being sold for $1 to raise funds to fix the Gun Club. In addition, the TPA was asked to provide a new dock for $250, which led to another card party on December 3, 1947 in the high school cafeteria.

As the 1948 season arrived, the Gun Club had begun looking like a new building, freshly painted outside, and restored inside. Members continued volunteer work well into the nights to finish the project. Everyone was involved in some way. Windows were replaced. Members were making curtains, and others were finishing the upstairs dressing rooms. At this point, the Executive Committee decided that beginning with the 1948 season, children eleven and under would continue using the old original bath houses below the play area, and those twelve and over would now use the Gun Club building—but more funds were needed.

The Beach Club, now thriving with volunteer action, had a restored building, and improved outdoor facilities, including a larger picnic area with fireplaces. New ideas for fundraising seemed to pop up every day. Even though the virtually new building had increased annual expenses, there was a reluctance to raise member dues. One idea: Why not host an amateur musical revue, open to the public, to raise revenue?

In August, Beach Club members performed a musical revue at George F. Baker High School in the Village. While they were amateur performers at best, many of the Club members, like my mother, aunts, and uncles had participated as children in theater arts and music at the school. When many of the older members were children, they would get together after school, and particularly during the summer, gathering at the beach or in someone's garage in costume to perform plays.

Upon George F. Baker High School's professionally designed stage, volunteers gathered and shared their talents during long hours of practice to make the show a success. The musical revue, *Even You*, was just that. The show was a hit!

THE TUXEDO COMMUNITY CLUB

presents

"EVEN YOU"

A MUSICAL REVUE

GEORGE F. BAKER AUDITORIUM · TUXEDO · NEW YORK

The performances were surprisingly good and entertaining. Mothers with young children, and fathers working full-time jobs, had recognized the importance of the community's needs, and so they came together to perform. After the revue, there was no letup in raising funds. Some Tuxedo Club members, including Mrs. George Amory and Mrs. H. P. Rodgers, continued to provide annual donations to the Beach Club. Other Tuxedo Club members paid the membership fee even though they never used the beach. Throughout the winter, club members held food sales during social events at members' homes in order to further fund the Beach Club's operating account.

With the approach of spring 1949, the members began working at night continuing to improve the beach club and putting the finishing touches on the Gun Club. After much discussion about overcrowding, a vote of the membership was taken and a majority approved raising dues to $10 for first-time members, and annual family dues of $5 thereafter. Membership was now approaching 200 members. Concern was increasing by property owners in Tuxedo Park, who were members of the Tuxedo Club, about the number of guest cars following members from outside the Park to the Beach Club. Membership requests poured in from throughout the Town of Tuxedo. A request from the Nurses' Home, a lodging facility for nurses at the hospital, to admit eight nurses was approved as a group membership since they were residing in the Hamlet.

As the summer passed, expenses continued to increase. It was decided to hold another performance of *Even You* to raise funds. A program was printed, local businesses were solicited for advertisements, and the Board decided the price of tickets would be seventy-five cents for adults and forty cents for children. Once again, on Monday evening, August 29, 1949 at 8:30 p.m., another revue was performed by the members of the Beach Club at the George F. Baker auditorium.

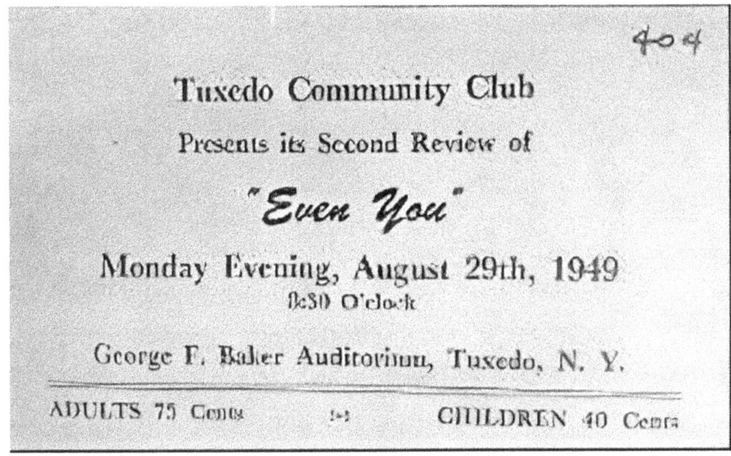

Admission ticket for Even You

The revenue helped improve the bank balance, as there were few expenses, but as was the case the year before, you could not put a price on the efforts of the members who gave of their time and talents making their own costumes, rehearsing, and performing.

The Tuxedo Community Club had become a focal point of activity for many residents who worked in the Park and now owned the many old stables, cottages, and carriage houses from the TPA. They were not members of the Tuxedo Club and did not live in the Hamlet. The area for swimming, parking, picnicking, and outdoor activities had grown five-fold from its humble beginnings fifteen years earlier. But with growth came problems as well. Membership issues and establishing written rules and regulations now took precedence over pulling out stumps in the picnic area and expanding the beachfront with a non-swimmer area. The Tuxedo Park Chief of Police, Edward I.

Greene, had the ultimate responsibility for controlling entry into Tuxedo Park. He was a fair-minded, even-handed keeper of the peace. Residents of the Park could rarely do wrong, and as to the Hamlet, he maintained a soft spot, particularly for the young boys and girls, as his wife was my first-grade teacher at the school and was much loved by her classroom children. He easily could determine the background of those outside the Park, as Mrs. Greene could provide information about the children, their families, and their home lives.

Chief Green reported to the Tuxedo Club and TPA, and so his responsibilities to the Tuxedo Club came first. He was often called with respect to complaints from residents of the Park, many of whom were uncomfortable with the growing popularity of the Tuxedo Community Club and the growing number of members from outside the Park. It was recorded in the Beach Club minutes of September 14, 1949 that Chief Greene had received ten complaints on one evening alone about swimmers using the beach after 9:00 p.m. At this point in time, it is doubtful that the complaints were coming from Mrs. Frelinghuysen, or from any original residents and members of the Tuxedo Club. The more likely source of the calls was the new generation of Tuxedo Club members, folks attempting to wrap themselves in the past traditions and carry themselves as Tuxedo Club elites. One could see the storm clouds gathering for a clash of cultures as the dynamic decade of the 1950s was about to begin.

Chapter 17: The Early 1950s

Picnic at the beach, ca. early 1950s

The United States entered the 1950s under the leadership of President Harry S. Truman, now well into his own elected term after assuming President Franklin D. Roosevelt's fourth term in 1945. The country was rapidly putting the Depression and World War II years behind it. Throughout the United States, major changes were taking place, and Tuxedo Park was no exception. Many Hamlet residents returning from the war were starting families and finding full-time jobs in industry. Concurrently, many of Tuxedo Park's elite were continuing to "downsize," a common word today, but a relatively new concept in Tuxedo Park at that time. Chauffeurs, butlers, cooks, housekeepers, and gardeners remained at some estates, but a house or grounds staff of twenty or so had long since disappeared. Children whose parents worked on the estates had grown, attended college, served their country, and were now leaving the area to start families of their own in the new suburbia beyond New York City.

The original men who had built Tuxedo Park had since passed on, and the early men and women who had long worked there and in the original village outside the gates, were now deceased, retired, or nearing retirement. To be sure, estates like those of George Grant Mason, George Amory, and a few others, continued as if nothing had changed other than employing fewer in-house staff. Many other estates were left vacant, had been torn down, had become the subject of accidental (or not) fires, and some had been donated to charitable organizations. The days of the Gilded Age were now truly long gone. Both my grandfathers continued as superintendents maintaining Renamor and Kincraig, but the Amorys and George Grant Mason spent little time there. The Tuxedo Club was no longer the bastion of elite society and enormous wealth that it had been thirty years prior. Despite all the changes, social division endured.

In May 1950, the Tuxedo Park Association announced a plan to sell off open areas of land and to allow for the subdivision of some of the large estates into smaller lots. This was done to increase the population, yet the announcement caused concern, as the price range for these new homes would be in the $25,000 to $40,000 price range. The TPA's developer stated that there would be approximately 100 new homes and asserted that the character of Tuxedo Park would not be changed. Of course, given the prices and lot sizes, the homes were more like those being built in the suburban developments popular in the expanding areas beyond New York City.

Social change was about to firmly establish itself in Tuxedo Park, just as the country was seeing extensive development brought on by the post-war years. [62] This would ultimately lead to a vote to incorporate Tuxedo Park in 1952.

Meantime, the Tuxedo Community Club at the beach continued to mature. Those who had used the original beach as children of the working class before the founding of the Beach Club were now parents themselves. In 1950, my mother, Margaret Barth McGregor, who was the first treasurer until relinquishing that position to my Aunt Marie, again stepped up and this time was elected secretary. Her minutes reflect that the first Executive Meeting of the decade was held on June 27. I was now five years old. After much discussion, household membership dues were raised to $10 for the season and all persons over 21 who were self-supporting, despite living at home, would have to purchase their own annual membership for $5. This was a difficult choice, which led to a caveat that if the Beach Club gate guard received an abundance of complaints about the increase, the decision would be reconsidered.

The Beach Club was asked to participate in an annual scholarship fund to send a deserving senior at George F. Baker High School to college. My aunt on my father's side, Marie McGregor McCarroll, now treasurer, was assigned to set up a committee to explore the request. This request came from the school principal and first president of the Beach Club, Louis Euvrard, and John J. Slocum from the TPA. With a report from twenty-eight members selected by Marie and very little discussion, the Beach Club agreed to make an annual contribution. After all, the probability was high that the lucky graduate would be the child of a Beach Club member. The children of Tuxedo Club members typically went to the private Tuxedo Park School, then matriculated to the elite prep schools to prepare for entry into the Ivy League colleges. There was little need for a scholarship fund as most were financially able to cover college tuition and costs. In addition, many children of Tuxedo Club members were what was known as legacies at the colleges, and many of the schools had endowments or buildings named for their ancestors. As children, my mother, Margaret McGregor, and my aunt Marie had grown up using the beach, which had motivated my grandparents to form the Beach Club. Now they were both married and had the responsibility to keep the Beach Club operating in good standing with the TPA so that my friends from the Park and Hamlet could enjoy the same experience.

Membership increased with this second generation of young members, whose own children would later become known as Baby Boomers. The ever-present subject of tennis courts moved up on the to-do list and many, led by James Barth, argued strongly that tennis should be a part of the club. There was room to the north toward the large old icehouse, where the stand for releasing the pigeons remained from the days of the Gun Club. The area was flat and would be easy to clear. A number of members volunteered to do the work. Although there was support for this activity, many were also concerned about the cost and the Tuxedo Club's reaction. The Beach Club decided to take a survey of the membership. Much of the opposition expressed by members was not about cost, but rather the concern that the sport of tennis should be reserved for the upper-class members of the Tuxedo Club. As noted earlier, changes that threatened Tuxedo Club's long-held class distinctions did not come easily.

When I discussed the Beach Club meeting minutes with my Aunt Marie, she recalled that into the early 1950s, there persisted a psychological barrier involving tennis; that is, some Beach Club members believed that tennis would be better left to Tuxedo Club members. They feared the plan would bring unwanted attention to the Tuxedo Community Club. In any event, in those years, horseshoes and bocce were much more popular than tennis with the Beach Club members.

With any controversial matter, the Beach Club tried to remain under the radar of Tuxedo Club members. Pigeon Point was, after all, owned by the TPA, and some Tuxedo Club members who owned TPA shares had not supported the original Beach Club plan, asserting that new tennis courts were not the best use for their property. Some Beach Club members worried that Tuxedo Club members would object to the expansion of activities at the Beach Club. During the early 1950s, remaining large estates were being gifted to charitable organizations, sold by their owners, or auctioned off by surviving family members and subdivided into smaller lots suitable for new development. The housing market at the time was not bursting at the seams for mansions containing large kitchens in basements and upper floors with multiple small rooms for "help quarters."

During this period, fear and rumors abounded that the beach area was for sale by the TPA. Every year the rumor would resurface that home sites were to be sold on Pigeon Point and at the racetrack, notwithstanding that they were originally planned and developed by Pierre Lorillard to remain as recreational areas. As a result, the proposed construction of tennis courts was again sidetracked. The Beach Club President, Mabel Tansey, entered into discussions with the TPA concerning these rumors. Mabel reported back to the board that both the racetrack and the beach (Gun Club) locations were described in the old deeds of Tuxedo Park as property for recreational purposes only. Notwithstanding the relief felt by everyone, there would be no

Beach Club tennis courts, but friction persisted between the members from the Hamlet who were concerned about the interests of Park residents, who were Tuxedo Club members, with respect to the operation of the Beach Club. However, spirits were generally high, and in keeping with a volunteer spirit, work nights were planned and well-attended. Women were expected to clean and repair the upstairs girls' dressing rooms in the old Gun Club for the new season. John Billie and my uncle Buddy McCarroll put together a basketball backboard and cleared an area which would have been part of the proposed tennis courts. Charlie Albanese, a highly regarded gardener in the Park, took responsibility for setting up the horseshoe pits and scheduling tournaments for the men and young boys. Tillie Henderson said she would approach Mrs. Amory at Renamor about donating a ping-pong table and some chairs that Tillie knew were not being used at Mrs. Amory's pool house for the first-floor area of the Gun Club. Several of the men were returning veterans and they attacked the task of improving the Beach Club as if they were on a wartime mission.

In 1950, my uncle, James Barth, who went on to college after World War II and became a teacher, was selected as senior lifeguard for the fifth straight summer. His tasks extended beyond beachfront duties at the Tuxedo Community Club, according to conversations with my uncle. Before the beach opened for the season, the senior lifeguard was responsible for preparing the beachfront area. Ropes had to be placed, the beachfront cleared, the raft had to be floated and secured, and the diving board had to be reattached. Opening duties also included burning and clearing the extension of the picnic area before brush started growing, painting the raft and the children's bath houses, setting up the swings, cleaning the clubhouse, and fixing the waterfront and sand area walls as needed. Lastly, each year a new mat needed to be placed on the diving board. It was my uncle's responsibility, but there were always many hands offering to help, even little ones like mine.

At the end of the season, the senior lifeguard was also responsible for closing the beach. That meant securing and storing all the equipment; cleaning, painting, and storing the picnic tables; cleaning out the bathhouses; taking down the diving board; and towing the raft to the TPA side of Pigeon Point where the TPA would remove it from the water. The lifeguard's boat would then be locked up in the girl's bathhouse. Of course, there was no lack of help in doing this work, and no need to ask for it. Volunteering was a key piece of the fabric that held the Beach Club together. Preparing the Beach Club for opening day, and helping secure it at the end of the season, was more than enough compensation for these eager volunteers.

Before and after each season, the Beach Club held a general membership meeting. As-needed, special meetings were called at other times. At the meeting following the 1950 season, my mother announced the treasurer's report, which noted a bank balance of $586.39. Jim Barth again suggested that tennis courts could be built before the opening of the 1951 season. This time the members considered requesting bids on the work. Other requests for improvements included tarring the road entrance and parking surface, thereby addressing the constant labor-intensive battle with weeds and dust. The plan was presented as a cost-saving measure that would provide "a more natural look." Tina Mottola asserted that tar was *not* a natural look and suggested grading and resurfacing the road and parking area with gravel. Tina's motion passed unanimously. As to tennis, once again Jim Barth had to tuck his racket under his arm and return home for another winter, knowing there would be no tennis courts the following year. My uncle actually had access to a tennis court behind the gardener's cottage where he lived with my grandparents. It was abandoned, but I hit balls there by myself on occasion. It was a fenced court, located just past the kennels where Mr. Armory kept his hunting dogs, and near the chicken coop that provided eggs for the Amorys. I believe my uncle Jim's real frustration was not so much the lack of a tennis court, but the lack of potential playing partners and an interest to be more like those who were members of the Tuxedo Club. In those days, tennis was considered a rich person's game by most Beach Club members, who viewed the sport as more appropriate for members of the Tuxedo Club. Those from the Hamlet had little interest in tennis and were much more passionate about their horseshoes, bocce, and baseball. In that same meeting following the 1950 season, the members also discussed the successful *Even You* show, agreeing to send letters of appreciation to Bill Trehy (the piano player), Mabel Tansey, and Jim Barth for staging the production. They held off making any decisions about future productions and a proposed square dance in August.

In the spring of 1951, it was time for the Beach Club to start planning for the new beach season. In April, the Executive Committee met to discuss concerns about the club's lease. Many discussions were held with the TPA to try to ensure continued use. Mabel was a fierce competitor and not about to back down from the Tuxedo Club members, some of whom actually controlled the TPA. She was a force to be reckoned with as the TPA had to report back to and satisfy the Tuxedo Club membership. For the Beach Club, this was a source of much concern. The members were making many improvements to the property but did not know from year to year whether they would be allowed to operate. Once again, the TPA offered the Beach Club the customary one-year lease at $1 per year. Other ambiguities persisted. For example, there was no guarantee that the Beach Club would receive proceeds toward any claim paid by an insurance policy funded with Beach Club fees. The Beach Club asked the TPA for a longer lease and other items that would provide some security and incentives to make improvements. Despite the many discussions, the relationship between the Beach Club and the TPA remained status quo, per Mabel's report to membership. The year 1951 would see another season of running the beach on a budget that depended on a membership fee that was reasonable for most of the members but could not cover increasing expenses. Additional funds would have to come from fundraising events and the hoped-for donations from those Tuxedo Club members who had supported the Beach Club in the past.

On June 10, 1951, the Beach Club held its annual membership meeting to elect officers and an Executive Committee that was similar to a Board of Directors. According to the meeting minutes, one member suggested opening a refreshment stand to generate funds. Although everyone was supportive, the startup costs and the lack of volunteers were concerns. At that point, Tony Mottola's name came up. Tony was from Sloatsburg, the town just south of Tuxedo, and despite his physical disability, was well-known for his hard work and his infectious, upbeat personality. Tony had expressed his interest to a Hamlet member, and when offered the opportunity, he became the Club's beach concessionaire. Tony set up a giant red Coca-Cola cooler under the shade of the white birch trees at the entrance to the picnic area. This was a welcome addition, especially to children like me. It was difficult for parents to say no to their children's cries for soda and candy when they came out of the water or when they ran from the play area to the picnic tables, as they always had to pass Tony's stand. I still remember being fascinated by the smoke coming off the dry ice when Tony opened the cooler to get me a frozen Milky Way candy bar, or when he let me reach into the separate section filled with regular ice to pick out my own soda—so long as I promised to bring back the bottle.

Tony Mottola serving food and snacks at the Beach Club, ca. 1951

Nancy Albanese, the star performer at the *Even You* revues, was named lifeguard. The usual list of what needed to be done to prepare the beach for the season was discussed, and a work night for "all" members was scheduled. Two of the many items were to replace curtains and construct wood partitions in the girls' dressing room.

The 1951 season of the Beach Club opened with a new gravel parking area and no weeds. Picnic tables and fireplaces stood within the shade of the beautiful strands of white birch trees. To the left of the parking area was a small informal basketball court and freshly mowed grass for throwing around a baseball. In the far corner toward the point were the horseshoe pits. These pits could have hosted a major championship, given the professional dimensions and manicured layout. A line of boulders separated the parking lot from the children's recreation area. There were two swings separated by a pull-up bar, freshly painted bright-red seesaws, and baby swings. A large sandpit was deep enough for the young ones to build tunnels and castles after carrying their buckets of water up from the Wee Wah. A slide in the back of the playground ended with a fall into the soft sand. At the beachfront, a slide into the lake beckoned children old enough to climb the steps below the play area. Those of us who were daring could slide down face first. The lifeguard stand was positioned close to the slide, giving the lifeguard a clear view of the diving board on the dock and of the raft. If given the chance, as boys we tried sliding quickly after the boy before us to try crashing into them in the water. Oftentimes, we would hear the whistle and the lifeguard giving a baseball umpire's "you're out" shout, which signaled a timeout from the lake. This was true of the diving board as well, where cannonballing the proceeding diver when their head appeared out of the water was a favorite activity. That was cause for another serious timeout.

The children's bathhouses were located near the tip of Pigeon Point. Constructed years earlier by the TPA for the enforced move to so called "North Beach," they required the most work. They had been cleaned and painted for the start of the season, but even so, the twenty-year-old structures were in deplorable condition. The boy's bathhouse was just a large room with benches along the wall. The girl's bathhouse had separate stalls and I believe a bathroom. The area around the bathhouses was like a swamp after a rain. A three-foot-wide space between the bathhouses allowed "someone"— a number of the older boys at that time—to carve peek holes into just about every girl's changing partition in their bathhouse. It was a wonder the wall was still standing. I was a very young boy at the time, but I recall the screams, followed by girls running from the bathhouse shouting for Mrs. Tansey, as we kids called her at the time. Even at seven years old, I knew that you did not want to be caught by Mrs. Tansey for lurking between the bathhouses. Despite the condition of the bathhouses, which were isolated from view, the beachfront was raked and the shorefront immaculate.

The season opened without incident, and the happy sounds of children are remembered most, mainly because I was one of them. I was seven years old. I had successfully learned to swim under the watchful eye of Mabel and her daughter, Barbara. I had long since made my first jump off the spring diving board at the end of the long dock protruding from the west end of the swimming area. The next step was to pass the raft test, which required swimming—using the Australian crawl—from the east end ropes across the entire swimming area to the west end ropes, then returning to the east end and finishing back in the middle where we had to tread water for one minute. I passed! This was all done under the watchful eye of the lifeguard. So, this was the year I started jumping off the board and swimming out to the raft like the big kids. I had graduated from the play area above the beachfront and the water area before the first ropes.

Of course, my friends and I continued to use the slides. The water slide was the most popular because you could go much faster with a wet bathing suit and make a big splash into the water. It didn't take long to organize a bucket brigade to bring water up the hill to pour on the landlocked slide, dramatically increasing the sliding speed. There were face-first sliders and contests to see who could land farthest from the end of the slide.

Nearby, on land, we marveled at the older boys and some girls who would try to "do the loop," a forbidden move on the swings. As the name implies, doing the loop meant swinging so high that you continued over the top bar, coming down the back in a circular motion, or dropping straight down. I must admit I never had the courage to try it. Another forbidden activity that we would watch with wide eyes and laughter was balancing on the seesaws, where one would stand on one end, another would stand opposite, and a third would try keeping their balance in the middle. A dangerous game on the seesaws occurred when the older boys convinced another to get on the seesaw. When he was at his highest point, the one on the opposite end would jump off the seesaw, leaving the other to slam to the ground. Fortunately, I never witnessed any serious injuries, but there were various scrapes and bruises, and more than a few tussles.

When the seesaw games grew dangerous, or after they had become boring, someone would yell, "First to the raft!" and there was a race to the diving board. No one wanted to be "last to the raft." That would result in those already on the raft jumping off in a tuck position known as a cannonball in an attempt to create waves for the last arrival. Another water sport was to bring a pinecone out to the raft and let it sink into the water. After a slow count to five, everyone would dive off, attempting to be the one to retrieve the pinecone. As with the cannonballs and the diving, bodies landed on each other, resulting in constant battles with the lifeguard. He or she would blow the whistle and call out the names of offenders who would then be summoned back to shore for a lecture and removal from the water until being told they could go back in.

Tom Salierno, a teenager at this time, and a future president of the Beach Club, commented on another game he and his friends would play on the lifeguard. As teenagers, some were able to dive off the board, hold their breath, and swim under water all the way to the raft, where they would resurface on the back side out of view of the lifeguard. Tom mentioned that my Uncle Jim, who was the lifeguard at the time, would go crazy as Tom and his friends never appeared on the surface after diving off the board. The first few times resulted in frenzied scenes, with Jim Barth running along the beachfront blowing his whistle in search of the lost divers who were laughing uncontrollably in the water on the back side of the raft. Soon an understanding was reached that this activity had to end.

The raft itself was a wooden structure supported by empty barrels that left open areas under the deck that were above the water level and out of sight. Per the rules, there was to be "no swimming under the raft," but once again, the swimmer would be in the open areas out of the sight of the lifeguard. Needless to say, this provision did not prevent teenage sweethearts from using these areas for their amorous adventures. All the while, my friends and I would be on the raft lying down looking through the cracks in the deck boards to watch the young lovers. In a few years, it would be my generation's turn.

Shortly after the season opened, the TPA told the Beach

Club's Executive Committee about numerous complaints from Park residents. Tuxedo Club members were complaining about the purported increased car activity among people who did not live inside the gates of Tuxedo Park. Mabel called for a meeting on July 16, 1951 to discuss the concerns and a request by the TPA that the Beach Club send a letter to its members. The resulting letter was simple: No guests would be admitted unless accompanied by a card-carrying member. In addition, there was to be no fishing or boating at the club, no using the lifeguard's boat, no dogs, and no parking in the picnic area. It pertained to all members, not just those who lived outside the gates. The conditions were followed, although Beach members were used to these complaints and they were mostly disregarded as unfounded. The 1951 season proceeded without additional community concerns.

In 1952, a major change to the governance of Tuxedo Park was approved. The Tuxedo Park Association, which originally bought out the Lorillard family's interests and managed the Park, was comprised of a small number of Tuxedo Club members who collectively owned all the non-deeded property in Tuxedo Park. When Tuxedo Park was created, the TPA originally fulfilled its responsibilities in accordance with the Lorillard family and other residents. Many of the resident shareholders served on the Board of Governors of the Tuxedo Club and had been given the opportunity to buy stock in the company. The property comprising the entirety of Tuxedo Park, including 355 acres of lakes, now operated as a public municipality under the laws of New York State. It was now called the Incorporated Village of Tuxedo Park. When an official of the Association was asked what changes this would mean for Tuxedo Park, he replied, "None." He said there was no difference in the essential private nature of the Park.[63] Lorillard's requirement that one must be accepted into the Tuxedo Club before they could buy a house or vacant lot had long since lapsed.

The Village then fell within the overall public governance of the Town of Tuxedo, Orange County, and New York State. As a municipality, it was now a public entity with an elected mayor and board of trustees. Prescott A. Buell was the assistant treasurer of the Tuxedo Club, treasurer of the Tuxedo Memorial Hospital, and chairman of the Board of Trustees of the Tuxedo Park School. He also chaired the annual meeting of the School District in the Hamlet. Prescott A. Buell was elected as the first mayor. All those elected were members of the Tuxedo Club, where the election was held. As a municipality, all property owners were now taxed for the public services they received. A budget was prepared and passed.

The Tuxedo Park Association owned the land on which the Beach Club was located, but decisions about the Tuxedo Community Club would now be made by the Incorporated Village of Tuxedo Park, its mayor, and the Board of Trustees. This was a result of the Village now having responsibility for and control over the water in the lakes. While there was the opportunity to lease the property from the new TPA, without permission from the Village to swim in and use the Wee Wah Lake, there was no "beach." In the end, however, there was little change. At this point, the elected officials of the newly incorporated Village were long-standing members of the Tuxedo Club who had supported the Beach Club's annual lease. Therefore, the Beach Club would essentially now deal with the mayor and Board of Trustees. The Tuxedo Park Association donated much property to the new municipality. However, the TPA continued to be the largest landowner in Tuxedo Park, as they owned and controlled much of the undeveloped property.

The Annual Meeting of the Beach Club on June 14, 1952 was brief. A motion to provide $200 to the recreation program passed unanimously. Next was another unanimous vote for the concession request from Tony Mottola, who was now a fixture at the beach in front of the beautiful strands of those white birch trees. The thorny issue that needed to be addressed involved guest privileges. The original policy was intended to cover "house guests" but was never defined as such. The guest policy was not tightly enforced, and this was always a source of friction between Beach Club members and Tuxedo Club residents. All guests would have to be accompanied by a Beach Club member, a rule that existed previously but was not strictly enforced. Locals from the Park and the village outside the gates (now formally referred to as the "Hamlet") who were "eligible" to become members and pay the membership fee could no longer enter as guests. Those living within the geographic boundaries had to become a member to use the beach. Those within the boundary could not use the beach as guests of a member. To demonstrate to the membership that the rules were to be enforced, checkers were instructed that there would be no exceptions, and the beach entrance was to be chained and locked except during regular hours.

The change to a municipal government in the Park initially did not affect the membership of the Tuxedo Volunteer Fire Department, as there was only one station, and that was in the Hamlet. This was a volunteer organization started in 1901 by Richard Talbot, a Park resident and member of the Tuxedo Club. He was joined by Charles Patterson, who served as the first Town of Tuxedo supervisor, among other volunteers. Over the years there was no shortage of volunteers, whether residents of Tuxedo Park or the Hamlet. The volunteer fire department was turned over to the Village of Tuxedo Park. Three years later, the fire department was finally included in the Town of Tuxedo and became the Tuxedo Joint Fire District, which continued to be comprised of volunteers. There was no class distinction in the Fire Department. A Tuxedo Club member might work alongside a man from Southfields (located in the township), or perhaps a man from the East Village who worked on an estate within Tuxedo Park. The July Fourth parade was a time for honoring the Tuxedo Fire Department, as well as the country's birthday. The firefighters wore their neatly pressed dress uniforms with highly polished accessories and were presented to honorable guests. Every year, they receive the loudest applause from the crowd. However, despite the celebrations and acknowledgments, volunteer firemen who did not live within the geographical boundary required for membership in the Beach Club were unable to join the Beach Club.

In front of the Tuxedo Club: Chief Robert Bentley, Commissioner Hunt Tilford Wagstaff, Commissioner David Black, Mayor Prescott A. Buell, Commissioner and Assistant Fire Chief George Zupko Jr, and U.S. Congresswoman Katherine St. George review the Fire Department, ca. early 1950s

Guest privileges remained a problem after the beach opened for the 1952 season. Members continued bringing more than houseguests. Many families living in the Hamlet now had other family members who lived outside the boundary lines but not far from Tuxedo. This question of geographical boundaries, memberships, and guests would continue to be a source of friction regarding the use of the beach by non-residents in the newly incorporated Village of Tuxedo Park. At a meeting on July 20, Mabel issued a directive that the Executive Committee supported. Members would be issued four guest tickets. Children under twelve were not to be counted. To acquire more guest tickets, members would need approval from the Executive Committee. Another serious matter was the bank balance: $94.64. While the records do not reflect any cash infusions, the club made it through the remainder of the summer season without a call for funds. As per usual, after Labor Day the chain was placed across the entrance and the area was locked up for the off-season.

Right on time, the 1953 season preparation started with a meeting on May 15. A work night to clean the beach area was scheduled. Mike Crisci, the pharmacist at the drugstore and later a Town of Tuxedo supervisor, suggested it was time for the Beach Club to invest in the future and buy a riding lawnmower. Mike had his facts ready for what became a spirited discussion. A power mower would cost $145, and could be paid for through installments, a concept many people were unfamiliar with. This was 1953. Beach Club members typically subscribed to the financial philosophy that if you wanted something, you paid in full at the time of purchase. But as manager of the drugstore in the Hamlet, Mike was quite familiar with business matters. He sold the idea based on season-long savings on expenses.

The general meeting was held on June 24, 1953, and, sure enough, Mabel presented a letter from Mayor Buell complaining about littering of the road, deemed to be caused by Beach Club members and "certainly not by any residents in the Park." The mayor advised that memberships would be strictly limited to Park residents, and to residents within the initial agreed-upon boundaries outside the gates. Apparently, a few exceptions had been made over time, and some residents of the Town of Tuxedo who lived outside the geographic boundaries had been allowed to become members. No one outside these boundaries would be permitted to join, and there would be no exceptions. The Executive Committee refunded membership costs to those who lived outside the membership boundaries as described by the Village of Tuxedo Park. Finally, my uncle, Buddy McCarroll, the de facto beach manager, provided the committee with a list of rules for the lifeguards to maintain the beach:

- Keep bathhouses clean
- Rake beach daily
- Put out garbage cans the night before collection
- Keep picnic area clean
- No fishing on beachfront, no firecrackers, no glass bottles
- Days off were Saturday or Sunday
- Report all "misdemeanors" to the Executive Committee
- Duties should be performed before beachfront duties
  With respect to finances, the members decided to impose a 25-cent guest fee. The entrance checker would work from 12 noon to 8 p.m. daily and be paid $5 per day.

Chapter 18: The Lake Is Empty

Wee Wah Lake, as it appeared drained in 1953. At this time, the Tuxedo Club briefly considered using the property to replace portions of the Tuxedo Golf Club taken by the State of New York to build the Governor Thomas E. Dewey New York State Thruway ca 1953

With the 1953 summer season in the books, the Beach Club closed, and the fall meeting wrapped up, but over the winter months, much was happening outside Tuxedo Park. As early as the mid-1940s, a plan for a major highway between New York City and Albany, a highway that would eventually stretch across New York State to

Buffalo and the Canadian border, was being considered by the state government. By 1949, the actual highway was incorporated into the Interstate Highway System. In 1964, the state formally renamed the highway the Governor Thomas E. Dewey New York Thruway, although the road, to this day, has always been known as "the Thruway."

In 1954, the portion of the Thruway through Tuxedo was completed. The roadway was built right through much of the open area in the Italian and Slavic sections of the East Village as it followed the Ramapo River, and the Erie Railroad tracks north. This was terribly disruptive to all the residents of the Hamlet as the Italian and Slavic villages fell under the same Hamlet umbrella. The town's original baseball field was now gone. During the 1920s and 1930s, several Wall Street tycoons who were Tuxedo Club members supported baseball teams of local youths. These spirited games became the focus of extensive betting activity. Some of the better young players were offered jobs on Wall Street. In one case, Bill Barth, my uncle, was not only given a job on Wall Street in New York City, but he also received a baseball scholarship to Northeastern University in Boston with the help of a Tuxedo Club member.

As the construction moved north, the next stretch of the highway went right through the picturesque holes of the Tuxedo Golf Club. Developed in 1898, the Tuxedo Golf Club was said by some to be the second oldest course in the country, after St. Andrews Golf Club, which was founded one year earlier in Westchester County across the Hudson River. St. Andrews is undisputed in golfing history, but as best as I can find in golf research, the next in order of oldest is subject to debate. Shortly thereafter came The Country Club in

Brookline, Massachusetts, and Shinnecock Hills Golf Club in Southampton on Long Island. Initially in Tuxedo Park, a course containing a few holes was developed on Blairhame that was the Blair estate, a large English Tudor residence at the top of the mountain on the west side of the Park. A new course, four holes just inside the north gate, was laid out at the north end of Tuxedo Park. Five holes were quickly added across the highway, the railroad, and the Ramapo River. Golfers would have to cross the road, the train tracks, and the river to play the course.

As golf gained popularity, matches were regularly covered by the *New York Times* and other papers. In New York, the August 31, 1896 edition of *The Sun* reported on a three-day tournament to be held at the new course: "The Tuxedo links are among the most picturesque and attractive in the country, the clubhouse has the facilities of a large hotel, the cottages are cozy, and the Tuxedo golfers are the soul of hospitality, so that visitors will have nothing to complain about."[64] The Tuxedo Golf Club was incorporated in 1897 with 100 members who were members of the Tuxedo Club as well. Additional holes were added, and by 1900, national matches were played on the eighteen-hole course. In the 1930s, with financial support from George Grant Mason, the course was again redesigned across Route 17. An underpass beneath Route 17 was constructed to avoid crossing the highway and railroad tracks with a crossing over the Ramapo River. It was a picturesque, scenic course nestled in the narrow valley with the mountainside to the east and the river bordering on the west. The land was purchased from the Palisades Interstate Park Commission, which had previously received an enormous donation of land from E. H. Harriman for public parks known as the Harriman State Park and Bear

Mountain State Park today.

When golf was first established here in the United States, it was played well into the late fall and resumed in early spring. Golf stories are famous for their lack of reliable quotes, but an American friend of mine playing during a summer golf trip in Scotland told me he was at St. Andrew's Old Course when his elderly Scottish caddy told him the sport originally was not played in the summer months. Surprised by this comment, my friend related that as they played down the well-cut fairways, his caddy said, "Look out there, laddie, [pointing to the Old Course], we didn't have nary a lawnmower in those days nor near enough sheep." One had to wait for the late fall and winter when the grass had died and the ground was barren. Pictures of golfers at these American clubs in the late 1800s show gentlemen in knickers and long coats.

By 1950, golf was a major Tuxedo Club sport, with competitions among the various top clubs in the area, including Rumson in New Jersey and Shinnecock in Southampton. The betting was big and bragging rights were good throughout the fall in Tuxedo, and from Newport in summer, to Palm Beach in winter.

Thomas E. Dewey, the forty-seventh governor of New York (1943–1954), was the Republican candidate for president in 1944 but lost to President Franklin D. Roosevelt in the closest of Roosevelt's four presidential elections. In 1948, Dewey was again the Republican nominee, and once again he lost to the incumbent president, this time Harry S Truman, in one of the greatest upsets in presidential election history. Dewey was an advocate for the professional and business community in the Northeast, which was later called the "Eastern Establishment." This group, although Republican, supported many of the social-welfare reforms enacted during the administration

of Roosevelt. Dewey remained governor of New York until 1954 and

was succeeded by a Democrat, W. Averell Harriman.

Thomas Dewey made his name as a fighter of organized crime

while a district attorney for Manhattan in New York City. When he

became governor in 1943, he was faced with a bill passed the previous

year adding a "general route" of a cross-state superhighway to the

state's official highway map, clearing the way for its design and

construction. On July 11, 1946, Governor Dewey broke ground for the

first section in central New York State. [65]

Tuxedo Park was certainly a bastion of Republican political

support, but it was much more conservative than the leaders of the

Eastern wing of the party during the late 1940s and early 1950s. As the

District Attorney in New York City and before running for governor,

Thomas Dewey resided outside the city in the Emily Post house #2 in

Tuxedo Park, socialized with Tuxedo Club members, and played golf

at the Golf Club. Interestingly, there is no record of his membership in

the Tuxedo Club books of members I viewed at the Tuxedo Public

Library, and I was not permitted access to the archives of the Tuxedo

Club. Furthermore, it is unclear whether membership applications still

exist from that time. In any case, for those running for public office,

the elitism associated with Tuxedo Park was not the best place to

gather support from the general New York State populace. In addition,

Dewey was a very public figure when it came to news articles as a

fighter taking on organized crime in New York City. Unlike many

presidential candidates over the course of history, Dewey actually

enjoyed the press. Although the Tuxedo Club membership had

changed, as a prosecutor and district attorney who enjoyed the spotlight, his notoriety did not jive with the history of Tuxedo Club membership, although I assume he was invited as a guest of a member numerous times. Mabel Tansey recalled giving swimming lessons to the Dewey children at the Tuxedo Club pool.

Dewey ran an aggressive office and was a crafty politician on the rise. One can only wonder how he handled one of the first items on his plate when he moved into the governor's office in Albany. There on his desk was a "general plan" for an across-the-state superhighway that easily could go right through the second oldest golf course in the United States. That golf course just happened to be the golf course of the Tuxedo Club. And so, the Tuxedo Club was faced with the loss of half its golf course! The TPA and Club members had to make some serious decisions. Is it possible that Governor Dewey had been refused membership in the Tuxedo Club and was exacting his revenge when routing the Thruway through Tuxedo? Governor Dewey signed legislation that established the routes of the Berkshire and New England sections of the Thruway in 1944. Six years later, on March 21, 1950, he signed the Thruway Law. As reported in Michigan's *Battle Creek Enquirer* on November 12, 1952, "Not only will the Thruway traverse Tuxedo, the National Geographic Society reports, it will commit the almost unbelievable desecration of bisecting the famous and ancient Tuxedo golf course with a double ribbon of concrete—a hazard never dreamed of by the men who laid out the links."[66] On May 27, 1955, the fourteen-mile stretch through Tuxedo from Harriman to Hillburn opened to traffic.

In February 1954, when the Village began draining Wee Wah Lake, the headline in the *New York World Telegram & Sun* read in bold letters, "Tuxedo Park 'Outsiders' Fight for Swimmin Hole." The article reported "that would leave 165 Community Club families high and dry when the hot weather comes."[67] By Memorial Day, May 30, 1954, the phone lines of Beach Club members burned as word spread as fast as you could post on the internet today. Those who happened to drive along Wee Wah Road that morning were in for a shock. Wee Wah Lake was still empty! Phones rang off the hook. Meetings took place in every corner of the Hamlet and Park. Mabel spoke with the TPA and called for a meeting of the Beach Club at the beach on Wednesday, June 9, at 7:30 p.m. Archer Brown, president and general manager of the TPA, attended the meeting and addressed the members. He began his remarks by stating the TPA passed a resolution on June 6, stating that a swimming pool should be made available adjacent to the proposed athletic fields to be constructed for the Tuxedo Union School District #3 for use by the community, and that the TPA would contribute to the cost of the pool. He noted that the Beach Club property was owned by the TPA and was for sale. He also reminded attendees that the property could not be sold to the Beach Club for recreational purposes, as it was not zoned for that. Of course, the proposed pool would be outside the gates of Tuxedo Park.

But why was the lake drained with no notice, and why was the TPA making such a resolution? What many had suspected was now out in the open. The Tuxedo Club was considering using the Wee Wah Lake property and Pond 3 as well. They were considering a plan to drain these lakes permanently to construct a new section of the golf course, as the Thruway was taking all the golf holes east of Route 17. Of course, the private golf course existed exclusively for the use of Tuxedo Club members. Mr. Brown said the pool would be supported by the town, school and the Community Club. Control over the pool would be worked out between the school and Community Club. The TPA would deed the property (they still owned property throughout the Village of Tuxedo Park and the Hamlet) either to the school or the Tuxedo Community Club. "The proposed pool would have nothing to do with the Wee Wah," as stated by Mr. Brown in the meeting minutes. As soon as the golf architect had finished his survey, Mr. Brown stated that the TPA and Village would replace the boards at the north dam that held back the water and allow the lake to be refilled.

The floor was open for questions. Many years later, my aunt and my uncles who were present at the meeting still remembered the tense scene. One could easily come to that conclusion simply by reviewing the meeting minutes. Mr. Brown was not prepared for either the well-reasoned questions that followed, or the lack of trust in the air. He continued to stress the idea for the pool as an asset to the community, while emphasizing that the pool was separate from the athletic field. Building them together would be cheaper, as the equipment would already be on site, and the fill from the pool could be used for the athletic field.

The first questions were more legal in nature. One question stated in the minutes went like this: "What about the reverter clause in the deeds for this property?" Mr. Brown explained that, as had always been the case, the school and property surrounding it were originally owned by the TPA and the property in question would revert to the TPA if it were no longer being used as a school. That sidetracked the discussion to the future of the school. Mr. Brown assured there would always be a school. Many Beach Club members were skeptical, as they were teachers who were well-aware of ongoing discussions about centralizing the school districts. If that became reality, Tuxedo children would no longer use the schools in town. Louis Euvrard, who was still the principal of the school and a Beach Club member, noted that centralization, should the matter come up, could be avoided if people in School District #3 voted against it. If there was centralization, the pool and athletic fields would be useless. Joe Salierno suggested that in the event the school was closed, it would make an excellent theater, due to the original design and the configuration of the auditorium and stage area. Mr. Brown expressed certainty that the school and TPA would continue to exist, and he seemed to have successfully changed the focus of the meeting from the empty lake to the school in the Hamlet.

Mike Crisci, as earlier stated, would later become the Town of Tuxedo supervisor. He managed the drug store in the Hamlet and was well-respected by all in Tuxedo. Granted permission to speak, He took the moment to focus the discussion back on the Beach Club. The Beach Club had never complained or overstepped its bounds and was perfectly happy at the Wee Wah. He called the plan a blatant attempt to take back the beach for property owners in the Park who were members of the Tuxedo Club. It is important to remember that the TPA was formed to service Tuxedo Park when the Park was populated solely by members of the Tuxedo Club, many of whom were shareholders in the Tuxedo Park Association. Others suggested that the TPA was working with the Village and Tuxedo Club with respect to the possibility of selling the land for a new golf course and was therefore stalling at filling up the lake. The Beach Club members believed that draining the Wee Wah was a violation of the original plan for Tuxedo Park.

Mr. Brown denied the suggestion and attempted to calm the

members by noting the TPA had decided not to put the property up for sale and that the Tuxedo Club had a beautiful pool of their own. In an attempt to conclude the discussion, he added that the Village of Tuxedo Park was responsible for filling the lake and that it would be done as soon as the survey for a potential expansion of the golf course had been completed. As the meeting got heated, further questions addressed the proposed pool outside the gates and the Beach Club property. Would town water be used for the proposed pool? Could the building lots near the pool tie into the water and sewer system that would have to be installed? The answer was yes, but owners would have to pay half the cost of running lines to their property. How much would the TPA contribute to this proposed pool project? Mr. Brown said he had no idea. He also acknowledged that the TPA might one day sell the actual Wee Wah property on Pigeon Point to potential Tuxedo Park residents, which would mean "the Beach Club would have to go." He continued that the beach property was now taxed about six times higher than in previous years. With Tuxedo Park now incorporated, taxes on the beach property had soared sixfold. As the owner of Wee Wah Lake water, the Village controlled its use and could prohibit swimming, fishing, and any other activities. The "old icehouse" was also highly taxed, and the TPA planned to move it. The inference was clear. This prime beach area could easily be subdivided into private waterfront residential lots.

Profit motives had now entered the discussion and perhaps other concerns were driving the TPA agenda. Was the TPA selling the property for residences? The answer appeared to be yes. The questions were pointed and reasonable, considering this issue Mr. Brown had brought to the Beach Club. The minutes contained a member's question: "If zoning changes can be made for a golf course, why not for a beach?" Joe Mottola Jr. spoke again, stating he believed that the Beach Club property had been originally owned by a Tuxedo Club member, Mr. Talbot, and deeded for "recreational purposes only." The tension rose again when Mr. Brown was asked who gave the order to drain the Wee Wah, and did the stockholders vote on the matter. Mr. Brown responded that the TPA Executive Committee was authorized by the 250 or so stockholders to make decisions without consulting them.

With everyone angry and tired, Mr. Brown told the group the TPA stockholders were meeting on June 26, and he was confident that after the meeting, he would be able to get the boards back into the dam and take ten inches of water off Tuxedo Lake to hasten the refilling of the Wee Wah. The membership voted unanimously to invite the TPA's Executive Committee to a meeting at the beach on June 27 or July 3, whichever was the most convenient for the TPA.
Mr. Brown took his leave, and the meeting was adjourned after the members returned to their usual beach business and agreed to donate $10 to the Tuxedo Scholarship Committee Fund.

It was not the normal happy return home for the members of the Beach Club. Word spread quickly that it looked like not only would there be no beach this summer, but the property had been put up for sale. The future of the Beach Club seemed bleak, but the Executive Committee was hard at work. Beach club members were on the phones and talking to neighbors. In the Park, those still working for Park families who were members of the Tuxedo Club and, in many cases, stockholders of the TPA, were told about Mr. Brown's remarks. Some Beach Club members were members of the Tuxedo Club as well and, in most cases, they supported efforts that benefited the entire Tuxedo community.

In early July 1954, the TPA chairman invited Mabel Tansey and Margaret Hilton to attend a Village of Tuxedo Park trustee meeting on July 3 to discuss swimming at the beach. In the hope the lake would be refilled, Beach Club members had already begun setting up picnic tables and otherwise preparing for summer activities.

But this was not the Fourth of July holiday weekend the Tuxedo Community Club had planned when the season ended the previous fall. There had been a general cleanup, but the lakefront was just an empty hillside of sand and dirt. The dock was still on shore. No diving board had been placed. No ropes to designate the swimming area had been put out. It was a beach club with a beach—but no water.

The fateful meeting with the TPA and the Village began shortly after 9:30 a.m. on Saturday, July 3. Trustee Clarence Bartow introduced everyone and said the Tuxedo Community Club had requested the meeting. Trustee Bartow was an investment banker and director of Drexel Firestone, Inc. He was a Governor of the American Stock Exchange and his father had been a partner with J. P. Morgan and Company.

Mabel Tansey then spoke with the intent on demonstrating the need for the beach. "Let's focus on the children of our community." She listed the hardships of the local children and said that supervised recreation had prevented "juvenile delinquency" in Tuxedo. In the 1950s, juvenile delinquency was a common problem in society, often reported about in newspapers and on television. The school grounds could not be used for the program because of a lack of shade and activities. Then a trustee interrupted Mabel with a comment stating "certain ethnic groups" were improperly being provided memberships and using the club facilities. Mabel reminded the TPA that the club had no policies banning any ethnic group, and that any problems should be discussed with Tuxedo Club members, because it was their "help" who were joining the club and using the beach.

Other complaints from the trustees were then brought up. Cars were speeding through the Park and taking shortcuts to the beach. A person from outside the Park was mentioned by name. Mabel said the individual in question was not a member of the Beach Club, and the Tuxedo Park Police, not the Beach Club—still officially the Tuxedo Community Club at this time—was responsible for keeping out trespassers. Every year the Beach Club provided a list of members whom the TPA had to approve. The list was given to the main gate so guards could allow entrance only to Club members from the Hamlet and their guests. A TPA board member said he had observed Rockland County, New York license plates on cars at the beach, proving they were from out of town as Tuxedo was in Orange County. Mabel explained that many locals, even Tuxedo Club people, had Rockland County license plates because it was more convenient to get them in New City, the Rockland County seat, rather than at the Orange County seat in Goshen. At this time, license plates included the county in which the plates were purchased.

Trustee Bartow attempted to move the meeting back to the main issue of a lake with no water, suggesting that Lake Sebago, the new state recreation facility in Bear Mountain Park, offered a nice beach for children and families. Mrs. Hilton countered that she had taken her two sons there recently and would not go back. "The water was dirty, the place overcrowded, and safety was a concern," she said.

Given this book's examination of social change, it is only fair to mention that Lake Sebago in Harriman State Park was a destination for many underprivileged families, mainly those from New York City. Mrs. Hilton may have been suggesting she would rather not socially mix with the visitors to Lake Sebago, although her reasons may have been due to the need for a long car trip when the Beach Club was within walking distance, as the Hiltons resided in the Park. Chairman Bartow said a plan was needed that would be agreeable to the entire community. Mrs. Hilton provided the board with a membership list beginning in 1936, a financial report, and a copy of the beach regulations. In addition to the in-town membership list given to the police gate, Mabel said she had given Mr. Boynton of the TPA a list of out-of-town members in 1953, though he said he remembered only one. Next, the earlier comment on "certain ethnic groups" became more specific. The discussion led to a comment that Mr. Freed, who owned the Red Apple Rest, and others from the Southfields community in the Town of Tuxedo, had been admitted to the Park to use the beach. Was the reference that Reuben Freed, who was Jewish, related to the earlier statement about ethnic groups, as there was a belief there were no Jewish residents in Tuxedo Park at that time who were members in the Tuxedo Club?

Reuben Freed and his family had long operated their very successful restaurant on Route 17 within the Town of Tuxedo just outside the Hamlet. It was conveniently located halfway between New York City and the resorts and bungalow colonies in the Catskills Mountains that were the summer retreat for a large segment of the Jewish population in New York City. Buses would stop to allow for bathroom breaks and food before passengers would reboard for their final destinations. Mr. Freed employed many of the local youth in the summer and was quite generous to the community. The Red Apple Rest was a landmark overflowing with crowds 24 hours a day. On many nights you might find a table of famous comedians, like Eddie Cantor, Milton Berle, Jackie Mason, Buddy Hackett, and Henny Youngman, trying out jokes around the table on their way to and from such resorts as Grossingers, the Concord, and Browns.[68] During these years before the opening of the Thruway, I remember going down to the drugstore across from the train station on Sunday to watch the traffic backed up bumper to bumper as vacationers from the Catskills returned to New York City.

Trustee Bartow said the membership "had grown out of all proportion." Mr. Adrian, another Trustee, recalled that originally the beach was only to be used by the "domestics" in the Park. Mabel corrected him, saying Village workers who lived outside the gate, as well as community shopkeepers, and others associated with the well-being of the Tuxedo Park community, had been allowed to swim at the beach. Mabel then reminded the board about the history of the beach area, alluded to the drowning at the north beach, and the return to the TPA beachfront that had led to the formation of the Tuxedo Community Club.

Mabel questioned whether the Beach Club should pay to fix the dock while the lake was drained and make other repairs to the rock wall and beachfront. The question went unanswered, and the meeting was adjourned.

After the meeting, the Beach Club's Executive Committee scheduled a membership meeting for July 14 to see if people were willing to pay dues for 1954, or whether they wanted to rejoin as new members, should there be a beach club in 1955. The fallout from the recent meetings with the TPA and the Village had created an icy tension between many Park residents who were members of the Tuxedo Club and people in the Tuxedo community, specifically those in the Hamlet who serviced the Park.

At the July 14th Tuxedo Community Club membership meeting, Mabel announced that the club had permission to use the picnic grounds for now. Should the lake be filled, the beach would be available as well. The boards had been replaced in the dam, but the TPA would only allow water from Tuxedo Lake to drain after a rain. She also relayed Mr. Brown's comment that the club should not spend any money on improvements or repairs to the dock and walls.

The issue was simple. There was no guarantee the club would continue if the property were sold. It appeared the TPA, Tuxedo Club members, and many property owners were using the draining of the Wee Wah for one of two purposes. Initially, it was done to consider expanding the golf course, which was closed due to the NY Thruway construction. Now it appeared this was a cover to secure the beach location for Village of Tuxedo Park residents and for Tuxedo Club members, thereby closing the beach to those living outside Tuxedo Park gates. Another concern was that TPA stockholders wanted to sell Pigeon Point for residential development. On the Beach Club side, the club treasury had less than half of what was needed to repair the deteriorated dock, but if repairs were to be made, the best time to do it was before the lake filled. My Aunt Marie, the treasurer for many years, reported a balance of $123.47, while the estimate to repair or replace the dock was conservatively around $300.

Club members were united in going forward with repairs and

improvements, despite Mr. Brown's admonition not to do so. But where would the money come from? If all 224 members renewed their memberships, the dues would amount to $1,120. There was considerable discussion. Some wanted to wait and see how many people would renew their memberships, since half the summer was over, and it did not look like there would be much swimming. Others believed that members might pay double the usual membership rate to cover the project's expenses. The Tuxedo Community Club's constitution stated: "A resident of Tuxedo shall attain membership by paying a $10.00 fee by July 1 for a first-year membership and $5 each year thereafter providing his membership is continuous." Mabel suggested that members who had not yet paid for 1954 should start as new members in 1955 and pay $10. This was a problem, as members had to be approved by the TPA, and if there ever was a time when the Beach Club needed to show continuous membership, it was now.

Robert Bentley said, "If you think you will get enough money, go get the work done!"

Mr. Euvrard followed, "The use of the picnic grove is worth $5.00!"

There was no need for a vote. Discussion then turned to the usual fundraising suggestions such as a raffle, contributions, etc.

At this point, Joe Salierno spoke up. He suggested the club get written permission from the TPA before any money was spent, and requests for dues should be sent out as soon as possible. Joe Salierno was not convinced Mr. Brown would keep his promise to fill the lake that summer. The TPA had not yet replaced the upper planks in the dam, despite assurances they were refilling the Wee Wah. However, the consensus was not to let the TPA deter the Club, and they agreed to go forward with the repairs. Joe Salierno then volunteered that his construction company would build a new cement dock for cost and overlook insurance and other overhead.

The next issue dealt with whether members who had not paid their dues should be notified that their memberships had lapsed, in which case they would have to join as new members for $10. Instead, members decided to keep the membership list as it was to show a positive attitude and present a united front.

With everyone now solidly behind the plan to move ahead as if Wee Wah Lake would shortly be filled, the members reelected the present officers and an Executive Committee. Since it was one of the main responsibilities of the Executive Committee to get the work done—and my uncle, Buddy McCarroll, had taken over many of the tasks—Mabel said the need for work nights would be best served by letting Buddy choose and lead a committee. But the members opted to go with nominations. Although five were usually elected, the members chose seven, to show the club's determination to face the challenges ahead. Elected were Buddy McCarroll, Charlie Albanese, Jimmy Venezia, Joe Salierno, Paul Murtaugh, Louis Euvrard, and John Mottola. These men were all respected throughout the Tuxedo community, and were well known to the Tuxedo Club members. According to the minutes, as they were about to adjourn, Mrs. Albanese asked about the rumor she had heard that the Beach Club had been accused of letting people of color swim at the beach. This incensed many who were present. "We are not allowed to segregate," Mabel said, but it was true a remark had been made about "ethnic groups" at the recent TPA meeting. Mrs. Tocher, who lived in the Hamlet, yelled that if the TPA had a problem, they should read the

U.S. Constitution. One should remember that most members of the Beach Club from outside the gates had come from a family history of discrimination and a rigid social class distinction when Pierre Lorillard created Tuxedo and Tuxedo Park.

Although the members were angry and upset over the attitude taken by some on the TPA and Village board, Mabel turned to setting a date for the annual picnic in August to show the club was continuing as if Wee Wah Lake would be filled. This was truly a call for action, even though she had not received a lease from the TPA since the first lease in 1953.

The picnic was set for the third Sunday in August, with a rain date of the following Sunday. The meeting was adjourned and everyone left with a renewed sense of vigor. Despite all the challenges, they remained determined to work together toward the enduring survival of the Beach Club. In fact, the prevailing attitude was to make the Beach Club bigger and better than ever.

At a July 19th Executive Committee meeting, Joe Salierno submitted plans for the dock, but the committee was concerned the dock would be too expensive. Joe wanted the committee to get outside bids, but they were committed to him and did not feel it was right to have someone come and give a bid knowing they would not accept it. Joe then sat down with Mabel, my Uncle Buddy, and my Aunt Marie McCarroll, as well as other officers, and agreed to do the job for a range of $500 to $600. Joe was told to start as soon as possible. Mabel said she would let the TPA know they were going ahead with "repairs." Joe Salierno moved quickly. Estimates and drawings were completed, the heavy equipment moved in, and work began in earnest. The old dock was removed, forms were erected, and a new, solid concrete dock was soon in place. Meantime, the Wee Wah remained empty.

An interesting side issue focusing on the Continental Road, also known historically as the Corduroy Road, was never discussed. The discovery of Washington's road traversing the now-empty Wee Wah was carried in papers across the country.[69] In today's environment, the historical aspects related to developing the lake bed would most likely have led to lengthy litigation that would have suspended any attempt to change the Wee Wah Lake into a golf course.

In 1777, Continental Army troops created this emergency military road in order to move supplies and men from New Jersey to West Point. The use of the Orange Turnpike could have alerted the British as there were many settlers in the area who supported the British at that time. They came right through Tuxedo Park, and on finding a swampy area (later the Wee Wah Lake), they set down a log road to support the men, as well as oxen and carts carrying supplies and cannon. These logs remained submerged and never rotted as the wood had never been in contact with the air. Once the lake was drained, the road appeared in much the same condition as it had nearly two centuries earlier. One can only imagine the uproar today if a decision was made to clear the property and destroy the remnants of a Revolutionary War Road for a golf course.

MILITARY ROAD OF 1777: Mrs. Elizabeth Garlick walks along what remains of emergency road built at Tuxedo Park, N. Y., by George Washington 177 years ago to guard against attacks by British. The Continental road was found when Lake Wee-Wah was drained.

Walking in George Washington's footsteps

On July 23, a general meeting was held at the beach. As a result of the uncertainty surrounding the future of the beach, Marion Mottola wrote a letter to Hans Christian Sonne of the TPA Board and a leader in the Tuxedo Club, asking for his advice. Mr. Sonne had always been concerned about the greater good of the community, and he was well respected for having a reasoned approach to solving problems. Marion read aloud the letter he had sent in response. He had

231

been to the beach and saw there was considerable work to be done, but added there was no cause for alarm. Any decisions regarding the sale of the property were five or ten years down the road. He had instructed the TPA to make certain the Wee Wah was filled by April 1 of the next year. He also enclosed a personal check for $100 to be used for repairs. On behalf of the TPA, he requested a copy of the rules & regulations, as well as an accounting of the present dues. The members, heartened by Mr. Sonne's response, decided to send a letter of appreciation to him.

Joe Salierno again requested the club get other bids for the dock. Mabel said the agreement that the work would be done for five to six hundred dollars was enough. The bank balance was $377, but letters for dues had not yet gone out, awaiting the night's decision. She had already told Mr. Brown at the TPA that the club was going forward with repairs. The meeting closed on a happy note when longtime secretary, Marion Mottola, was nominated to run a fundraising raffle for a basket of liquor. That's what you get when you do a good job: more responsibility.

By the August 27 Executive Committee meeting, the dock was completed, along with other waterfront projects, all with the help of Joe Salierno's crews. And there was more good news: 115 members had paid their dues, increasing the club's account balance to $744.88. Joe submitted his bill for $600, along with the detailed expenses showing the job actually cost him $1,181.36. The committee was excited and appreciative of his generosity. Final plans were made for the annual picnic. Police Chief Greene was called with a request to hire an off-duty officer to check those entering the Club "at the beach" for the picnic to be sure they were members. This would be in addition to the check at the main gate entrance in order to satisfy the Village of Tuxedo Park. Chief Greene declined, explaining he did not want himself or his men involved.

The new dock was in place, the water was slowly coming back into the Wee Wah, the picnic was a huge success, and plans were made to purchase new swings and seesaws for the play area, as well as new barrels to support the raft for the next year. Work nights were occurring frequently as the fall approached. When Buddy McCarroll and his crew, together with many other volunteer members, placed the chain across the entrance with the leaves changing all around, they could look back at a beautiful, well-kept clubhouse and a defined weedless, white gravel parking area. It was surrounded by a large open field play area, playground equipment, and large sand area for the children separated by a stone wall with benches along it. From the benches, a gentle slope covered in sand led down to the walled beachfront with a new dock as well as a slide awaiting the rising water. The picnic area was covered with grass, shaded by beautiful white birch trees. The area was filled with stone fireplaces surrounded by tables. One would be hard-pressed to find a weed. This created a perfect setting for enjoying the views. As Thanksgiving approached, many in the community, especially the children, sat at their dining room tables giving thanks and saying a little prayer that the lake would be refilled, and that the Beach Club would continue to exist next year.

Chapter 19: 1955

A Weekend Day at the Beach, ca. 1950s

The Village of Tuxedo Park, recently incorporated back in 1952, was taking a more active role in managing and governing the Park as a municipality by elected officials who were referred to as trustees. Much effort was made to refer to the Park as an incorporated village. This required an individual and community rethink to call the "Tuxedo village" outside the gate something else. The "Hamlet," a description from the turn of the century, seemed appropriate and served the purpose of separating this community from Eagle Valley, Southfields, Arden, and other areas within the Town of Tuxedo. Of course, much of the undeveloped property in the Park, or now the Incorporated Village, was still owned by the entity called the Tuxedo Park Association and its stockholders. The governance of this property, now a municipality, was subject to the laws, rules, and regulations developed by the trustees and mayor who were elected by the Village residents, and the TPA was required to pay property taxes.

While class warfare was not visible, tension was in the air in the early spring of 1955. The now locally named Hamlet community was energized, as were residents of Tuxedo Park who were not members of the Tuxedo Club. The talk centered on what would happen to the Tuxedo Community Club. These groups, not members of the Tuxedo Club, were focused on their quality of life as it related to "their" Tuxedo Community Club inside the new Incorporated Village of Tuxedo Park. The trustees were virtually elected by residents, most of whom were members of the Tuxedo Club. The Community Club was also increasing membership from within the Park because of the newly constructed smaller homes by the Tuxedo Park Association's plan at the beginning of the 1950s. Many of the new residents were not joining the Tuxedo Club, but they were availing themselves of the opportunity to join the Beach Club.

The 1950s was a time of tremendous economic growth in the country. Those returning from World War II and Korea now had the opportunity to further their education under the GI bill. Good paying jobs were plentiful. Tax rates were more proportional, briefly exceeding 90% over a certain level of income for those at the top of the income scale, under the Republican President Dwight D. Eisenhower. This resulted in the ability to create national job growth through plans like the Interstate Highway System. Mass production housing created new suburban communities where home ownership, a car, and television were within reach of what was fast becoming known as "the middle class." Longtime divisions of society between the "have's" and "have nots" were blurring. However, the distinction between Tuxedo

Club members and nonmembers (many of whom had purchased property within the Park themselves), and others in the community outside the main gates, remained.

After all, most Beach Club members who lived in the Park viewed the incorporation of the Village as a positive development, as its status was now better defined, and no matter the size of one's house or bank account, each resident had a vote. Although the Park was now a formal municipality, in the first two years, there wasn't much change, as the elected trustees of the Village were longtime members of the Tuxedo Club, and the Village was still in the hands of its largest landowner, the TPA which controlled significant undeveloped real estate in the Park. These shareholders were also longtime members of the Tuxedo Club. Elections in the Park were virtually predetermined by Tuxedo Club members who outnumbered the non-member property owners. In addition, there was no choice in voting, as candidates who were running for office typically ran unopposed.

On May 2, 1955, Mr. Hans Christian Sonne, Chairman of the Executive Committee of the Tuxedo Park Association that owned the Pigeon Point property that included the Beach Club, received a letter from Mayor Buell regarding a report prepared by The TPA "On the Use of the Lower Lakes," making it clear that the Village had an interest in the lake and lake property of Pigeon Point pertaining to health and protection. Mayor Buell indicated that the Village had certain rights to withdraw water from these lakes and could terminate any activities conducted on the property. The mayor also required all persons, not Park residents, using the facilities enter only through the main gate and would not be allowed entrance through the North Gate or the South Gates from Eagle Valley. He closed with an admonition that "all [Tuxedo Park] ordinances will be enforced; your attention is invited to past criticisms of litter left on the premises and along the roads." The letter deserves to be reproduced in its entirety, as it is a precursor to issues that persisted over the following sixty-five years: veiled attempts on many occasions to restrict, if not destroy, the Wee Wah Beach Club.

TRUSTEES
Anzonella K. McVickar
Matthias Plum
Alexander H. Tomes
James A. Cathcart, Jr.

opy

VILLAGE OF TUXEDO PARK, N. Y.
Incorporated 1952

Hon. Trescott A. Buell, Mayor

H. K. McVickar
Treasurer and
Village Clerk

May 2, 1955

Mr. H. Chr. Sonne
Chairman of the Executive Committee
The Tuxedo Park Association, Inc.
Tuxedo Park, N. Y.

Dear Mr. Sonne:

The Village Trustees and I have reviewed your letter of April 25, 1955 including the report of the Advisory Committee "On the Use of the Lower Lakes".

At the outset, we wish to make completely clear the Incorporated Village should not and will not participate in the negotiations and arrangements concerning this situation for the reason that the problem is one relating to private property and to an activity in which the Village has only an indirect interest.

The Village could be affected, as we see it, from two standpoints; namely, health and protection. Inasmuch as the Village has certain rights to withdraw water from the subject lakes, any arrangements that may be made should include its termination in the event the Village determines to withdraw such waters for Village use.

Insofar as police protection is concerned in order to make this more effective it is requested that persons using the contemplated facilities enter and leave the Village only through the main gate.

While, of course, all ordinances will be enforced, your attention is invited to past criticisms of litter left on the premises and along the roads. We trust appropriate supervision to eliminate this problem will be provided.

While the Village Police are always available to protect and assist when necessary residents and property owners, we are sure you will agree that it will be up to the contemplated organization to furnish its own supervision and see to it that its rules are adhered to.

Sincerely yours,

/s/ T. E. Buell

Mayor

238

In May 1955, Mabel Tansey phoned the secretary at the Village office, instead of the TPA, to request the water be turned on at the Tuxedo Community Club on June 1. The Executive Committee of the Beach Club met and called for a "work night" on May 26, and set the Annual Meeting for Sunday, June 5 at the beach. Mr. Sonne's assurances given to Marion Mottola and other members the previous summer appeared to be the reality. In fact, at the first Executive Committee meeting on May 22, Charlie Albanese made a motion to give Mr. Sonne the title of Honorary President. Although there was great support, thanks to Mr. Sonne's efforts on behalf of the Beach Club, after much discussion, the matter was tabled.

At the Annual Meeting, Mabel read a letter from the TPA Advisory Committee of the Village suggesting certain rules be adopted if they were not on the books already. Mabel had signed the lease with the TPA, as the TPA still owned the property. She stated the lease was too long to read but available for any who wanted to see and read it. Mabel discussed the Beach Club's involvement with the State of New York recreation program for children—which the Beach Club had joined—and again appropriated $300 for membership. This was a net positive for the Beach Club, as the state then paid $350 back to the Club to pay for lifeguards and counselors for the program.

I was much younger then, but I recall that this was a wonderful, well-received program. My friends and other children from the Park who were not members of the Tuxedo Club would be dropped off at the high school in the morning where we would be involved in arts and crafts with the other children from the town. As was popular at the time, the girls made woven plastic bracelets, and the boys made wallets. We participated in art contests, archery, and a variety of other sports and creative activities. After lunch, we were bused to the beach for sports activities, including swimming and diving lessons in the afternoon. Some of the children, especially those from outside the Park, would return to the school on the buses. But for those of us whose mothers lived inside the gates, belonged to the Beach Club, and enjoyed time at the beach themselves, we could remain for a great cookout dinner when our fathers arrived at the beach after work.

Dues were raised to $10 for existing members and $15 for new members. Those serving in the armed forces would be charged $10. The lifeguard salary was raised to $45 per week. Guests eleven years and older would be charged 50 cents, guests under eleven would pay 25 cents, and each member would be allowed a maximum of five guests who "must" live outside the boundaries designated as eligible for membership. Requests for additional guests would go to the Executive Committee. Finally, a $10 donation was approved for the Tuxedo Scholarship Committee.

My uncle, Buddy McCarroll, continued as beach superintendent, and was put in charge of the grounds and maintenance, with his group of young men doing most of the labor. Work nights for the membership would continue. Lifeguards were hired, and Tony Mottola would continue to run his concession stand for the season. The July Fourth picnic would return as usual. Elections were held and the officers and the Executive Committee were unopposed, much like the Village of Tuxedo Park elections, although there were instances of write-ins or a contest for Village positions. Here they were by unanimous vote. The Beach Club agreed to let the American Legion use the beach for a children's picnic on July 2 and discussed plans for the annual picnic in August. Before adjourning the meeting, members considered Charlie Albanese's suggestion to make Mr. Sonne an honorary president in appreciation of his support of the Beach Club. After considering whether such an honor would create problems for Mr. Sonne, as he was a prominent member of the Tuxedo Club, they unanimously voted to make Mr. Hans Christian Sonne an honorary lifetime member.

The Tuxedo Community Club was now operating with increased formality. Rules and regulations were mailed to members. The gate checker enforced the rules for guests and made sure only members were admitted and guest passes were collected. Insurance inspections found the need for more improvements. Buddy and his crew were not just maintaining and repairing, but building improvements, such as raised lifeguard chairs. A new boat was purchased. Signs, such as "No Diving off the Dock," were printed and posted. Upon arrival at the entrance, one would have no question that this was a "beach club" in the Incorporated Village of Tuxedo Park.

After the Annual Meeting on June 5, the beach opened. There were smiles on the faces of members, and children's laughter could be heard all around the lake. And indeed, the Wee Wah was once again a lake. Over the winter and spring, it had been refilled to its normal level. The waterfront was a beehive of activity with the addition of a new concrete dock with a ten-meter diving board and lifeguard chairs. No longer would the old dock with its boulders be a haven for the water snakes that were common, and disruptive, when they came out for a swim. Sand had been added to the beachfront and to the play area. The playground and the picnic area had been enlarged to accommodate the beach's younger members with growing families.

Indeed, the 1955 Fourth of July picnic was an exciting event.

The sight of children laughing, playing, swimming, and surrounding Tony Mottola with his big red Coke cooler was just as it should be. Families at the picnic tables talked and laughed as the charcoal in the grills burned bright, with hot dogs and hamburgers sizzling under the restful shade of the birch trees. Serious competitions were taking place at the horseshoe pits. There were lines where children waited for their turn on the swings, slides, seesaws, and diving board. Little ones played in the sand running up from the beach front with water buckets to create castles and moats.

After the picnic expenses and other bills were paid, my aunt, Marie McCarroll, gave a treasurer's report stating the bank balance was $1,897.05, a far cry from the year before when the account balance was less than $400 and the beach needed a new dock. Everything was running smoothly at the beach, but behind the scenes, not all was happy at the Village office. On July 8, 1955, Mr. Sonne received another letter from Mayor Buell on behalf of the Village of Tuxedo Park.

Not surprisingly, in July, members received word that Mabel Tansey had received a rather formal letter of concern from Archer Brown, the TPA's vice president and general manager. At a general meeting on July 20, and after a letter was read from H. C. Sonne expressing his thanks for being made a lifetime honorary member, Mabel addressed Mr. Brown's letter. It expressed grave concerns over allegations of "crowded conditions, unlimited guest privileges, and cars with foreign [in other words, non-local license plates] at the beach as reported to the trustees of the village by Tuxedo Club members." Complaints had been made at a taxpayers' meeting in the Village of Tuxedo Park. Mrs. Hilton, who attended the meeting, told the members she had attempted to rebut the allegations, and that all the "foreign" cars either belonged to summer residents who were dues-paying members, or belonged to guests of Beach Club members. One of those cars could easily have belonged to my parents, as we had "foreign" New Jersey license plates. My mother and father were no longer members, nor were they eligible to have a family membership. Due to the number of our relatives living in Tuxedo Park, we had no problem obtaining guest passes. In addition, I was usually living with my grandparents and uncle for extended stays, and I suppose I was considered to be under someone's family membership.

Mrs. Umdenstock volunteered to write a letter to Mr. Sonne explaining the situation and asking how to put the matter to rest. Mabel and the Executive Committee could see for the first time that the Incorporated Village of Tuxedo Park, still controlled by members of the Tuxedo Club who, due to their majority, elected the trustees, was starting to exert its control even though the TPA owned the property that the Beach Club had leased for many years. However, the Village owned the lake, and Tuxedo Club members controlled the Village officials. The social distinctions continued to create pressure over the use of Wee Wah Lake by Beach Club members who lived outside the gates in the Hamlet.

The annual picnic in August was a great success, the summer concluded, and fall gave way to the last cleaning of the beach and storage of the recreational equipment, among other preparations for winter. At the last Executive Committee meeting, my uncle, Jim Barth, who lived in the Park, made a motion to hire Joe King in the winter to clear ice from the existing swimming area for ice-skating, as this was historically allowed on Tuxedo Lake and Pond 3, but that was only for

Tuxedo Club members. Although the lease to the beach for the beach property was for a designated period, typically from Memorial Day to Labor Day, Beach Club members thought this was a great idea and embraced it, although it was not within the lease period and anyone other than Village residents using the beach area would be considered trespassers. Later that winter, Mr. King cleared the ice for skating, but few used it, as there was no indoor enclosure with a large roaring fireplace—as there was for Tuxedo Club members on Pond 3—and it was difficult for Hamlet residents to get through the main gate of the Village. Therefore, the winter season did not materialize, and thus the Beach Club avoided a new confrontation with the trustees of the Village.

Chapter 20: Guest Privileges

A Day at the Beach, ca.1955

The mid-1950s were a time of tremendous growth for the country. President Eisenhower was on his way to reelection in 1956. The Northeast experienced increased population expansion. The farms of northern New Jersey and the fields of Long Island were being transformed into suburban communities and shopping malls. Many of the larger estates of the former Gilded Age class in the metropolitan region had been sold and purchased to be rezoned by developers. New schools, hospitals, and other infrastructure necessities opened, and thousands of miles of new and upgraded highways were built in a frantic effort to keep up with the burgeoning population. The Ramapo Mountains on the west, and the narrow valley with the state parks on the east, left little room for development in the Route 17 corridor from

Sloatsburg to the south and Monroe to the north. This did not mean that families were not growing in the Town of Tuxedo, but the population was not on pace with the rest of the metropolitan area. The third generation of many original families were now in their teenage years. However, membership in the Beach Club increased steadily as these extended families grew larger. Many of the second generation that had moved on did not move far away. Requests for guest privileges soared as families continued their tradition of family gatherings on weekends. In the summer, a good number of those using the Wee Wah lived outside the geographic boundaries and were admitted as guests of their parents and grandparents, many of whom lived in the Hamlet.

In the spring of 1956, the Beach Club was increasingly becoming a focal point of concern for the Village trustees. There were many reasons and rumors. These were the same as the days when Tuxedo Club members opposed allowing anyone from outside the Park, including non-members from the Hamlet who were staff within the Park, to use the Wee Wah for swimming. There were rumors of a thinly disguised effort to take over the beach property and provide exclusive access to Village residents. After all, the TPA owned the land and paid the taxes, but the lake was owned by the municipality. This was a beautiful recreational facility in the Village, so why couldn't they restrict its use solely to "Village" taxpayers? This position developed, notwithstanding that those who lived in the Incorporated Village of Tuxedo Park, whether they were Tuxedo Club members or not, could join the Beach Club. It was simply a matter of requesting a membership application and paying the annual dues. The membership list was still provided to the TPA, but now the list was required to be provided to the Village trustees for approval as well. No one who lived in Tuxedo Park had ever been denied membership. It was never talked about, but all knew the underlying issue. It was believed that many Village of Tuxedo Park residents who were Tuxedo Club members used the Tuxedo Club facilities and were not interested in joining a recreational facility such as the beach club where they would have to share the water with their landscaper or grocery store clerk who did not live in the Park.

Mabel Tansey received a letter from the TPA with a request that the majority of the Executive Committee of the beach reside in the Village of Tuxedo Park. From its inception, the Tuxedo Community Club Executive Committee was elected by the general membership, and any member was eligible for the position. The Executive Committee moved forward without responding to the request, and according to the original minutes, the matter does not appear again during this period. After all the repairs in the fall of 1956 were completed, and after all the bills had been paid, the Beach Club had only $261.80 in the bank.

There was much work to be done for the 1957 season. Buddy McCarroll called for two work nights prior to opening the beach. One important compliance item (fortunately, this was something simple and relatively inexpensive) involved properly checking entry to the Beach Club. It was not so much for security as it was to present an image for anyone driving by the entrance. Until this time, access was allowed by showing one's membership card to a checker who would then lower a rope. This year, they would replace the rope with a gate that the checker could raise to allow entrance to those providing proof of membership or a valid guest pass. It accomplished the same purpose but appeared more formal.

The 1957 Annual Meeting was held at the beach on May 27, and the officers were unanimously re-elected. Buddy was recognized for his efforts. A new Executive Committee was selected, and the usual $300 was approved for the state recreation program (with the provision that the Beach Club would get back the funds, plus additional money to cover the lifeguard expense). Tony Mottola would return to run the concession stand. Although there were many issues regarding the relationship with the Village, such as dues and who were members and guests, the focus was on getting the beach ready for opening. As no one other than JoAnne Mottola applied for the job, she was hired as the official checker. These positions tended to be filled with children in families who were active, original members. Requests for picnic days by the Methodist Church and Daughters of the Eastern Star were approved without objection. These requests were not forwarded to the Village trustees. The officers remembered how the request for the nurses who lived in the annex of the Tuxedo Park Hospital had been declined many years ago. And since the inception of the Beach Club, the clergy of both St. Mary's-in-Tuxedo Episcopal Church and Mount Carmel Catholic Church had also been "given" annual memberships.

I can recall spending most of July with my grandparents and my Uncle Jim Barth as I secured a job as a caddie at the Tuxedo Golf Course. As was usual, my parents would drive up from New Jersey almost every weekend to visit with my grandparents and my aunts and uncles. I lived less than an hour away in New Jersey, and had remained friends with many kids I had originally started school with in Tuxedo. I was about to become a teenager. There was only one major activity and meeting spot. That was the beach. It started there. Those who lived within the Park, but didn't belong to the Beach Club, could walk down to the drugstore in the Hamlet and meet others outside the main gate. As to a guest pass, I must admit that many assumed I was a family member, and perhaps more significantly, I knew the checkers who were young girls we all partied with and knew for years. Teenagers always seem to find ways around the system.

The summer of 1957 certainly appeared to be a wonderful season, or perhaps it was just a great summer for me. It was still a time in Tuxedo Park where, if I was walking back and forth to the Golf Club to caddie or downtown to the drugstore, if someone came along in a car, they would stop and offer me a ride.

Based on the minutes, the beach opened and everything ran smoothly at the Wee Wah Lake. Picnics were frequent. As usual, the Beach Club closed after Labor Day, children returned to school, and the members responsible for their tasks needed no instruction to accomplish them. Nothing further came of the letter from the TPA concerning the make-up of the Executive Committee or the existence of the Beach Club.

In March 1958, as the spring thaw was beginning, the Executive Committee conducted its seasonal gathering at the club to walk the grounds and identify projects that needed to be done before opening in June. They determined that Buddy and his crew had done a fantastic job of keeping everything clean and in good order. Fresh paint, new picnic tables, new playground equipment, re-sanding and painting the surface of the raft, and new sand for the play area had all helped prepare for the opening of the 1958 season. Other items involved finances, dues, memberships, and any other matters to be addressed at the Annual Meeting in May or June. The minutes reflect

that everyone agreed that the club was in "the best shape ever."
However, Mabel injected the reality of how fragile the club really was
due to the continuing tension with the trustees of the now Incorporated
Village. At a meeting she was asked to attend with the TPA, Mr.
Sonne explained that while the TPA owned the land, the club was
subject to the control of the Incorporated Village of Tuxedo Park, as it
retained the water rights to the lakes. He advised Mabel that Village
Mayor Buell said there was too much traffic on the Park roads and that
tighter controls over Beach Club membership would be forthcoming.

Before incorporation, going back to the inception of
Lorillard's Tuxedo Park, the TPA was simply the management
company that would interact with the Tuxedo Club to enforce
decisions made by the Board of Governors of the Tuxedo Club. Now,
the elected officials of the newly incorporated Village were all
members of the Tuxedo Club. There was little, if any, change in social
status.

The mayor supported requiring a new constitution for the
Tuxedo Community Club, one that defined Park residents as "resident
members of the club." All others would be "out-of-town members."
Although against the rules, apparently there were some "special
exceptions" through the years that met approval review by the TPA.
Any current members who lived in the Town of Tuxedo who had been
allowed as exceptions from Sloatsburg, Eagle Valley, or Southfields
were to be dropped. He requested that a complete list of members, and
the guest book, be presented in two weeks.

Despite many efforts from original Beach Club members to
explain the history and practices of the Beach Club, Mayor Buell and
the Village trustees held firm. During the second meeting, the Village

imposed its rules for the club, without discussion. The new rules for the Beach Club as reported in the minutes would be:

- Hamlet residents would be allowed to join, but *would not* be allowed to bring guests.
- Village of Tuxedo Park members who joined the Beach Club *would* be allowed four guests per week.
- Residents in other areas outside the Park and the Hamlet geographic boundaries would no longer be allowed to join.
- Tony Mottola must be considered an employee of the club.
- Hamlet members must place stickers on the right side of their windshield, visible to the club gate checker, in order to be admitted at the front gate.
- Only three groups would be allowed to have picnics: The Fire Department on July Fourth, one church group, and the American Legion.

There had always been a vast difference in social standing in these separate Tuxedo communities—emphasized by the imposing main gate that kept Tuxedo Park private. The strict division between the classes continued to exist, but much had changed as a result of the Great Depression and World War II. This change continued into the late 1940s and early 1950s. Efforts had continually been made to bring about social change and blur the distinction between the Hamlet and the Park. Looking as far back as 1945, the Tuxedo Park Association described its efforts in its annual report to shareholders (many of whom were original families of Lorillard's Tuxedo Park) regarding the relationship between the Park and the Hamlet (at that time called the "village"). Section E of the report describes the efforts of the TPA to improve conditions in the East and Slovak villages.

"The 'Village' [Hamlet], which is the responsibility of the Association no less than the Association's responsibility to the Park is to assist your officers in discharging this responsibility. Key residents of the Village are being consulted on Village matters and your officers and intend to lay stress on measures affecting the social and financial welfare of the people of the town."[70]

These new rules imposed by the mayor and trustees were an unexpected setback after the previous great summer. All the new work done in the fall and spring to get ready for this year's opening seemed unappreciated by the Park trustees. Art Tocher, a respected resident of the Hamlet and longtime member of the Beach Club, resigned. A new constitution would have to be drawn up, and the members would have to be notified to meet to adopt the document. Mr. Euvrard, the school principal, was directed to make sure all the children in the school were notified of the new rules and told to inform their parents.

On May 3, 1958, the Annual Meeting of the Tuxedo Community Club (now commonly referred to as the Beach Club) was held at George F. Baker High School. In all, 185 members reflecting two groups had sent in their dues. One group included the original members who had lived in the Park or Hamlet and who had worked from the beginning to support Tuxedo Park and its Tuxedo Club members. The other group of members were their children, now grown with homes in the Hamlet and families of their own, along with new residents of the Hamlet. My Aunt Marie described to me how several original members who attended that 1958 meeting shared vivid memories of the social distinctions of the times, from Tuxedo Park's beginnings in the 1880s through the end of World War II. Even though it was 1958, this was a reminder that many people opposed the social changes taking place throughout the country and were attempting to pass on their elevated lifestyles within private communities like Tuxedo Park. Since the Village of Tuxedo Park was now incorporated and indeed was *their* (the resident's) community, the elected officials had the power to impose their will. Granted, the mayor and trustees' positions were easily defended and did not violate anyone's rights, but the matter could have been handled more tactfully. What initially was extended as a privilege some thirty years prior, back when the Tuxedo Community Club was formed, had become thought of as a right by many Tuxedo community members who lived outside the Park gates. The Beach Club considered the limit on membership to mean "only" the original geographical boundary that encompassed the Hamlet outside the gates. This membership right was now under attack.

There was much discussion, and some of it became quite heated, but no alternative seemed advisable. If there was to be a Beach Club, they would have to comply. A new constitution would be drawn up incorporating the changes. With respect to guest passes, Mabel said she would talk with Mr. Sonne to see if something could be done. Officers were unanimously reelected. New members of the Executive Committee included Village of Tuxedo Park residents, such as Ann Mottola, wife of Dr. Sam Mottola, who was a member of one of three Mottola families that had grown up outside the gates. Dr. Mottola was now a well-respected physician who lived with his family in the Park in the house originally built for Dr. Rushmore, Tuxedo Park's first physician. Next was Tillie Henderson, who lived and worked for years as the personal maid to Rene Carhart Amory at the Renamor estate. Mrs. Amory was a Carhart, and grew up at the Villa Blanca estate, which had views down to the Wee Wah, but it was demolished in the 1940s, except for the separate Ballroom at the end of the gardens built for her debutant coming out party at the Autumn Ball. The Villa Blanca estate was located up on the hill near the Frelinghuysen estate. George S. Amory was on the Executive Committee of the TPA, an original trustee of the new Village of Tuxedo Park, and a long-time officer in the Tuxedo Club as well. Tillie's husband, Alec, was the houseman for George Amory. Also elected was a Park resident, and owner of one of the new TPA homes, Sally Fay, the mother of a childhood friend, Peter and his brother, David Fay. Today David is the retired executive director of the United States Golf Association (USGA) known for his TV commentary at PGA major golf tournaments and noted for his expertise on the rules of golf. None of the Village of Tuxedo Park residents elected were members of the Tuxedo Club. The usual $10 donation was approved for the Tuxedo Scholarship Committee and $300 for the recreation program, as well. Beach club checkers were hired and would start after school closed and the Beach Club opened. In fact, not much changed with the new constitution. The club had the windshield stickers printed and carried on business as usual. Tensions remained, but the Beach Club operated as it had in the past, and it did not appear the Incorporated Village of Tuxedo Park's new rules were given much consideration. The Beach Club persevered through 1958 calmed by another summer of rest, relaxation, and recreation.

The next Annual Meeting of the membership was held June 1, 1959. The matter of "guest privileges" was still causing resentment.

The Beach Club had worked around most of the conditions imposed by the Village of Tuxedo Park. Some "unwritten" compromises had been worked out over the winter, as the preceding summer had been without any problems. The officers were again reelected unanimously. However, in keeping with the requirements of the Village, the Executive Committee continued to be made up of both Park and Hamlet residents. Park residents elected included Tillie Henderson, Sally Fay, Iris Appleton, James Barth, Charlie Albanese, and Ralph Hellum. They were from families long associated with the working class and were not members of the Tuxedo Club. Those elected from the Hamlet included Ralph Napolitano, Jim Venezia, and Tom Melillo (all from early established families and well respected in the Hamlet). In a letter, Ken Koran at St. Mary's, the Episcopal Church Center inside the Park, requested memberships and they were accepted but without the ability to have guest privileges. Honorary membership cards were sent to Reverend Cooper of St. Mary's, Father Hannifin and Father Monaghan of Our Lady of Mount Carmel, and Mr. Sonne.

Tuxedo Park Police Chief Sam Mottola was asked to set up a telephone line from the beach to the police at the main gate. This was approved and installed during the summer. It was now basically a repetition of following past policies. Everyone knew their role. The beach was prepared for its opening with lifeguards and checkers. Buddy McCarroll was performing as expected. Calendar pages turn quickly. Not just the months, but the years as well. There was sadness that spring of 1959 when all in both the Village and the Hamlet learned Tony Mottola had passed away. I can still remember the first taste of a frozen Milky Way that came out of Tony's large red Coca-Cola cooler filled with sodas and smoking dry ice in addition to those chilled candy bars. The business of the Wee Wah Beach Club had to go on, and so the Executive Meeting took place. Dan Winfield and Marion Crisci, children of original members, were hired as checkers. Marion was the daughter of Mike Crisci, a fixture behind the counter at the drugstore in the Hamlet who later would become the supervisor of the Town of Tuxedo. Mike was known to all, and a tireless vice president, as well as a member of the Executive Committee for many years. The lack of guest privileges for Hamlet members was a source of continual resentment, but requests to the Village trustees for reconsideration were repeatedly denied. To make matters worse, the TPA asked that employees of the TPA and the Tuxedo Club be allowed membership in the Beach Club, despite some living outside the geographical boundaries set by the Tuxedo Park trustees. Mike Crisci arranged a meeting with Howland Pennington "Pen" Rodgers, a young, prominent Tuxedo Club member who was also involved with Village politics. Pen Rodgers was well-liked and respected. The results of the meeting, as reflected in the minutes, stated Rodgers said he understood there were only two employees who wanted to join, and it would be best to play it down, although they did not live within the boundaries.

With the 1959 season concluded, the 1950s were coming to a close, and transportation issues persisted. Recreation at the Wee Wah had grown substantially, and buses leased by the school could not hold all the children. As a result, parents who were not from the Hamlet and did not have a sticker showing membership in the Beach Club were stopped at the gate driving their children to the beach, creating an access issue. The main flash point between the Village and the Beach Club had always been the matter of privacy and security for those who resided behind the imposing gates of Tuxedo Park. The Beach Club members from the Hamlet were an exception. Any deviation from the rules restricting entry to members could cause repercussions with Park residents. The trustees would then hear the usual litany of complaints: too many cars that don't belong, speeding on the roads, garbage left along the roads, etc. Some things change but many things remain the same, and these complaints were repeated well into the new decade.

Soon it was time for the children to return to school. Cool autumn breezes cast a chill on Pigeon Point. If you were not in the sun, even in the middle of the day the breeze under the shade of the white birches in the picnic area would require a sweater or light jacket. A peaceful quiet settled over the Beach Club, and it was time to enjoy the changing of leaves and the beginning of preparations for winter.

Chapter 21: The 1960s

Bocce games at the Wee Wah Beach Club, ca. mid-1960s

Many traditions remained, but a new era was upon us, and you could somehow feel change in the air. In March 1957, the *New York Times* reported that the days of high society with staff in the dozens to serve the household were long gone. It referenced a family in Tuxedo Park who, facing a servant problem, thought they had found the answer. "The Tuxedo family thought it had solved the servant problem by hiring a refugee couple. But it took the refugees only two years to become aware of the facts of American life. They now work in industry, have their own home and car, receive free medical and dental care from their employer, and have a promise of pensions when they retire."[71] Jobs were plentiful. No longer a new concept, suburbia continued spreading throughout the area and across the country. John F. Kennedy, an inspiring young Democrat, was in the White House. Trescott Buell was still mayor and a member of the Tuxedo Club, as were the other trustees of the Incorporated Village of Tuxedo Park. Yet the social fabric of Tuxedo Park and what was now called the "Hamlet" outside the gates had experienced many changes in the preceding decade.

In the Park, although huge homes still were lived in and reflected the incredible work of architects and builders from the Gilded Age, none of the large estates remained fully operational. Time, taxes, and ease of travel had taken their toll. Some of the large houses were unoccupied and left to the elements. Villa Blanca was torn down in the 1940s. Estates such as Kincraig had been subdivided and auctioned off in the mid-1950s. The large garage was a separate parcel. The potting shed undertook a major renovation to become a home by new owners, who had also acquired the extensive garden portion of the Kincraig property. Even a sectioned lot with the water tower was sold and converted into an unusual home. Others were donated to charitable organizations. Chastelux and Renamor, two other large estates, were now operated as a Catholic girl's school known as the Academy of Mount St. Vincent. The Tilford estate, originally constructed for H. W. Poor, founder of Standard & Poor's, was now an Episcopal conference center and its garage, gardener's cottage, and gardens were subdivided into separate properties. Household staff no longer lived in the larger houses. Butlers, chauffeurs, lady's maids, and cooks were now a part of storied history. Many of their children remained in the Village and had purchased the smaller homes such as former stables or staff cottages that had been zoned into separate lots in the Incorporated Village. Others found homes in the Hamlet. Gardeners, who were more aptly called "horticultural experts," were now deceased or were no longer required. Large vegetable gardens and flowers, as well as ornamentals that had been the focus of competitions, were no longer regularly reported in the national press. Most landscaping work now involved general upkeep contracted out to landscaping companies from outside the gates.

The manicured gardens were gone, and outbuildings had been rezoned and sold off. Zoning changes in the 1950s had allowed for the construction of smaller tract-like homes, and with that came more new families with children, or young businesspeople without the means or the social acceptability to become members of the Tuxedo Club. However, as many of the new owners were financially successful, which was now more important than family pedigree, these new residents sought and gained the prestige and history associated with the Tuxedo Club. All appreciated the reclusive beauty of Tuxedo Park. As a result of the new construction, the Village population almost doubled. The original water and sewer lines, as well as the roads built in the late 1800s, were now archaic when one thinks of the improvements in design, materials, and construction methods employed in the ensuing decades, but to the credit of the expertise of those early laborers from the Hamlet and the East Village, the infrastructure continued to serve the community.

To be sure, there were still residents who could trace their family to the early days of Tuxedo Park. They continued to guard the original intent of the founders to preserve the unique, private community. Most social activities of the Gilded Age were long gone, although some traditions such as the Autumn Ball continued to serve as the coming-out party for daughters of prominent society families with large houses in Tuxedo and expensive apartments in New York City.

In 1962, Mrs. Crawford Blagdon was appointed the chairman of the ball committee by the Board of Governors of the Tuxedo Club.[72] Changes were made from the early days, as there were just not that many debutantes of members. On October 21, 1962, a *New York Times* headline reported, "More than 120 Debutantes Attend the 74th Tuxedo Autumn Ball, 12 Young Women are Presented at Annual Event." There was a difference between "attending" and "presenting." Presenting was actually making their debut, one of whom was Amanda Jay Mortimer, granddaughter of Mrs. Stanley G. Mortimer. Typical of older times, Mrs. Mortimer gave a large dinner at her home for her granddaughter, who was an "official debutante," along with others with last names such as Phipps and Baker, which harkened back to Tuxedo Park's Gilded Age. By 1970, the Autumn Ball had only three debutantes.[73] It would be the final time. An annual tradition that had lasted eighty-one years slipped into history.

Meanwhile, court tennis, squash, and racquets were still time-honored traditions for national and international tournaments held at the Tuxedo Racquet and Tennis Club. At the time there were approximately eight "court tennis" courts in the United States, with most built around the turn of the century. These could be found in Philadelphia; Boston; Newport; the former Lakewood, New Jersey estate of Jay Gould; Aiken, South Carolina; and New York City. Exclusive to the very wealthy and old society clubs, and referred to as

Royal tennis in England, "court tennis" dates back to the early 1500s. It was played within the castle walls using a heavy, dead ball similar to a tennis ball with wooden racquets that resemble those used for lawn tennis in the early 1900s. The courts today are indoors and continue to have one side that was fully walled. The other sides had slanted top galleries protected by netting, all of which were in play.

With skyrocketing property taxes and a need for urban planning, Tuxedo Park became less desirable, which affected real estate prices. Commuters traveled by train into New York City that terminated on the New Jersey side of the Hudson River at Hoboken. From there, one would take the ferry, or the Hudson PATH tubes under the river, to reach the office in Manhattan. There was also bus service to the New York Port Authority station at Forty-second Street in the city. Across the Hudson River in Westchester and Connecticut, there was direct train service into Grand Central Station. These communities had become more attractive to affluent families, who now resided permanently outside of New York City. The "old money" was gone, and people with "new money" from New York City were opting for Westchester County towns like Bronxville and Scarsdale, as well as Southern Connecticut towns like Greenwich, which had town centers, exclusive country clubs like Tuxedo Park, and, of most importance, quick and easy transportation into New York City. The population of the Village of Tuxedo Park was not growing, and real estate prices were in decline. Something had to be done. Eyebrows were raised, and many cynical articles were written in national magazines and the top newspapers, when Mayor Buell and the trustees sought federal aid for the approximately four-square miles that had once been one of the country's most exclusive communities.[74]

In the summer of 1960, I was a young teenager dividing my time between my parents' home in New Jersey and continuing to spend time with my uncle and grandparents in the Amory gardener's cottage while working as a caddie at the Tuxedo Golf Club. The Amorys' wills had left the cottage and grounds to my grandparents to reside in for free until they passed away. The years had passed quickly from the mid-1950s, when my friends and I would watch the older boys coming into the Beach Club and carrying on, as I mentioned previously. It was now our turn to try diving off the board and swim underwater to the back side of the raft where the lifeguard could not see us. It was our summer of awakening to try getting a girl to go under the raft and come up together into one of those tight open spaces, while the rest of the boys would quietly watch through the seams in the boards above.

For me, looking back, it was at this time when summer romances and exploration flourished at the beach. What started as fun and games for the teenagers at the raft took on a more advanced tone. The raft still consisted of a wooden deck structure supported by several floating barrels. This left openings below the deck that were just large enough to accommodate two bodies by swimming beneath the outside frame and emerging within the empty cubicles. The objective was clear. Once a boy and girl agreed to occupy the space, there was no room for anything other than "romance," to use a polite word. Boasting and denials were left for later in the day. Looking back, the odd thing was that the lifeguards, including my uncle during this period, would blow their whistles and use the megaphone to yell some version of "Everyone out from under the raft … now!" These under-the-raft cubicles on the back side were not visible from the beachfront, so we often wondered how the lifeguard knew someone was beneath the raft.

Years later, I questioned my uncle about his knowledge of what was going on. It was a simple answer. He said one only had to look at the raft and see the group of young teenagers on deck of the raft. The girls would mostly be sitting in groups, while the boys would all be lying on their stomachs with their heads together in a line. Of course! You see, there was a gap between the boards making up the top of the raft, and when one of the girls agreed to join one of the boys in the cubicle underneath, we would all silently lie down with heads together to look through the cracks and observe whatever romance was taking place. Who knew that the Wee Wah Beach Club had its own peep show long before they became the scourge of Times Square in New York City, although whatever I was able to see or participate in would be PG-rated today.

These summers were aptly captured in Paul Anka's big 1960's hit "They Called It Puppy Love" that he wrote for the cutest Mouseketeer, Annette Funicello, on TV's popular *The Mickey Mouse Club.* Some of the boys boasted of taking things a bit further, as there was another so-called private place on the north side of Pigeon Point where the Department of Public Works was located in the old icehouse. It was beyond the horseshoe pits and through the woods. Work ended at four o'clock, leaving the DPW facility deserted. This was the location of the old north beach, where a small fishing dock still jutted out from the shore. There was also a bench and a nicely maintained grassy area under a strand of trees. On occasion you would see "two lovers" disappear through the woods and head for the spot. There was no need to discuss it, as there was an unwritten code that no one was to follow or sneak up to observe what was going on. I can only say I was not one to boast.

These were summers where the group I was part of were hanging out at the drugstore or at the Beach Club when not working, cruising Greenwood Lake bars at night as the New York drinking age was 18 (which really meant 16 at many spots), or having wild parties at the original but now-abandoned golf club by the also abandoned North Gate. If the local girls were babysitting in the larger homes in the Park, you could be sure we would show up at the house and search out the liquor cabinet. While social lines had blurred, the group I was friends with mostly did not mix with boys or girls whose families were members of the Tuxedo Club. More than once the police came to my grandparents' home to question me as to where I had been the prior evening, creating a sick feeling in my stomach. Truth be told, I certainly was not where I had told my uncle or grandparents I was going the night before, but it certainly was not around the Tuxedo Club. However, each time my friends and I later found out that all the Tuxedo Club deck chairs had been thrown into the pool, or that some other teenage prank had occurred. Each time we would learn that it was the Tuxedo Club kids, the Parkies, who were responsible for the mischief. Of course, nothing happened to them.

By the early 1960s, the quaint and serviceable Beach Club had come a long way from what was once a small informal swimming and recreational area. The old, repainted Gun Club, with its unique design, now served as the entrance to the Beach Club, with cars entering beneath the portico. It added a historic touch to the area, though unused but for the Beach Club, and looking like a shell of its former original beauty. Still, it presented an impressive view upon entering the beach grounds and it served as an example of the history of the original Lorillard plan—and it conveyed how the original Tuxedo Club lifestyle had declined over the years. Now serving as a Beach Club community center, the old Gun Club provided comfortable changing areas for the adults and shelter for waiting out thunderstorms. The picnic area had now been extended well back to the cove separating it from the main road. The children's play area and grass recreation field had also been expanded, with a large sand play area that led to the beachfront. Two lifeguards in raised chairs overlooked the water and a beautiful stone wall met the water at the shore. Wide stone steps leading to the concrete dock, diving board, and raft provided a picturesque scene that instilled in the officers and the Executive Committee a sense of pride and accomplishment.

Membership had grown to almost two hundred. Members now in their sixties could remember the original beach and the beginning of the Beach Club in the early 1930s. They had come a long way and overcome many obstacles. The best part was that the effort had involved everyone in the community who had neither the interest nor the connections or money to gain acceptance into the Tuxedo Club. The Beach Club was established with minimal annual dues and had always been run by volunteers. The primary concerns involved the continual objections by many residents of the now-incorporated Village of Tuxedo Park. These residents maintained that the Beach Club was not truly a Village entity. Of course, this was a veiled reference that this was Village of Tuxedo Park property and that only "residents of the incorporated Village and invited guests" should be allowed access to Tuxedo Park and the Wee Wah Lake.

And then, it happened. At the Annual Meeting on May 15, 1960, the minutes reflect that Mabel Tansey announced that the TPA, which renewed the $1 lease for one year, was nonetheless proposing another recreation area for the Beach Club. The TPA suggested no more money be spent on improving or maintaining the beach. The lease raised questions about whether the trustees of the Incorporated Village had input into the matter of maintenance and improvements as the Village now owned the water rights to the Wee Wah Lake. There was no sense having a beach if the Village planned to prohibit swimming. Having been through this before, the membership discussed attempting to get a longer lease, or, alternatively, purchasing the land from the TPA. Purchasing the land was a good suggestion but a non-starter as the ownership of the lake was controlled by the Village. Despite the TPA suggestion, the Executive Committee forged ahead with improvements. They raised dues to $15 for established members and $20 for first-time members. They supported the same donations and approved a beach picnic for St. Mary's. The officers were unanimously reelected, and the new Executive Committee was elected with the now requisite majority members from the Park. Village of Tuxedo Park resident member, Mr. Skvarla, requested and received permission to form and chair a committee that would approach the TPA in an attempt to secure a longer lease—or to buy the beach property. The committee included Mr. Gordon, Mr. Ebberson, and Mr. O'Leary, all of the TPA. Another issue was that Sterling Forest owned by City Investing, west and north of the Tuxedo Park boundary but within the Town of Tuxedo, was developing a residential area in the Town of Tuxedo, and the Beach Club received its first application for membership from a resident in this community. It was denied and left to the TPA and Village to deal with this issue.

At the next Executive Committee meeting, Mr. Gordon requested approval for a letter drafted by Mr. Skvarla's committee. It was quickly decided that the letter (for which, no copy remains) would only create more friction. Two weeks later, on July 1, Mr. Skvarla presented a more conciliatory letter to the TPA, which the committee tentatively approved while calling for a special meeting so all members could have input.

In other business, Frank and Alice Rigby, two longtime members of H. P. Rodgers' household staff, as well as the Methodist minister, were approved for complimentary memberships. The Rigbys were a true service couple in the old sense of English aristocracy and very close friends of my maternal grandparents. Frank Rigby was an English butler married to Alice, an Irish cook. They were born and raised into service and had no children when they came to America to work for the H. P. Rogers family in Tuxedo Park. They could easily have been the inspiration for the characters of Mr. Carson and Mrs. Pattmore on the award-winning series and movie *Downton Abbey*. A cook extraordinaire, Alice had always kept her own recipes in a single book featuring her special desserts. That book was sought out by everyone in the community, including Tuxedo Club members. We have no record that it was ever passed on, and if it was, no one admits to having it. Frank Rigby, well into his 70s, could set out a formal place setting of china plates, silver and five glasses for a nine-course dinner in less than a minute. Then he could seamlessly remove the used pieces as the courses were served. They were always invited for weekend dinners and the holidays by my maternal grandparents for as long as I could remember and well into the 1970s. Frank would always serve the tea and there were numerous delicious desserts prepared by Alice.

One interesting fact that will always stay with me occurred on each Christmas Day. Alice and Frank would be present with the entire Barth family late in the day at the gardener's cottage to exchange presents. At around four o'clock in the afternoon, Mr. & Mrs. Amory would come down the drive to stop in and say hello. We all knew they were arriving, at which point, Frank and Alice would leave their seats and go into the pantry between the dining room and the kitchen, where they could neither be seen nor heard. Mr. Amory would go into the kitchen to have a drink and give my grandfather, "Barth," as he called him, a Christmas check. Mrs. Amory would chat with my grandmother and express her admiration for the tree and good wishes to the family. They stayed not more than fifteen minutes and then Frank and Alice would return. Old habits of "servants were not to be seen or heard" were hard to break.

In 1961, the Beach Club membership roster dropped to 142. This was mainly due to the restrictions and whims of the Village trustees who reviewed the applications and requests. A request to hold a picnic for hospital employees was rejected, coupled with the suggestion that the employees apply for membership. The application of Alfred Stevens, a long-time sexton at St. Mary's-in-Tuxedo Episcopal Church inside the gates and the place of worship for the original founders, was rejected because he was neither a resident of Tuxedo Park nor, any longer, a resident of the Hamlet. This was in accordance with the strict rules required to control membership by the trustees of the Village of Tuxedo Park. The TPA wanted the Beach Club to reconsider the hospital request, requiring another meeting three weeks later. Mr. Fredericks of the TPA also "suggested" the application for Mr. Stevens be accepted as an accommodation, as these were people who "served" the Park, and that had been the original intent for membership. This was now viewed by the Beach Club members as the Village interfering when it suited them to include those who did not qualify for membership. Contention around such issues was rising often now among the Tuxedo Community Club, the Village of Tuxedo Park, and the TPA. This was beginning to affect the operation of the Beach Club.

As the Executive Committee met to tour the grounds on May 12, 1961, there was much more on everyone's minds than the condition of the beach, which, by the way, needed serious attention. Over the winter, many sections of the wall on the waterfront had collapsed, and a large amount of the beachfront sand had washed away. Both lower bath houses needed painting and the raft was in disrepair. The annual battle against poison ivy, which continually invaded the borders of the play areas, would need to be fought again with heavy spraying in the upper beach and picnic grove. In the 1960s there was less concern over the effects of chemical spraying than with the pain and itching associated with poison ivy. As they walked the beach, the unspoken issue on everyone's mind was that more work needed to be done and that more money needed to be raised; otherwise, the Beach Club might not be allowed to continue. Mabel told the committee that the TPA had sent her a one-year lease, for the seasonal rent of $1, on the condition that the same rules and regulations remained in effect. It was getting dark, and everyone agreed on the to-do list, including running an advertisement in the paper for a lifeguard, a reserve lifeguard, and checkers. They also selected a date for the Annual Meeting. Discussion continued until it was completely dark, at which time, the exhausted members returned to their homes.

The Annual Meeting was held at the beach on Sunday, June 4,

1961. Moving quickly past the fact that the TPA had not responded to Mr. Skvarla's letter, Mabel discussed the repairs needed to the waterfront and suggested the Tuxedo Community Club request bids to repair the wall. The members decided to donate some extra boats to the fishing club on the north side of Pigeon Point.

The hiring decision as to checkers and lifeguards was now left to the Executive Committee. Donations of $30 to the Tuxedo Scholarship Committee and $300 to the recreation program were approved. Rather than give the fire department a cash donation for the July Fourth picnic, the Beach Club instead decided to provide an additional lifeguard free of charge. In the past, the fire department was required to pay the Beach Club the same amount as the donation for an additional guard on the day of the picnic.

The Executive Committee met the following Wednesday at the beach to consider the bids on the beachfront wall work. The bids averaged around $1,200, which was more than the Tuxedo Community Club could afford. Four members stepped forward and volunteered to repair the stone wall from the dock to just beyond the slide. From that point to the end of the beachfront, they would use cinderblocks and cement. They would only charge for materials, not their labor. Betty Zupko was selected as the head checker, with Honey Mottola and Janice Lippiello as substitutes. All were daughters of original Beach Club members. Three weeks later, work on the beach wall was completed. The cost of $485 provided a sixty percent savings over the original bids.

Meanwhile, the surrounding area saw continued development. Like the previous request from the Sterling Forest development, people from the new community of Maplebrook in the Town of Tuxedo, just outside the south gate of Tuxedo Park, were interested in joining the Beach Club. Maplebrook was another of three communities developed by City Investing Company, which had bought eight thousand acres of Town of Tuxedo property, a section known as Sterling Forest, from the Harriman family. In the nineteenth century, the forest was the location of a thriving iron industry. The property was bought in 1895 by the Harriman railroad family, which sold it for $750,000 in 1953 to a real estate developer that set up the Sterling Forest company. The company developed homes for 250 families and offices in scattered park areas but ran into financial difficulties and was trying to unload the larger property for years.[75] This was no longer a "request" for the memberships with a review by the TPA. The TPA was now "informing" the Beach Club that Maplebrook residents "are" eligible to become members. It appeared that the TPA (which still owned significant property in the Park) approved the "Maplebrook" request due to that community's proximity to the Tuxedo Park boundary line and its location between the south gate entrance and the new Tuxedo Club golf course—built in the 1950s on land purchased with funds from the TPA. The golf course was actually in the hamlet of Eagle Valley, outside of Tuxedo Park's southern boundary. The Beach Club did not question this decision, as it would provide a needed increase in membership. However, this situation was another example of how the TPA and the Village of Tuxedo Park trustees altered Beach Club membership restrictions to suit their own needs.

The July Fourth event was a success and the 50/50 raffle brought in some much-needed funds to cover the wall repair. The raffle winner received half the proceeds, with the balance going toward the construction work. Membership stood at 158 on July 13, and the bank balance was exactly $1,368.63. The annual picnic was scheduled for August, bills were paid, and $20 was approved as a donation to the Tuxedo Volunteer Ambulance Corps. I recall the weather was very pleasant that summer and the beach was in great condition. Everyone was enjoying a carefree summer of swimming, games, and picnicking. A local chapter of the Republican Party's request for a picnic was granted. Miss DiMicielli ("Dee" to all and known as the head of nursing at the Tuxedo Memorial Hospital) asked to hold a picnic for the Camp Fire Girls, and her request was granted. Mayor Buell's no-picnic rule was being overlooked.

When the Beach Club closed for the winter, the lifeguard and helpers performed the usual end-of-season cleanup. My Uncle Buddy took care of winter maintenance with the help of the Executive Committee and volunteers. When the gate was closed and Buddy looked back, his smile and pride resonated through the Park and the Hamlet. The property had never looked better. The leaves were changing and the cleared picnic area, with the strands of tall white birch, the lake, and the older, large remaining homes such as Mrs. Frelinghuysen's perched up on the mountainside, looked like a postcard scene. The swings and seesaws had been put away. The raft had been towed in and pulled onto the shore. The ropes, the lifeguard stands, and the diving board were locked up for safekeeping. The clubhouse was clean and quiet, but if you closed your eyes, you could hear the screams and laughter of the children, as well as the friendly arguments and jesting between families at the picnic tables. You could smell the charcoal burning and the hot dogs, hamburgers, and sausages on the grills in the fireplaces. The 1960s had begun and, in summer, Wee Wah Beach was the place to be.

Chapter 22: 1962, Double-Barrel Shotgun

The Tuxedo Community Club (formerly the Gun Club), 1949

Mabel Tansey was reviewing her Beach Club files to prepare for another summer season. It was early on a Saturday morning in June of 1962, and she was excited about the progress that had been made and how well the members were working together. She heard the phone ringing and wondered who would be calling at this time. When she was given the news, it must have been hard for her to catch a breath. She sank back into her chair, and I am sure tears came to Mabel's eyes. Was she still sleeping, and was this a nightmare? During the night, a fire broke out at the beach. The old Gun Club, which the Tuxedo Community Club had lovingly restored, and which now served as the center for the Beach Club, had burned to the ground. This was a devastating blow to everyone, and to make matters worse, the resulting investigation, which surely seemed to be arson, was inconclusive.

Spirits were low. It was hard to hold back the tears when you passed by the entrance and saw the charred remains of the restored beach clubhouse. However, Mabel and others were up to the task of carrying on. Despite the initial shock and sadness, summertime was coming soon and everyone turned their attention to how the Beach Club could move forward. The minutes reflect that the Executive Committee met on Tuesday, June 5, at the beach near the charred foundation of the clubhouse. The leaders had already discussed one issue with the Village of Tuxedo Park trustees and the TPA. Beach Club members would need bathrooms and a place to change when the beach opened for the summer. The committee found solace in many of the improvements that had been made over the winter. Spirits began to rise as they toured the beach property and made notes about additional repairs and improvements they could make in preparation for the fast-approaching summer of 1962. Despite the great loss caused by the fire, everything else seemed to be in fine condition.

Mabel held up her hand to make an announcement. From the look on her face, it seemed as if a big storm cloud was sweeping across the Wee Wah Lake from the Village office. As if the fire weren't bad enough, Mabel shocked committee members with the news that Village Mayor Buell had taken the opportunity to provide the Beach Club with a new lease. After twenty-plus years of paying a nominal rent to the TPA, the Village would now be the lessor and was increasing the annual rent from $1 to $2,400. The rent was to be paid in two installments: $1,200 on July 1, well before the Beach Club had received all the membership dues, and $1,200 on August 1. It was a clear message to the assembled members that the Village trustees were using the loss of the Gun Club as an opportunity to utilize changing the terms of the lease and thereby coerce this unique and adored Tuxedo Community Club toward closure.

For some, it felt like the Gun Club fire was the first round from the shotgun, and now came the second blast to finish them off. There were no tears, but there was now growing anger and a long discussion. Mabel had no answers to the many questions about why this was happening. Many felt that, once again, those in the Park who were members of the Tuxedo Club felt members from the Hamlet outside the gates were infringing on their claim to privacy and exclusivity. Mr. Ebbersen, a taxpayer from the Park, commented on the timing of the rent increase and the fire, expressing what others were thinking regarding many of the Tuxedo Club members. Mabel was asked to call Mayor Buell immediately to request a meeting with the Village trustees, and the officers and Executive Committee of the Beach Club. A meeting with the mayor was set for Thursday at 8:30 p.m. Mabel said the mayor had suggested raising the dues to $25 and allocating $10 from each membership payment for the rent. That would not even come close to covering the rent increase. Mabel encouraged committee members to think about questions for the mayor. The Annual Meeting was set for Sunday after the meeting with the mayor.

Discussions among members of the Executive Committee continued as they prepared to present the news to members at the Annual Meeting. The meeting of the Executive Committee, the mayor, and trustees on Thursday at the Village office would be brief. However, the mayor agreed to attend the Annual Meeting at the beach and address the membership. Everyone had been respectful and calm during the Village office meeting with Mayor Buell and the other trustees. The underlying reason for the meeting had not been resolved.

The proposed $2,400 lease was substantially more than the Beach Club could afford. Coming at this late date, it might not be possible to raise the money, members might balk at renewing at the higher fee, and the Beach Club could find itself without a home. Also, under the surface lurked the continual suspicion that this was just another attempt to force out members who were not residents of the Park so the residents of the Incorporated Village of Tuxedo Park could take control of the property. Many residents of the now Incorporated Village of Tuxedo Park who were Tuxedo Club members were upset that this lakefront property used by the Beach Club was not available to them during the summer months "unless" they actually joined it even though it was Village property.

The membership assembled Sunday afternoon in the beach picnic area, with one non-member conspicuously sitting beside Mabel. She stood up and announced that Mayor Buell had been invited to the meeting and would like to address the membership. The mayor thanked Mabel and those present. He remarked that he was hopeful all would bear with him until he finished. He first voiced his utter disgust with what had happened to the bathhouse but stated that it was in the past and all should look to the future. Fire insurance proceeds to the Beach Club had amounted to approximately $3,000, and he hoped to receive an additional $2,700 from the Village's insurance company. Getting to the important news, he said that after meeting with the TPA, they had reached an informal agreement to amend the beach lease and return to the customary TPA $1 rent for the 1962 season. A local contractor had offered to build a rectangular one-story cinder block building with a cement floor that would house changing spaces, lockers, and two toilets. The building could easily be expanded in the future. The cost would be about $4,300, including plumbing, and the work could be completed within three weeks. He added that the Village had formed a committee to raise money for the project and that "all" residents in the Park would be approached for contributions. He further stated that both the trustees and Congresswoman Katherine St. George fully supported this effort. This was all possible because the Village had previously entered into an option agreement to purchase the beach property from the TPA. The TPA had now agreed to hold the two-year option open for the Village. Mayor Buell emphasized that the Village trustees wanted the Beach Club to run efficiently and smoothly, in complete harmony with the Village. He wanted to avoid controversy and have open lines of communication. He could not speak for future trustees, but he and the sitting trustees could offer their full cooperation. The mayor answered a few questions and asked the members to please consider raising dues. He thanked everyone for allowing him to speak, and Mabel expressed her thanks to Mayor Buell. Members respectfully rose from their seats and applauded as he concluded his remarks.

Once the mayor had left, the members expressed their views. During the past two decades, it had become increasingly apparent that the Village of Tuxedo Park viewed the Beach Club as an entity that did not fit the profile of such an exclusive and private enclave. By now, half the membership was comprised of Hamlet residents, most of whom were descendants of original families that worked in the Park. There were a few members of the Beach Club who were also members of the Tuxedo Club, but they spent little time at the beach. Most Beach Club members in the Park were not members of the Tuxedo Club but were residents of the Park. They were now living in restored homes that at one time had been carriage houses, stables, and gardener's cottages. Most were raising children who attended the public school in the Hamlet. While many residents in the Park who belonged to the Tuxedo Club and owned much larger properties, such as the Sonne family, were community oriented, an unspoken tension was growing between Beach Club members from the Hamlet and many residents, both old and new, who were Park residents and members of the Tuxedo Club.

After Mayor Buell departed from the meeting, many key questions arose, most notably, "Who were the people who were not satisfied with how the [Beach Club] was being operated?" Mabel tried to calm everyone, saying that if the Beach Club continued to operate as it had for over twenty-five years, no one would have anything to complain about. If you knew Mabel, one only had to see her expression to know what was next. Enough! Move on! She proceeded to call for the first order of business to select new officers and the Executive Committee. It was a tough job getting order, but all officers were nominated, seconded, and elected by unanimous hand and voice vote. Mabel, Mike Crisci, and my aunt, Marie McGregor McCarroll, were reelected for the eleventh consecutive year. Buddy McCarroll was selected as beach supervisor. Executive Committee members from the Hamlet included the so-called three musketeers: Ralph Napolitano, Jimmy Venezia, and Tom Melillo. For the past four years on the committee and for many years before that, these gentlemen had volunteered their time and services. In addition, they were highly respected in the Hamlet and very knowledgeable about the feelings and concerns of those outside the gates of Tuxedo Park.

The Village was represented by my uncle, Jim Barth, long a

fixture on the waterfront and one of the first lifeguards. Another Village resident and long-time member on the committee was Tillie Henderson, who had the ear of Mrs. George Amory at Renamor. Mrs. Amory and her husband could always be depended on to help all in the Tuxedo community. Also elected were newcomers Kathleen Burris, Tom Cahill, and S. Karkula. The treasurer's report was read by Marie, and Mabel brought up the suggestion to raise dues to $25. She pointed out how the Beach Club needed to operate more efficiently and that they should anticipate an increase in the rent next year. Also, it was prudent to have a working balance at the end of the season. To show good faith and have an argument against a future rent increase, a portion of this increase in dues could go toward the cost of the new bathhouse building. A motion was made and passed without discussion. Mabel now could offer some good news. As part of the negotiations with the Village at the Thursday meeting, additional guest privileges would be extended to the Hamlet members, and these members could bring four guests per week, as had been the case in the past for members from the Park. Guest passes were set at $1 for adults and $0.75 for children.

As they moved on to new business, Joe Salierno introduced Mr. Gans and asked if he could say a few words. The membership was concerned with Mayor Buell's remarks concerning the TPA's potential sale of the property. Mr. Gans, a Beach Club member and Village resident, told everyone that Pigeon Point was to be sold by the TPA to the Village for $40,000. He was trying to get a company in the city to buy the property from the TPA, rather than see it sold to the Village. He asserted that the proposed building was inadequate and that proper facilities for a men's and women's locker room should be constructed.

He felt Mabel was on the right track suggesting contributions on behalf of the Beach Club members and believed the insurance money would cover the expenses of the new facility on the site of the burned Gun Club building. Joe Salierno expressed his opinion that they needed facilities for the recreation program, and that this proposed building would serve that purpose and could be finished quickly. The members had a lot to consider, but before Mabel adjourned the meeting, there was one more item of interest. She had been informed that the Village trustees had overruled the TPA, meaning that Maplebrook residents could no longer be members of the Beach Club; therefore, the Beach Club could no longer count on an increase in membership and dues from that community.

Two days later, on June 12, the Executive Committee and officers met again. After discussing the proposed new building, they agreed to contributions of $300 to the recreation program, $20 to the Tuxedo Scholarship Committee, and $30 to the Ambulance Corps. Mabel would meet with a local contractor and make some suggestions about the building. Any contribution by the Beach Club would be discussed later. In July, the committee decided to build steps at the wall beside the dock and remove the ladder next to the diving board for safety purposes. Because of the lack of a bathhouse, the annual Beach Club picnic was canceled.

The replacement bathhouse was quickly completed on a portion of the foundation of the Gun Club. It was located within some trees in an attempt to soften what was a basic dark-green one-story cinderblock building. It contained an open men's changing room and bathroom separated by a wall down the middle from a similar women's section with partitioned changing spaces. The checker would now sit at a card table under an umbrella at the entrance to the Beach Club. Previously the checker was stationed inside the old clubhouse at a window facing the entrance portico where she could see who was coming in and raise the gate.

Bathhouse on the site of the destroyed Gun Club, ca. 1980

The following year, in April 1963, the officers and Executive Committee received the news they had anticipated. Mabel had received a new lease calling for a rent of $2,500 from May 1 to September 30. Marie McCarroll reported a bank balance of $1,476, as a result of the increase in dues the previous year. A review of the beach indicated everything was in good shape, so expenses could be kept to a minimum. They decided to accept the lease without pushing back against the Village. A letter would go out to members informing them of the increase in rent. The proposed payment deadline for membership dues was June 1. After some discussion, the date was extended to June 15. Those who did not meet the deadline would have to reapply as new members at the increased membership rate. The Village office requested all new applications be submitted to them as soon as they were received by the Beach Club. Applications for two picnics by the Republican Club and for the Fourth of July were approved. A request was also received by the Cub Scouts to have a picnic supervised by parents. The lease was accepted, the election of officers held, lifeguards and checkers appointed, and seasonal dues remained at $25. The annual donations were approved. Roddy Farningham replaced Tillie Henderson representing the Park on the Executive Committee; Tillie was no longer living in the Park over the Renamor garage because Mr. and Mrs. Amory had left the Park and Renamor, another of the great estates, which, as previously stated, had been donated to the Academy of Mount St. Vincent, a private Catholic school For girls. The 1963 swimming season was uneventful, but the joyful users of the Wee Wah Beach Club had no idea what awaited the country several months later.

Chapter 23: 1964 – 1969

Let the races begin! Final recreation day of the season, ca. 1964

As the snow melted and warmer weather lurked around the corner, there was a sense that the winds of change in the country had shifted—and not for the better. By the beginning of 1964, you could see it on the national news every night. Newspaper headlines stared you in the face when you stopped for coffee at the drugstore. In November 1963, the nation had received a body punch that brought it to its knees with the assassination of President John F. Kennedy. Still suffering from the effects of the blow, the country was now being pummeled with right and left hooks of racial unrest and a growing conflict in Vietnam. The first members of the Baby Boom generation (those born in the late 1940s, soon after World War II) were coming of age. As youngsters in the mid-1950s, they had watched older brothers and sisters rebel with the music of Elvis Presley. Values were openly questioned at the dinner table. This independent thinking and challenge of authority brought changes in every aspect of the culture. The Beatles came to the United States in 1964, and along with them, a new generation in their late teens began to question every facet of life. Imbedded in the social consciousness of the nation—with the threat of nuclear war with Russia starting in the late 1950s and continuing with Vietnam to allegedly prevent the spread of Communism—a shift in social standards had developed. Family gatherings and dinner conversations were strained. America seemed to be maturing, a middle class had emerged, and opinions were mixed on where the country was headed under the unexpected leadership of President Lyndon Johnson. Across the country, and particularly in the Southern states, highly visible political upheaval over civil rights collided with stubborn, long-held norms that were ripe for change. These states were now traditionally democratic, as it had been President Lincoln, a Republican, who had freed the slaves. Women were now an accepted presence in the workforce and continued to raise their voices for equality.

Locally, much was changing as well. The Incorporated Village of Tuxedo Park was just over ten years old. In 1924, the original Tuxedo Park Association, formed by Pierre Lorillard to hold title to the property, was sold to the Tuxedo Securities Corporation by the estate of Peter Lorillard, a son of the founder. The shareholders of this company were, for the most part, property owners of Tuxedo Park and longtime members of the Tuxedo Club. It continued to perform the services originally provided by the TPA until the incorporation of the Village of Tuxedo Park in 1952. The TPA was now basically a real estate holding company. The company was no longer involved in the Village management. The Park's infrastructure and maintenance was now the responsibility of the Public Works Department of the Village (DPW), but Tuxedo Park Associates, which owned significant undeveloped land within and outside the Park, remained powerful. Not actively involved in the day-to-day affairs, it was nonetheless the largest property owner in the Village. The DPW infrastructure involved employees who, in many cases, were former TPA employees.

Tuxedo Park had changed over the past ten years and not for the better. Income taxes, inheritance taxes, property taxes, advances in travel, and the decline of an active social society scene had all contributed to declines in local revenue, and the Park infrastructure such as walls and roads were showing wear. Nonetheless, Tuxedo Park was still an idyllic spot, and although the biggest estates were gone, many large Gilded Age homes remained and continued as well-kept residences.

In 1954, George Grant Mason's estate, Kincraig, had been subdivided and auctioned off as building lots. By 1964, the long gravel driveway, raked every day when Mason was in residence, had become a rutted dirt road. The formal Italian gardens were overgrown with weeds. The large vegetable, flower, and fruit gardens on the northwest were fallow, and the fruit trees, ravaged by pests and disease, no longer bore fruit. Lastly, the garage and courtyard, roughly the size of a football field, where I grew up in one of four large corner apartments, looked more like a rundown building in an inner city. Unlived in but for one apartment facing the road, it was used by the new owner for repairing old cars, trucks, and trailers that littered the outside and matched the derelict building. It was defended as a hobby because no businesses were allowed in the Park. In the early years, such an eyesore would not have lasted a week. However, the years had taken a toll, and properties on the market could be purchased for way below the asking price during this period.

As for the Beach Club, the Incorporated Village had taken complete control from the TPA. The Beach Club never fully recovered from the catastrophic loss of the historic Gun Club-turned bath house. Membership declined, as there was no longer a large number of staff with families working in the Park. That generation, for the most part, was deceased, and many of their children who had received the benefit of education and fulfilled the duty of war service, had long departed for better jobs and affordable homes in new communities. The surrounding communities were also suffering. Many manufacturing jobs had left the narrow valley in Orange County, New York. The area was fast becoming a long ribbon of ghost towns along State Road Route 17.

At the 1964 Annual Meeting, members followed the time-honored procedures in preparation for the beach opening. Discussing the 1960s with my Aunt Marie and my Uncle Jim Barth, at her retirement party in July of 2005 as treasurer of the Beach Club after 57 years, both recalled the tension between the Beach Club and the Village trustees during this period and believed there would always be friction with the Village government over the membership of the Beach Club. Per the minutes of the Annual Meeting, Marie explained that they could not operate with dues at $25. She suggested a $5 increase. After much discussion, the members rejected the increase and agreed that any working children living at home would not be considered members under a family membership but could be allowed to join for $10. Requests for picnic dates had been received from St. Mary's, the Tuxedo Teachers Association, and the Republican Club. With little discussion, they were approved. Notwithstanding the precarious financial condition of the Beach Club, annual donations made to organizations in the past were approved. The beach was ready for opening although the workload was now falling on far fewer members, most of whom were the sons and daughters of original members. They were raising families of their own and had remained in the Hamlet or had bought the smaller stables and garages in the Village. Summer 1964 came and went. By closely monitoring repairs and foregoing improvements, the Beach Club navigated the year successfully. However, the many changes in our world were having their effect. As a great statesperson, Tip O'Neill, once said: "All politics are local."[76] You could see the result of the national pulse by spending a day at the Beach Club. Social tensions remained between many old and new Park residents belonging to the Tuxedo Club—and those who lived outside the gate.

When the membership meeting took place prior to the 1965 summer season, a noticeable algae growth had invaded the lake. A new raft was needed, and Bill Sahler, a longtime local builder, was given the contract to build it. Over the winter, many overtures were made to the Village concerning the state of the Beach Club, and many discussions took place with individual trustees and Beach Club members—without formal presentations at regularly scheduled Village meetings. For many in the Village, the cultural and social divide remained, and the Hamlet membership continued to be a source of irritation for some, including many who were new to the Park. In her treasurer's report, my Aunt Marie said the Village indicated it would lower the rent to $2,000. In return, the trustees requested a reduction in the dues for residents of the Park to $15. Marie determined the reduction in dues would place the club in a deficit, even with the rent reduction. At the end of 1964, there had been sixty-eight members from the Park and seventy-eight from the Hamlet. Of the sixty-eight Park members, fifty-three were taxpaying homeowners (the vast majority were not members of the Tuxedo Club) and fifteen were renters. There was only $538.94 in the bank. The previous year expenses were $4,310.75, and receipts were $3,944.78. The club was on the verge of insolvency, and it appeared they would be unable to operate the beach. Members looked to the past and considered their fundraising options. A raffle was approved on the spot, and Sam Burris, a Park resident, donated a basket of liquor (commonly referred to as "cheer" for the raffle winner). "Cheer" was certainly needed.

Despite these financial challenges, the 1965 season did open as usual, with discussion about the Village "request" continuing. On July 10, the Executive Committee met with the Village trustees. In addition to the financial problems, the new bathhouse had been vandalized. No progress was made on the money issues, but the trustees agreed that locks could be placed on the bathhouse doors, with the police locking up at night and opening in the morning. Buddy McCarroll, Pat Cahill of the TPA, and the police would have the only keys. The algae problem was also discussed, and water samples were sent out for testing. As the summer passed, the club was struggling but survived. Over the winter, the Executive Committee discussed ways to change the appearance. The thinking was that a more attractive beach would bolster people's feelings and create a forward-looking, positive approach. It would hopefully increase membership and soften criticism from those Tuxedo Club members who asserted that the beach was not in keeping with the Village's image. Much of the discussion was really to bolster the morale of those who felt the burden of trying to keep the tradition alive.

The Beach Club was barely scraping by at the beginning of 1966. I had graduated from college and was no longer living in Tuxedo Park. I was working in New York City, but most weekends I would come out to Tuxedo for the weekend and family dinners at my Aunt Marie's or at my Uncle Jim Barth's. The Annual Meeting minutes indicated the skeet traps were to be taken down, the area cleared, and barbed wire was to be installed at the northeast side of the beachfront to prevent vandals and trespassers from entering after hours. Bonny Damato, a young woman we will hear more about, was selected as checker. Bill Iannone and Tom Salierno replaced Ralph Napolitano and Jim Gregerson on the Executive Committee. Tom, a resident of the Park and a contractor like his father, was generous with his time and efforts. His parents had been active Tuxedo Community Club members since their move to Tuxedo Park. His father was an Italian immigrant who grew up and established a successful general contracting business in New York City that worked on many projects for the Catholic Church. One involved a project north of Tuxedo off Route 17, and his father became interested in this exclusive, private property behind the big gates when he travelled past it. He saw it as a future home for his growing family outside the changing city neighborhood in East Harlem. He purchased property across from the Tuxedo Club and built a beautiful home. Of course, at the time, the issue of becoming a member of the Tuxedo Club was not available to him due to his ethnic and social background.

Members unanimously approved picnic dates for first graders and the Girl Scouts/Brownies. The summer passed with fewer members using the beach and there were no incidents of note. There were also picnics, the annual July Fourth gathering of many of the original members' families, and recreation days. There were occasional heat waves in August, but the shade and a cool breeze off the lake was always available.

Throughout the country, but especially on the East and West Coasts, 1967 was called the "Summer of Love."[77] The younger generation had captured the attention of society, but many parents and older generations did not embrace these new ideas and behaviors.

Needless to say, the Village continued to exert increased pressure and influence on the Beach Club in 1967. At the Annual Meeting, Beach Club members recommended that each member pay a $5 guest fee for fifteen guest passes for the season, with the passes valid on weekends only. The Village was to be informed of all decisions made by the Executive Committee and requests were now made to the Village office. As for use of the Tuxedo Community Club, the Village could direct if and how it would be used for non-membership activities. As an example, the Village "informed" the Beach Club that the fire department had been granted permission to use the beach on the Fourth of July. In the past, use was first requested of the Beach Club, and if the Beach Club approved, it would then be requested of the Village. Whatever the Village wanted to do, the Beach Club was powerless to deny it. Due to the involvement of both sides of my family in Beach Club governance, the various tensions between the Beach Club and the Village served as continual topics of conversation whenever I visited Tuxedo Park.

During this period, the Beach Club was expected to comply with many new state laws. Water-testing samples and beach inspections by the state were two of many requirements. Insurance rates were increasing, and there were more exclusions in the policy that required changes in the beach operation. One such requirement concerned the maximum number of bathers who could be in the water at one time. This was determined by a complex formula based on the square footage and the depth of the water in the boundaries of the swimming area. The boundaries had to be defined by ropes with buoys attached. Although the club had cordoned off the entire swimming area with ropes, and it had divided the shallow areas from the deep water with additional ropes, the regulations now defined how many swimmers could be in these areas. Trustees of the Village were adamant that the beach club keep count of the number of bathers in the water to comply with the law, and they asked the Beach Club to revise the rules to ensure compliance. Once opened, the club ran smoothly, and another season concluded without incident.

In 1968, things were looking brighter for the Tuxedo Community Club, thanks to the careful administration of expenses and volunteer work by many members. A new member, Charlie England, was appointed to the Executive Committee. Roddy Farningham was helping Buddy McCarroll almost daily in maintaining the beach and picnic areas. As an aside, and a testament to the uniqueness of Tuxedo Park, the advent of the 911 telephone emergency number also resulted in requiring homes to have a numbered street address. Prior to 1968, large homes and estates were identified either by the original owner's name, or by another given moniker. Other residences were identified by the road they faced. If you were visiting in the Park, you would need to be sure you had directions.

As to the beach, more health regulations were implemented, including regular measurement of the water depth at the diving board and raft. Due to insurance requirements, the slide from the water's edge was moved to the sandy area. Membership was now increasing again, and in August, my Aunt Marie reported the bank account was up to $2,573.76. All members of the Executive Committee were breathing easier about the future of the club, but were also exhausted from their efforts. Uncle Buddy was always on hand with a smile and a laugh as he worked to make the grounds attractive.

Of course, in 1968, the Vietnam war, the assassinations of Martin Luther King Jr. and Robert F. Kennedy, as well as all forms of civil unrest, served as flashpoints for the hotly contested presidential election. But for the most part, political discussions were left for places outside Tuxedo Park, a quiet community that served as a respite from the realities of the outside world. This was a small town, and it wasn't difficult to know where each resident stood on many of these national issues. In the early years, when all property in the Hamlet was owned by the TPA, voter rolls indicated the working class were substantially recorded as Republican. That was no surprise, as all the workers served at the pleasure of the Tuxedo Park residents and leased the property. A democratic vote could cost them their home and job. By this time, however, much had changed, and although the members of the Tuxedo Club were still overwhelmingly Republican, most Hamlet residents now supported the Democratic Party. The generational change was more apparent when the younger family members, the third generation, arrived at the beach, mostly in groups sporting bright colors, long hair, and "bikinis." Really, bikinis! Indeed, 1968 represented a new era for the Wee Wah Beach Club.

The Beach Club was thriving once again, as new homes were built in the Hamlet and the third generation of original families now had children of their own. The East Village was now a typical suburban community of attractive, well-maintained one and two-family homes, although the lots were very small. This added to the membership roster, but rumors resurfaced that the Village would take over Pigeon Point and close the Tuxedo Community Club. Mike Crisci noted that this rumor was heard year after year and that members should continue taking an active role in maintaining and improving the Beach Club.

In June 1968, the Village trustees held their monthly meeting, and a number of the residents were present to talk about the Beach Club. Doris Crofut, a resident of the Park, spoke about the desire of many to see the Wee Wah Beach area improved for the taxpayers [of the Village] as an area of recreation for the people who lived inside the Park. The minutes of the meeting reflect the mayor's response. Mayor Buell said he would "not" go along with the idea of making the Wee Wah Beach an area of recreation for the Village of Tuxedo Park alone. He said this area had been used for years by the people of the Hamlet, long before the Village was incorporated, and until such time that the children of the Hamlet had somewhere to go for swimming and other water sports, he would not under any circumstances prevent their use of the area. He said that if this were in the minds of those present, he could tell them that an open upheaval and great anger would be caused from our little neighboring community. He suggested that those present who wanted to do so could go to Town of Tuxedo meetings and suggest to the Town Council an area in the Township should be found for the Hamlet people, but that while he was mayor—and he said he could speak for the trustees as well—the people from the Hamlet would not be turned away from an area that they had used for so long that they called it their own.

Questions were then raised regarding the cost to Village taxpayers, and the mayor responded that any equipment needed over there was purchased by the Village, and the only thing the Beach Club had asked for that year was sand. Those present appeared to want to continue the discussion, but the mayor once again reiterated that he would not, so long as he remained mayor of the Village, force nor expect children in the Hamlet to stop using the facilities until they had their own beach.

Another agenda item related to a request from Jerry Magurno for permission to allow him to become a member of the Tuxedo Community Club. Jerry's parents were long-time residents of the Hamlet and Jerry had grown up as a member of the Beach Club, worked on the Mason estate in the gardens in the past, graduated from Tuxedo High School, and worked on Buddy's crew at the Beach Club during summers. He was now residing with his own family in Suffern, a nearby community, where he was a teacher and baseball coach. He was also employed by the Town of Tuxedo as the Recreation Director for the summer months. The Board requested the Clerk respond to Mr. Magurno to state their regrets, but since the Tuxedo Community Club residency requirements could not be met, the request was denied unless it related to his activities for the recreation program. Continuing to address the Beach Club, it came to their attention that some parents from outside the Park whose children were attending the recreation program in the Hamlet were coming to the beach to pick up their children. The Board authorized the clerk to write to the Commissioner of Recreation of the Town of Tuxedo, reiterating the mandatory requirement that all children be transported to the beach area by the school bus and transported back to the school in the same manner to be picked up by their parents.[78]

The results of the meeting of the Village's trustees, and Mayor Buell's comments, were welcome news to the members of the Beach Club, but tension within the community simmered. The beach was back in good shape. The lake had been drained once again over the winter, which gave the club the opportunity to repair the dock. The occasional draining of the Wee Wah always created rumors that the Beach Club was on the verge of losing its right to exist the following year. Volunteers also cleaned the ground in the shallow end that filled with small rocks, and they added sand to the shoreline. Lastly, a new baby pool was created on the west side of the dock to make it easier for parents to monitor their young children playing in shallow water. I was drafted into the Army at the age of twenty-four in the fall of 1968, and after basic training I was stationed at Fort Gordon in Augusta, Georgia. As a draftee, this was quite a transition from my early days of wearing a suit and tie with a good job on Wall Street. Fortunately, I was reassigned to Fort Dix, New Jersey in July 1969. This gave me the opportunity to visit my parents at home in New Jersey, spend time at the Jersey shore with old high school friends, and return to Tuxedo Park to visit relatives at—where else—the Beach Club! There was so much domestic conflict during these years, and during this time, my personal contact with Tuxedo was limited, but for occasional weekend visits during the summer.

In 1969, I am told that the highlight of the summer was the Woodstock event in August. The actual location of the famed concert was in Bethel, New York, which is not that distant from Tuxedo. Many concertgoers took the NY Thruway or State Road 17. For older residents outside the gates in the Hamlet, the intense traffic brought back memories of summer weekend bumper-to-bumper traffic headed to the Catskills. For the younger residents, it was quite a unique scene, with traffic at a standstill. Vehicles were packed with occupants resplendent in the styles of the so called "hippie generation." Woodstock became a national news event that changed a generation. It was also the talk of the town and at the Beach Club. For my younger cousins who witnessed the crawl of music and smoke-filled vehicles, the experience was as if an alternate version of the Ringling Bros. and Barnum & Bailey Circus had invaded the outskirts of our community. Woodstock has long been anointed as a "cultural phenomenon," and as the saying goes, "If you said you were there, you probably weren't."

Chapter 24: The Early 1970s

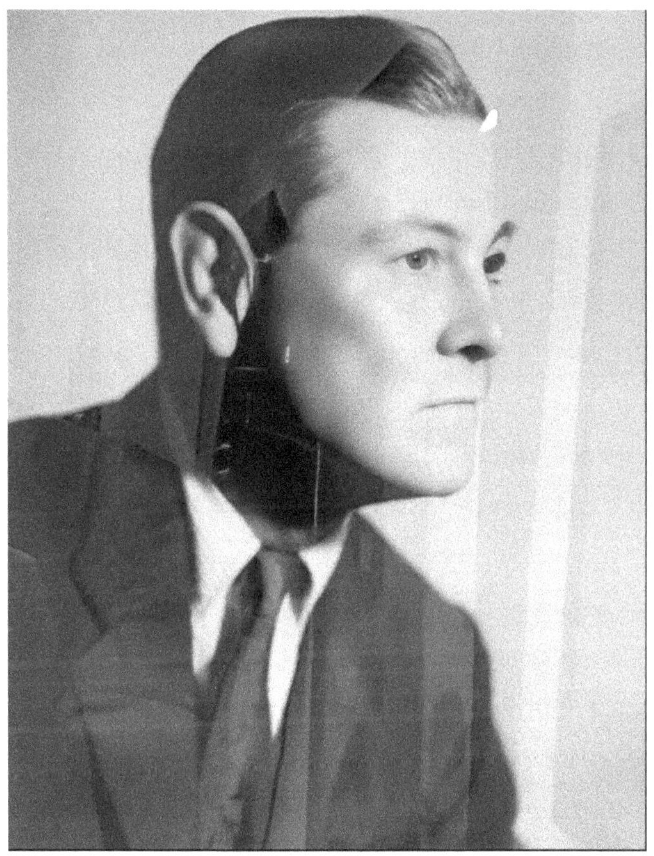

Crawford "Sonny" Blagdon, ca. 1970

By this time, my visits to Tuxedo Park were limited to
holidays with family, and infrequent summer days enjoying the Wee
Wah, where I caught up on conversations concerning Tuxedo
happenings. Tuxedo Park seemed somewhat immune from the far-
reaching societal upheaval of the late 1960s and early 1970s, as the
chaos of the outside world virtually vanished upon your arrival at old
Pigeon Point when you entered the Beach Club. Then again, the 1970s

would be a decade of maturity for what would soon officially be renamed "the Wee Wah Beach Club." During this time, there seemed to be a formalization of philosophies and policies that had developed over the first thirty-five years; much of that was confirmed when I spoke with people who remembered the time, and when I researched archived materials for this book.

However, at the April 9, 1970, Executive Meeting, there was bad news right from the start. Mabel Tansey reported that the Village would be raising the rent from $2,500 to $3,000, a twenty percent increase. There was presently $900.53 in the account. The Village now had a new mayor, Crawford "Sonny" Blagden. He was born on June 29, 1912, and attended Croton School and then Harvard College, where he joined the Harvard Club. He was a tireless worker in Tuxedo, not only regarding the operation of the Tuxedo Club, including his tenure as president, but also in the local community. Blagden was well-liked and keenly interested in the sporting activities outside the confines of the Tuxedo Club membership that would be available to all in Tuxedo. He had a special interest in sport trap shooting. He'd grown up when the Gun Club was still active and often hosted many matches with other clubs of social note.

Crawford Blagden married Mary Kernochan in 1934. Mary Kernochan was the daughter of the Chief Justice of New York's Court for Special Sessions. Justice J. Frederic Kernochan was a good friend of President Franklin Delano Roosevelt. Blagden's father-in-law was sitting next to Roosevelt in Miami during the attempted assassination on February 15, 1933. Mary Kernochan's family was well-established in New York society. They were related to the Pell family and were members of the list of Mrs. Astor's Four Hundred back in the day.

James P Kernochan had married Catherine Lorillard, whose brother Pierre founded Tuxedo Park. Both the Kernochan and Blagden families were longtime members of the Tuxedo Club and maintained residences in Tuxedo Park, as well as fashionable addresses in New York City. The Justice passed away at Tuxedo Hospital in 1937.

When World War II was declared, Blagden followed in his father's footsteps and served in Italy. A decorated veteran of WWII, he was awarded the Silver Star, the Bronze Star, and a Purple Heart. After the war, Crawford Blagden was a vice president at Benton & Bowles, Inc., a prominent advertising agency in New York. Prior to his election as mayor, Blagden first held four terms as a Village trustee and served the Tuxedo Fire Department as its president from 1946 to 1955. The volunteer fire department had always been a place where distinctions between a Village resident and a Hamlet resident disappeared, to a great extent. It was an opportunity for people to get together and serve the community as a team. Politics and social station were not a primary focus. Blagden was well aware of the social division in Tuxedo and had the respect of the townspeople. Together with his wife, Mary, he was also instrumental in forming the Tuxedo Volunteer Ambulance Corp and had encouraged townspeople and residents of Tuxedo Park to contribute toward the purchase of the first ambulance, a new 1956 white Cadillac.

Mabel called the new mayor to urge the Village to reconsider its position, as both sides knew the issue of rent increases could effectively shut down the Beach Club. Crawford "Sonny" Blagden had been elected mayor of the Village of Tuxedo Park in June of 1969, succeeding Prescott A. Buell, who retired after leading the Village since it was incorporated in 1952.

The Blagden family represented "old money," with significant banking and Wall Street interests. Blagden's father, also named Crawford, was born in 1881 in New York City and married Mary Hopkins in October 1911. Soon after his wedding to Mary, she passed away and left him with a small baby boy, Crawford "Sonny" Blagden. The senior Blagden was well liked in Tuxedo, both inside and outside the gates, and was active in the community, participating with the young men in the local football games held at the field in the East Village outside of Tuxedo.[79] He had no problems mixing in with the folks in the Hamlet, and was known to have instilled in his son, Sonny, the same values of competitiveness, service, duty, and of most importance, respect for everyone.

Crawford "Sonny" Blagden faced no opposition in his 1969 run for Mayor of Tuxedo Park. This was not unusual. A ticket would be announced, typically with the support of the Tuxedo Club members, and it would appear unseemly if someone were to challenge the choice. Although a number of property owners were not members of the Tuxedo Club, the numbers were modest, and residents expressed little concern over the availability of additional candidates. With no opposition, only 150 votes were cast out of 370 eligible voters. Mayor Blagden was joined on the board by Henry Maresi, who had been the village assessor for three years, as well as executive vice president of Tuxedo Memorial Hospital. Also reelected as a trustee was John Kennedy. John also had previously served as a tax assessor and was also a member of the zoning board of appeals and secretary of the Tuxedo Park School.

Mayor Blagden, who would serve until 1975, was supportive

of the Beach Club's concerns about rent and agreed to put the matter onto the Tuxedo Park agenda. Alas, the mayor's position on the rent increase did not change the outcome, as the mayor only had one vote. A simple majority of Village trustees confirmed the rent-increase decision. However, Mayor Blagden convinced the other trustees to reimburse the Beach Club for their costs for fresh sand to the beachfront, along with any Beach Club expenses dictated by the trustees, and even for expenses related to state regulations. Mabel's committee decided dues would have to be raised. The committee also presented a request to the trustees to repair the beachfront wall.

The Annual Meeting was held at the high school on April 21. Marion Hekl, who by this time had served as the lead checker for many years, applied for the position yet again. Her letter of application, which was read aloud, included her request for a raise. Each year, Marion would apply with a written letter and a request for more money, a recurring action that was now considered customary. Joe McCormick replaced Arthur England on the Executive Committee, and members approved a $5 increase in dues. All officers were reelected.

At the next meeting the committee addressed the issue of picnics. Requests had increased to a point where guidelines had to be drafted. Mrs. McKay had requested a date for the Tuxedo Hospital staff to have a picnic. It was approved but for "one year only." In addition, the hours available for the picnics were shortened, and applicants were required to provide their own lifeguard and picnic tables. The next request was for the Democratic Club picnic, which was approved. Guest passes, as always, were an issue. There was discussion of including additional members from Sterling Forest, and once again the Maplebrook development outside the south gate to the

Park was considered. The committee was concerned about complaints that blamed the Beach Club for outside vehicles using Tuxedo Park roads. To that point, the committee wanted the police to take more responsibility for cars not eligible to come into the beach, and to distinguish between Town of Tuxedo residents, Tuxedo Park residents, and unauthorized vehicles from other locations when violations were recorded. Mabel was not optimistic about the police request, but she was not about to give up without exploring all options. She agreed to discuss all these matters with Mayor Blagden.

Other issues to discuss with the mayor in 1971 included defining the boundaries of the Hamlet and the Village of Tuxedo Park as well as eliminating the need for membership applications to be sent to the Village office for final approval. Mayor Blagden and Mabel forged a cordial and productive working relationship, but the members felt the beach club should have more autonomy. Mayor Blagden came to the beach on May 10 for the Executive Committee meeting and expressed his personal feelings and agreed that all matters would be brought before the trustees. He believed that Maplebrook and Sterling Forest residents should not be eligible for Beach Club membership. Guests were to be defined as persons visiting members from outside Tuxedo Park and the Hamlet to prevent residents of the Hamlet not joining the Beach Club but coming with neighbors as guests. The police would be responsible for cars in the Park. He also believed that the rent increase would not be renegotiated by trustees. However, he had promised beach improvements in return for the rent increase in 1971. The Village would supply sand and help the Beach Club with repairs and maintenance. At the Annual Meeting of the Beach Club, all officers were reelected, and Frank Damato was elected to the

Executive Committee. A new guest pass system would be enacted, and guest fees were raised to $10 per guest. Buddy McCarroll needed a new lawnmower, and typical of the club's custom, a 50/50 raffle was suggested to fund this expense.

In 1972, the Annual Meeting was held on May 8, and once again all officers were reelected. Ten dollars was donated to the Tuxedo Scholarship Committee. It was business as usual. Marion Hekl faithfully submitted her application for checker, and again she asked for a raise for the checkers, this time to $1.75 per hour. After much discussion and much good-natured ribbing of Marion for these annual requests for increases, the raise was unanimously passed. A report was read regarding the purchase of a new lawnmower, concluding with a recommendation of the Sunbeam model for $325, versus a fancier model priced at $525. The cheaper model was approved and ordered. Buddy requested an addition to the bath houses to store beach equipment, and a decision was made to purchase materials and use volunteer labor. The health department had made their inspection and added more regulations. Each year, the Beach Club was required to comply with more and more regulations from the various state and county departments concerned with water recreation, and this year, they were required to provide mechanical hand-towel dispensers in the bathrooms, and to use disinfectant when cleaning the bathhouses. The Executive Committee approved picnics for the senior citizens and the St. Mary's church group. Going back to the well one more time, Marion Hekl requested a raise for herself as "supervisor" of the checkers, and the Executive Committee approved her twenty-five cent increase to two dollars per hour.

The fifty percent increase each year in rent paid over the last two years had taken its toll on the Beach Club's financial stability. Although many of the expenses required as a result of new state laws had been closely monitored, membership dues were insufficient to balance the books. At the close of the 1972 season, the Beach Club was left with a deficit. They were operating on a shoestring budget, and without the number of volunteers for much of the work required as occurred in the past, the threat of closure was real.

At the Annual Meeting in May 1973, the 1972 officers were reelected and dues were once again increased by $5. Then began the usual discussion over the lease. Mabel spoke of her attempts to secure a lease term longer than one year. She argued that without such a commitment by the Village, it was difficult for the Beach Club to do any long-term planning for improvements. The Village trustees rejected a longer lease but agreed to contribute $140 toward additional sand for the beach and the much-needed paint for the bathhouses, but only "if" the members did the painting. As was usual during this period, the improvements were accomplished due to the generosity of Tom Salierno, who continued to volunteer countless personal hours and his construction experience, as his father had done before him. Other members volunteered their labor for finishing work. In short order, an addition was built to the bathhouse to store the maintenance equipment formerly kept in the shack where a basketball and volleyball court sit today.

In 1974, the Village increased the rent to $3,100. New York State and Orange County regulations were becoming increasingly burdensome. One example was the health department requiring hand dryers in the bathhouses just two years after mandating the costly towel dispensers. One way to solve the problem with memberships was setting the same dues for all members. For years, Hamlet residents had paid substantially more than Tuxedo Park residents, due to the demand of Mayor Buell and the former Board of Trustees of the Incorporated Village of Tuxedo Park.

Equality was the theme of the Annual Meeting. A motion was passed that the dues be the same for all members pending approval by the Village trustees. Mabel said she was hopeful an understanding could be reached based on the financial projections for the coming year. The meeting continued and followed the typical annual agenda. Of course, Marion Hekl was re-hired as the head checker. Lifeguard applications were requested, and St. Mary's was approved for its church picnic. My Aunt Marie presented her budget for the coming year, and it looked like dues would need to be increased yet again no matter the result from the request to equalize the dues for all members. All existing officers and Executive Committee members were nominated and unanimously reelected without opposition. The beach would open with a new sign, and Tom Salierno was formally recognized for the excellent work on the new building addition.

Shortly after the Annual Meeting, Mabel met with Mayor Blagden concerning the dues for the club, and the plan was then presented to the trustees. There was not much discussion. The club's request was denied. Despite the critical funding situation, the existing membership came together and the summer season passed without any additional serious problems. The gate was closed in the fall with a collective sigh of relief. Members acknowledged valid concerns for the viability of the club in 1975, but for now, everyone paused to enjoy the incredible vista of the leaves changing and the joy of early autumn in Tuxedo Park.

Somehow the Beach Club managed to balance the books ahead of the 1975 season. The bathhouse with the additions and the grounds were looking much better. The children's area and beachfront were well maintained and membership numbers were stable. There was enough money in the bank to make the insurance payment and other early expenses needed for the club to open. Projected membership fees would provide the necessary revenue to keep the club operating throughout the 1975 season. The Executive Meeting and Annual Meeting followed the customary agenda. Over the winter there had been some vandalism, and Mabel would bring it to the attention of the police and the Village to see how this issue could be addressed during the summer and beyond. The club provided an attractive setting, and many more requests for special events from outside organizations were coming in. Although the "only three" edict from the Village remained in effect, there had always been ways around it by treating an event as a member request and then using the member's guest passes. In addition, many organizations were now going directly to the Village trustees and, if approved by the trustees, there was little the Beach Club could do about it. The annual request by St. Mary's and the firemen's July Fourth picnic were approved. The firemen's picnic was first requested through the Village trustees, as firemen came from areas such as Eagle Valley and Sterling Forest, which were in the Town of Tuxedo—but outside the Hamlet boundary for membership.

Another event that moved to the beach was the hospital dance. This was no small affair, as it was a first-class event that raised significant money for the hospital. In the early years of Tuxedo Park, the dance had been held at the racetrack. It was always attended by many Park residents who were Tuxedo Club members, as well as those from surrounding areas of Tuxedo. Tom Salierno volunteered to be the Executive Committee member who would work closely with the hospital dance committee, which was comprised of Tuxedo Club members, to finalize arrangements. Everything ran like clockwork. As the meeting progressed, a motion was made, seconded, and passed that senior citizens who were former Beach Club members would no longer have to pay dues to be allowed into the beach area.

Perhaps the most eventful point in the meeting came from Mabel, asking for quiet before closing the meeting to make an emphatic announcement. The "peace and love" era of the late 1960s and early 1970s had, of course, crept inside the gates into Tuxedo Park. There were many instances where people were not following the rules and regulations, such as bringing their pet dogs to the picnic area, which had always been forbidden. More upsetting were rumors of young people skinny-dipping after beach hours and throwing late-night parties. This had to stop, as it could jeopardize the club's existence, despite the common knowledge that many young non-member Village residents were using the beach to enjoy these late-night swims. Skinny-dipping in the dark was one thing, but Mabel was never in favor of bikinis. Bikinis first started making their appearance in the late 1950s and were popularized by the hit song, "Itsy Bitsy Teenie Weenie Yellow Polka Dot Bikini" in June of 1960. The fashion led to general acceptance, beginning with teenagers. With the cultural revolution of the late 1960s, this fashion trend went mainstream nationally, and the bikinis got smaller. For the past few years at the Beach Club, many high school girls and younger women were arriving at the beach during the day wearing bikinis that had become a bit more "itsy bitsy" from prior years. Many of the older members, mostly women I can assure you, felt the style came very close to, shall we say, overexposure. My Aunt Marie recalled the meeting where Mabel announced in a very loud, gravelly voice: "As to the Tuxedo Community Club, the rules will be 'FULL BATHING ATTIRE ONLY and NO DOGS.'" While no one was quite sure what was meant by "full bathing attire," there was no misunderstanding that Mabel was not enamored of this new swimwear trend, and she would follow Justice Potter Stewart's 1957 U.S. Supreme Court (Roth v. United States, 354 U.S. 476) ruling regarding obscenity and the First Amendment to the Constitution free speech protections: "I know it when I see it."

The 1975 season closed, and the Executive Committee looked forward to the next year. Several years earlier, the big new expense, besides increased rent, had been the lawnmower. For 1976, it was the raft. The cost of these items might seem small expenses by today's standards, but they were major expenditures for the Beach Club, which counted its pennies and relied on its members, many of whom likely ran their households on strict budgets. The existing raft was originally built in 1955 and needed replacement. It had been refurbished in 1965 at a cost of $575, but now, the boards could no longer just be sanded and repainted. In addition, the old,empty oil drums used to support it were no longer serviceable. This was a major expense that had to be budgeted for and completed ahead of the 1976 season.

Chapter 25: Movie Night

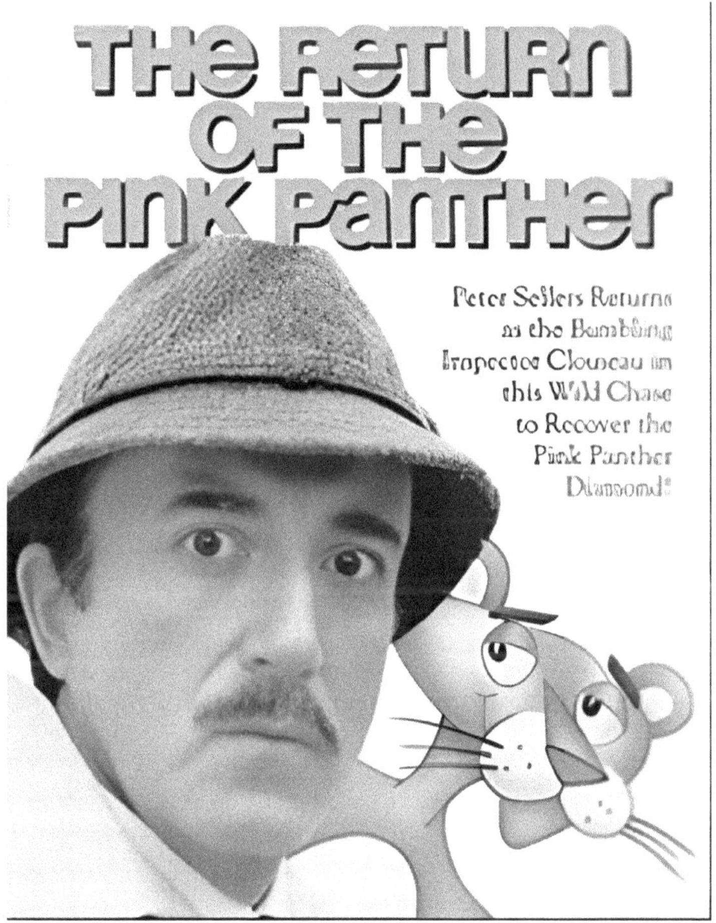

Movie poster advertising the fundraising event, 1976

By now, you surely know the customary format was to hold the Executive Committee meeting in the spring, followed shortly thereafter by the Annual Meeting. It was also common knowledge that the finance report would cause concerns about the ability of the Beach Club to fund its operations. Unforeseen expenses could jeopardize the

Beach Club's season. At the close of 1975, it had been decided to retire the original raft, and in keeping with his usual, above-and-beyond volunteering effort, Tom Salierno agreed to build the new raft. Tom and his two brothers, Joe and Louis, had continued their father's successful general contracting business. In keeping with his father's example, any work for the beach was performed for cost. Volunteers were also ready to join in when help was needed. Rather than the customary "raffle" to help pay for it, the Executive Committee decided to have a "movie night" in early July. Following the usual discussion and approval, a committee was formed. They selected the recently released Peter Sellers film *Return of the Pink Panther,* which would be shown with a short cartoon. Admission would be $2.00, and the movie would be screened in the high school auditorium. Volunteers made posters and placed notices in the paper for the July 10 event. My Aunt Marie would collect tickets at the door. Randall McCarroll, my cousin, and Dave McGrady would operate the projection equipment. This was exciting to many original members who recalled the annual fundraising events. All went smoothly at the movie night, and the club made a small profit, but it was noted in the minutes by Marion Mottola (who recalled the "sold out" audiences for the plays of the early years) that there was "poor attendance by members."

This note was a portent of the future. Membership was decreasing, but expenses kept increasing, and operating and maintaining the club was becoming more time-consuming. In addition, the volunteer spirit long associated with the club was fading. A few were now doing the work of many. Membership clean-up nights were replaced by my Uncle Buddy's small crew and the usual active members of the Executive Committee. Major changes in American life from the 1960s and 1970s were now firmly entrenched. Most original Beach Club members had since passed away. Now the membership consisted mainly of the children and grandchildren of those who had formed the club in 1936, along with new residents of the Hamlet who had purchased homes from those who originally worked in, or serviced Tuxedo Park in its formative years. Most young mothers now worked outside the home to make ends meet. Many fathers no longer left home in the morning and finished their work at 5 p.m. to return for a family dinner. Employment no longer required a strict nine-to-five job and overtime was always accepted if available. There was little time left for families to prepare for a cookout or picnic dinner at the beach during the season. However, despite the dearth of volunteers for Beach Club projects, thanks to the small profit from the movie and careful control over expenditures, the 1976 season ended with the new raft in place. Another Tuxedo Community Club summer was in the books.

In 1977, Marion Hekl was once again selected for the job of senior checker, and in keeping with her tradition, she waited until the end of the meeting before requesting and receiving her raise. The membership this year was expanding. New families were joining the Beach Club, notwithstanding societal changes in everyday life that had recently hindered growth. The beach remained a vital, enjoyable attraction, and if you lived in the Hamlet you joined, even if you couldn't spend as much time at the beach as you might have previously. The membership fees were so low that no one in the Hamlet wanted to be denied access to enter the gates into the Park to show off the Park to guests and enjoy a swim or a leisurely day at the beach.

The Beach Club was still facing increasing regulation from

state agencies and from the local Village governing body. The Village had hired a new police chief who met with the Executive Committee to become familiar with the rules regarding Hamlet members and guests. He was cooperative and had excellent suggestions for the committee. The Village was concerned with restricting the people entering the Park and the Beach Club, ensuring only Beach Club members and their guests came on the beach property. At this time, the rules and regulations included:

- Swim at your own risk when lifeguards are not present.
- Children of members are not allowed to swim when lifeguard is off duty "UNLESS supervised by parents."

There was also the unwritten, time-honored parental rule for children: "No swimming for at least an hour after eating lunch!"

The Annual Meeting was now typically attended by members from the Hamlet, and thus held at the high school. For many years, picnic requests were approved despite concerns about liability, expense, and the effect on members' access on picnic days. This year picnics (Senior Citizens, St. Mary's, and the Brownies/Girl Scouts) were only approved for weekdays, as members wanted weekends for themselves. These requests now had to coincide with the recreation program to avoid any conflicts. The Village of Tuxedo Park allowed the Town of Tuxedo Recreation Department, for a fee, to use the beach for swimming and activities through the beginning of August. Dues were again increased by $5, and 50/50 raffle tickets were sent out to members to be sold in the community with the hope that members would be generous in purchasing them as well to try to raise extra revenue to cover expenses. At Mabel Tansey's request, the Village supplied three new grills (instead of sand, as had been the case in recent seasons). Honey Hall, a third-generation member from the Hamlet and daughter of Marion Mottola, was made temporary chairman to conduct elections. As usual, after a motion and second, the entire slate of officers and the Executive Committee were unanimously re-elected. Danny Winfield, now in his early thirties and a second-generation member from the Hamlet, was added to the Executive Committee.

The members continued their efforts to improve the facilities, but they had little money to do so. My uncle Buddy McCarroll brought up a request to build a full basketball court; presently there was just a backboard and basket erected in a cleared dirt area. A request was also made for a volleyball pit. Of course, all work would be performed by members. Both requests were tabled as this would have to be approved by the Village. Normal business was concluded without any major issues, but one item continued to be a source of discussion that prevented the meeting closing. For some time, there was always a problem with beach entry, even though the vehicles would have to pass the checker. In prior years, the checker would ask the name, check it against the member list, and note if there were guests. Guest vehicles without a Beach Club sticker on the windshield would remain outside the gate in a small parking area off the main road to ensure enough parking spaces for members. The checker would see a sticker and the car would be waived in. The club still had no way of knowing if the car contained members, guests, guests using member's cars, etc. In addition, there was no way of tracking use of the beach other than collecting the guest passes, which relied on members providing the proper number of passes. Forty years had passed. The minutes do not reflect who made the suggestion, but one can only imagine the light bulbs going off. A member was recognized and said, "How about a sign-in book?" Voilà! The problem was solved, and the sign-in book that began in 1977 continued from that point forward.

Chapter 26: A New Mayor

Howland Pendleton "Pen" Rodgers (1922–2014), ca. 1975

In 1978, the Executive Committee attended a meeting on May 9 with the Village trustees at the Village office. The former mayor, Crawford Blagdon, had been succeeded by Howland Pendleton "Pen" Rodgers in 1975. Mayor Rodgers was born in New York City on July 11, 1922, to Henry Pendleton Rogers Jr. and Gladys Pell. He grew up in New York City and Tuxedo Park. His mother's side of the family was entrenched in the history of the early United States and is well-recognized today for the Pell Grants for higher education. His ancestors included Elbridge T. Gerry, a signer of the Declaration of Independence and the fifth Vice President of the United States; Nathaniel Pendleton, an officer in the Continental Army who was Alexander Hamilton's second in his duel with Aaron Burr; and Albert Gallatin who, as Secretary of the Treasury under Thomas Jefferson, financed the Lewis & Clark Expedition and later was a founder of New York University. A graduate of the Brooks School and Harvard University, Pen joined the Army in 1944 and served as a member of the 32nd Infantry Division in the Pacific. He was honorably discharged with the rank of Captain. Returning to Tuxedo Park after the war, he helped revitalize the greater Tuxedo community, including beyond the gates. He would assume key roles including Police Commissioner of the Village of Tuxedo Park and President of the Board of Trustees of the Tuxedo Park School.

Rodgers was very active in the Park, acting as the Tuxedo Park School Board President from 1962-1972. There had always been a private school for families with young children. The Tuxedo Park School was a feeder school for the Northeastern prep schools that provided the majority of students to the Ivy League colleges, mainly Harvard, Yale, and Princeton, where their parents had graduated in years past. This new school property and mansion, Blairhame, was the residence of John Insley Blair, an early resident of Tuxedo Park. Blairhame was built by the famous architects, Carriere & Hastings, in the early 1920s. It was also the site of the original Tuxedo Park golf course. It was donated in 1957 by the family when an earlier school building on the east side of the Park had become antiquated. In 1967, with Blairhame filled to capacity, Rodgers tirelessly led a campaign to build an additional wing, upgrade the facilities, and establish an endowment fund. The Tuxedo Park School dedicated the wing to Howland P. Rogers in 1944.

Rather than take up the trustee's time, Tom Salierno, now on the Executive Committee, made a motion accepted by those attending that the trustees meet with the Executive Committee at the beach the following week. All agreed, but word came back to the Executive Committee that the trustees wanted to hold the meeting at the Village office. The trustees did not want to actually visit the Beach Club, and why would they? They clearly had no interest in discussing business sitting around an outdoor picnic table. If there was to be another meeting, it would be in their chambers where they could sit behind their trustee table and receive proper deference with respect to any discussion. The social distinction between those living in the Park, and the Beach Club members who were not members of the Tuxedo Club and lived outside the gates (with the notable exception of Tom Salierno), remained, as always, the elephant in the room.

An idea had been circulating over the winter about changing the name of the Beach Club. There were now 185 members, including clergy and senior citizens for whom fees were waived. The idea was to end the confusion and annual concerns over who could become a member by changing the name from "Tuxedo Community Club" to something that would give the Beach Club an identity that distinguished it from the "Tuxedo" community that now included many sections of The Town of Tuxedo beyond just the Hamlet and the Incorporated Village of Tuxedo Park. For years there had been understandable confusion between "Tuxedo Community Club," and the formal and highly exclusive "Tuxedo Club." The goal was to adopt

a new name that would no longer be misinterpreted by residents of the
Town of Tuxedo. Also, a distinctive new identifier might be more
palatable for Village of Tuxedo Park residents who wished to retain the
exclusivity of living behind the gates. One suggestion stuck: the "Wee
Wah Beach Club."

Another issue was the annual firemen's picnic that was
becoming "too large" for the beach to handle. At the last picnic, a
fireman sustained injuries from a fall in the picnic area. Despite the
large quantity of beer he was alleged to have consumed, and the nature
of the terrain, this fireman, who was from outside the gates and
Hamlet, had stepped into a hole where a stump had been removed. He
then filed a lawsuit against the Tuxedo Community Club, the
individual Executive Committee members, my Uncle Buddy, who was
the unofficial beach manager, and the Village of Tuxedo Park. In the
past, lawsuits were few in this community. However, litigation, which
was exploding on the national scene, had now found its way inside the
gates of both the Park and the Beach Club. The carefree days of
children riding around Pond 3 on the fire engines after the July Fourth
parade were long since over. The slide at the beachfront into the water
had been moved up to the play area. Of no less concern was a report
that sewage from homes on the hills outside the club was seeping into
the lake. The working relationship with the new Mayor, Pen Rodgers,
and the trustees seemed solid, so this was an opportune time to have
these discussions. Tom Salierno and Pen Rodgers, although in different
social circles, were good friends. Other beach matters were discussed
including the basketball court and volleyball pit. The meeting was
cordial, but no further action was taken. Mayor Rodgers was now the
third mayor elected for the Incorporated Village of Tuxedo Park

formed in the early 1950s. Beach club members were acutely aware of these changes in the governance of the Village, not just regarding the mayor but the trustees as well. There was always the unspoken issue of the continued existence of the Beach Club and its use by those from the Hamlet. Those in the Hamlet had no vote in these elections and the residents who were members of the Tuxedo Club had a controlling block of votes for the resulting trustee elections of Tuxedo Club members to govern the Village of Tuxedo Park.

The Beach Club Annual Meeting of 1978 was well attended at Tuxedo High School. It was a year of change. Mike Crisci stepped down as vice president of the Beach Club, and Tom Salierno was elected to replace him. Tom continued to be very active in the Beach Club. He also built a number of homes in the Village of Tuxedo Park. Tom had an excellent reputation dealing with the Village that led to a good relationship with Mayor Rodgers and the trustees. The Village had raised the rent by $200. The insurance company was requesting some costly improvements and modifications. The retaining wall by the water was badly in need of repairs, the lawsuit was a major concern, and the question of changing the constitution and bylaws to reflect a name change to better define membership was on the table. This led to the usual discussion of the use of the beach by members and their guests.

The officers, with Tom Salierno now vice president, and the other Executive Committee members, were re-elected and got right down to business. Louis Euvrard Jr. continuing the Euvrard family service, was selected from the applications to be lifeguard for 1978, and a decision was made to limit guest passes to 20 adult passes per season for each membership. Over the years, despite agreements with the Village trustees and the Beach Club, the actual number of guest passes varied, as members could always request more if they ran out. Exceptions were liberally applied. Proposed expenses for the coming year included the repair of the beach wall, and new picnic tables were discussed. Tom volunteered to supply the equipment, the members could handle the labor, and Tom said he would encourage the Village to pay for the materials. The club, now thirty-two years old, continued the tradition of volunteer work to improve the beach and avoid the expense of outside contractors and labor costs.

An unexpected request was described in the 1978 meeting minutes. The item under discussion should bring a smile to your face; it was a reminder of the technological advances in the world that had taken place over the course of the Beach Club's existence. My Uncle Buddy made a report on the state of the beach maintenance, including a request for the purchase of a "Weed Eater," the now-familiar device used by homeowners and landscapers. Sure enough, "Weed Eater" was placed in quotes in the meeting minutes by Marion Mottola, the longtime secretary and Buddy's sister. Despite the weighty issues mentioned above, my Aunt Marie recalled this stopped the meeting in its tracts. Just what the heck was a "Weed Eater"? Was it a goat? Where would they keep it? What did it look like? Who would be responsible for it? How much does a "Weed Eater" cost? Apparently, you had to be there. "Weed Eaters," was, and still is, the trade name of a manufacturer of string trimmers that had been introduced in the early 1970s. By 1978 they had apparently become a somewhat "have to have" piece of yard equipment for those "in the know," along with lawnmowers and edgers. The Weed Eater string trimmer company was founded in 1971 in Houston, Texas by George C. Ballas Sr., the inventor of the device. The idea for the Weed Eater lawn trimmer came to him from the spinning nylon bristles of an automatic car wash. He thought he could come up with a similar technique to protect the bark on trees that he was trimming around. After much discussion as to the absolute necessity for spending money on a "Weed Eater," a motion was made by Bill Iannoni, seconded by Roddy Farningham, both of whom helped Buddy with maintenance of the beach and were anxious to get their hands on this new device. The membership voted to approve the purchase of a professional top-of-the-line "Weed Eater" for the club. The meeting closed with approval to go forward with the name change of the Beach Club. They amended the constitution and bylaws, and they agreed to do whatever was necessary to comply with the insurance requests.

As was true of many of the original members of the Beach Club, Mabel Tansey was now at a point where her children were grown and no longer living in the local area. Mabel was retired from George F. Baker High School. Her husband, Joe, was also retired and a highly regarded horticulturalist. Together, although not rich in the Tuxedo Park sense, they followed the pattern of many of the early, richest residents of Tuxedo Park with respect to real estate. The Tansy's had lived their lives recognizing how wealthy families always seemed to have several residences in upscale communities to enjoy the best of the weather in summer, fall, winter, or spring. Joe Tansey recognized that his family could now afford to do this as well, but on a smaller scale. Rather than mansions that were simply out of their price range and social position, when given the opportunity, they purchased a small cottage on Stable Road inside the gates, and thus they continued as residents of Tuxedo Park. Next, they purchased a cozy little house in Delray Beach, Florida along the scenic Intercoastal Waterway and a short walk over a bridge to the Atlantic shoreline, about twenty miles south of the grand winter mansions in Palm Beach constructed by wealthy families in the early 1900s, many of whom had been residents of Tuxedo Park and members of the Tuxedo Club. Lastly, rather than Newport as a summer destination, they purchased a small cottage closer to Tuxedo Park at the New Jersey shore on Long Beach Island, one of the most exclusive summer beach islands in New Jersey and a short drive for their visiting children and grandchildren. Mabel and Joe were now spending more of their time during the summers on Long Beach Island at the New Jersey shore and wintering in the house they had purchased in South Florida. Tuxedo Park was home for the spring when trees blossomed, and in the fall when leaves changed and fell. Spring and fall are the most beautiful seasons in Tuxedo Park. Tuxedo Park was still home for the Tanseys, but much like how wealthy residents spent their time enjoying the best of nature in multiple beautiful locations, Mabel and Joe had made excellent choices. In the 1980s, my wife and I rented Mabel and Joe's Tuxedo house for the summer months. I could walk to my Aunt Marie's house down the street, and my uncle Jim Barth was about one mile away.

With Mabel away much of the year, Tom Salierno took more control of Executive Committee meetings, which were now held monthly at Tom's house from late August through mid-October. To comply with the club's insurance policy, they agreed to purchase ropes, a new rowboat for the lifeguard, ladders for the raft, buoys, signs for the beachfront, and ladders and railings for the dock and steps. History and habit still had their place. When the replacement of worn picnic tables came up for discussion, the committee members agreed they should purchase the hardware and the lumber separately as well as save money by designing and building the new tables themselves. The lake water was typically lower in September, so repair work began on the retaining wall.

As noted above, late in the fall of 1978 a new constitution and bylaws had been drafted and approved, with help from the Village attorney. To that point, there was little question that Tom Salierno was bringing renewed energy and a more businesslike approach to the Beach Club. At a meeting in Tom's home on February 6, 1979, they formally agreed to change the bank account names immediately to reflect the new entity: the Wee Wah Beach Club. A letter was sent to Mayor Rodgers requesting a status meeting about the Wee Wah Beach Club and to outline proposals for repairing and updating the beach facilities. This included the beachfront retaining wall, gates, bathhouses, and a concrete shed for equipment.

On April 17, 1979, the Executive Committee and my uncle Buddy met with Mayor Rodgers and the trustees at the Village office. The new constitution and the name change were presented to the Village without discussion. The outcome of this meeting resulted in a vote by the Village trustees to provide $1,400 to the Wee Wah Beach Club for repairs, and to supply additional sand to the beachfront. The trustees also approved a rent increase to $3,500. Picnics were approved for Park School, St Mary's, and Tuxedo Hospital. The annual Fourth of July firemen's picnic was also approved. The issue of membership for those outside the Park was not discussed, but everyone knew that it remained a source of concern.

A month later, the Executive Committee met again at Tom's house with my Uncle Buddy, Roddy Farningham, and Joe McCormack to make plans for the Annual Meeting. My Aunt Marie, still treasurer, who recalled these meetings and confirmed the Beach Club minutes I reviewed as source material for this book, was asked to look into reducing the cost of stickers for member's vehicles. The Wee Wah Beach Club would now have formal rules and regulations printed up and handed out with the membership cards when dues were paid. Seasonal dues were raised to $50, but the initiation fee and guest tickets would remain the same. Lifeguards were to receive $140 per week for thirty-five hours, and would be on duty from 10:30 a.m. to 8:30 p.m. daily; the same schedule was assigned to the checkers. The formal beach opening was set for June 9. As was customary, lifeguard applications for 1979 were accepted by the Executive Committee, and Dan Winfield would interview and assess the candidates. Once again, Marion Hekl applied for the checker's job along with R. Hoffman. No need to interview Marion. The job was hers. Surprisingly, there was a welcome break in tradition. Marion did not request a raise this year!

The 1979 Annual Meeting was held at Tuxedo High School on May 7. The first order of business was to explain what had transpired over the winter with the name change, the new bylaws, and the new rules and regulations. There was some confusion as to the senior citizen membership, so it was spelled out: all residents of the Hamlet or of the Village of Tuxedo Park who are, or have been, members of the Beach Club and have reached the age of 65 may ask for the elimination of their dues. New members 65 or older may join the Wee Wah Beach Club for the first year with no initiation fee; thereafter, they were eligible to request a senior citizen waiver. What had been the quaint, sleepy, and somewhat tired Tuxedo Community Club was fast evolving. The newly minted Wee Wah Beach Club was energized and actively preparing to grow and expand for years to come. Relations with the Village trustees appeared to be improving. As the meeting came to a close, Mabel announced she was stepping down as president but offered to remain on the Executive Committee. She explained that she was spending much of her summers on the New Jersey shore at her home on Long Beach Island. There was little discussion as to an election of new officers. Tom Salierno was elected president, and Dan Winfield took over as vice president. Marie McCarroll and Marion Mottola were unanimously re-elected treasurer and secretary. The Executive Committee consisted of long-time members Roderick "Roddy" Farningham, Jane Cattrell, Joe McCormack, Bill Iannone, Florence Damato, Nina Matthews, Mabel Tansey, Tina Kusion, and Joe Heater. My Uncle Buddy McCarroll was again appointed to be Beach supervisor by acclamation.

The summer of 1979 passed with few incidents, and attendance was up. Outside the gates, a gas crisis was gripping the Northeast. Long lines and high prices at the pumps made people think twice about planning long trips. At the Beach Club there were the usual issues of members bringing guests without passes and young people sneaking onto the beach after dark. As the decade of the 1970s closed out, Beach Club membership stood at 203, an all-time high. The grounds were well kept and many improvements had been made. Rules and regulations were tightened up as to membership and guests. Additional regulations were being imposed by the Orange County Health Department with regard to lakefront and bathhouse/bathroom facilities. The relationship with the Village of Tuxedo Park trustees appeared harmonious, as there were no recorded complaints to the trustees from the Park residents. It appeared the newly named Wee

Wah Beach Club was about to enter an era of friendly coexistence with the Village and was well positioned for the future. The age-old distinction between social classes appeared to be easing.

Thomas Salierno, ca. 1970

The 1970s opened with the ongoing Vietnam War, which finally ended in 1975. Concurrently, America endured the Watergate scandal, which led to the resignation of President Nixon in 1974. On a positive note, in 1976, America celebrated its Bicentennial, but throughout the decade, the country dealt with staggering inflation and fuel shortages; new trends in fashion, music, and television programming; and perhaps most visibly, roads filled with smaller, more efficient, albeit less comfortable and less attractive vehicles. The tumultuous decade of the 1970s concluded with a protracted hostage crisis in Iran, not resolved until early 1981. Closer to home, Tuxedo, largely a refuge from the day-to-day stress of the outside world, faced its own local challenges. Fortunately, the relationship between the Wee Wah Beach Club and the Village of Tuxedo Park appeared to have settled into a less confrontational period. There was less focus upon social stations in Tuxedo, and it was clear the vast chasm between the attempted social aristocracy created nearly one hundred years earlier, and the rest of society, had been narrowed through wars, the Great Depression, taxes, and a rising middle class. Newport, Rhode Island mansions were now, in many cases, derelict shadows of their former grandeur—as well as tax burdens—on what had begun as a Navy port. Remaining testaments to the opulence of the Gilded Age were in peril.

Social change was underway throughout the country. In the 1980s, one would be hard-pressed to find a family that traced its heritage back to the original residents of Tuxedo Park and to early members of the Tuxedo Club. Old line society had long taken a back seat to the nouveau riche investment bankers and later, the hedge fund managers of Wall Street who saw their success compounded, courtesy of President Reagan's tax cuts. The disparate compensation between corporate executives and the employees of the corporations they led was exploding.

Thanks to all this new money, Tuxedo Park was slowly seeing a resurgence. The Village had been subject to many articles over the years, with many more to come in newspapers such as the *New York Times* that gave prominent front-page space on its real estate sections, exclaiming Tuxedo Park to be an extraordinary, beautiful place a mere hour from New York City. The older mansions were finding buyers, and the money to restore or rebuild was not a problem. Tuxedo Park represented "the perfect weekend or summer residence," featuring a "close commute to the city." A reverse in living styles now meant that the primary residence was often in Tuxedo Park, supplemented by a luxury apartment in New York City. The Fifth Avenue mansions of the early residents of Tuxedo Park were replaced by large apartments and cooperatives. Old Gilded Age "watering holes" in Newport were now historical travel destinations. Corporate and private jets, as well as large yachts, made the world an oyster for those who could afford to splurge. Concurrently, many of the newly rich ventured west, snapping up ultra-condominiums and custom homes in small, private ski resorts in Vail and Aspen, Colorado; Park City, Utah; and other pristine locales. Seemingly no desirable destination across the United States or anywhere in the world seemed out of reach—for the fortunate few.

In the 1960s, approximately one third of the largest Tuxedo Park houses were unoccupied. This once ultra-exclusive private enclave had effectively been reserved for the super-rich, but now a cultural change in the relationship between the Village and the Hamlet was underway. That said, symbols of separation between the "haves and have nots" from the turn of the century remained as physical and psychological barriers. The imposing fortress and Main gate reminded all outsiders that entry into Tuxedo Park remained restricted to residents and guests. In a somewhat backhanded slap at the current residents, Rick Hampson in the *Los Angeles Times* reported his interview with 78-year-old Pierre Lorillard Barbey. Barbey, the last "Lorillard" remaining in Tuxedo Park, was quoted as saying, "Nobody lives here [in Tuxedo Park] anymore who amounts to a row of beans."[80]

However, economically successful families and those coming from old money were finding this location incredibly beautiful, affordable, and within a reasonable commuting distance to New York City. The great houses that were left, and there were many, were renovated. In addition, construction of new high-priced residences on undeveloped property and converted barns and carriage houses was helping restore the unique character to Tuxedo Park. In the 1950s, zoning codes were passed to require a minimum of two acres for new residences. Now, however, zoning was expanded to four acres in order to emphasize the grandeur of Tuxedo Park and prevent the building of smaller tract homes. A new generation of Tuxedo Club members were no longer vetted on family, social hierarchy, and distinctions between "old money" and "new money." Similarly, distinctions based on fashion, cars, and manner of speaking between the Park and the Hamlet had all but disappeared. There was a new spirit in which many residents, from both sides of the main gate to the Park, worked to improve the lives of all who resided in the community.

In the 1980s, one thing remained a constant. If you lived in the Hamlet, you would be stopped at the main gate to Tuxedo Park unless you could provide the name of a resident and had been invited in. At the Beach Club, the 1980s opened with a new sign and an imposing swinging metal gate as you entered the old Pigeon Point bathing area.

The Wee Wah Beach Club was poised for change, but traditions built up over forty-five years, mostly under the original name, "Tuxedo Community Club," remained intact. Membership had increased significantly, and with this renewed interest, many new faces, new issues and formalities had to be considered. Continuity in leadership and a commitment to volunteerism remained at the core of the club. Mabel Tansey had stepped down, but Tom Salierno, with a keen sense of history and purpose, had stepped up.

The first Executive Committee meeting of 1980 took place at Tom's house in the Park just up the street from the Village Office on March 2. Tom had a practice of attending Village meetings, and he was not afraid to voice his concerns on Village issues. He was also intent on making sure the needs of the Beach Club were expressed to Mayor Rodgers and the Village trustees. Tom reported to the Executive Committee of the Beach Club that the relationship was good, but after speaking with Mayor Rodgers, another increase in the rent would probably be called for and approved by the trustees. After his talk, he hoped that the increase would be minimal, perhaps $200, with consideration paid to the Wee Wah Beach Club's 1980 budget that they would provide to the Village. My Aunt Marie, still treasurer, reported the Wee Wah bank balance was $3,104.07, a vast improvement over those prior years where they struggled to start the season with just enough money to pay the insurance bill and perform minor repairs. My Aunt Marie stated that in 1979, the club had a total of 204 members. My uncle Buddy, and Roddy Farningham, who grew up in a coachman's house on Stable Road next to my aunt and Buddy, stated they would report on the condition of the beach premises at the next meeting once the weather warmed up. As an aside, my wife Jean and I later purchased Roddy's parents' home next to my Aunt Marie's in the early 1990s. There was discussion that the Wee Wah should acknowledge longtime member Jerry Nardella, for all he had done during the changeover to the new organization. A motion was made, seconded, and there was a unanimous vote to provide the Nardella family with a free membership for the new season.

Executive Meetings were now being held monthly. One thing that didn't change was the application of Marion Hekl, which was received at the next meeting in April. Once again, Marion expressed her desire to remain as senior checker and now, once again, asked for a raise! As usual, there was little discussion. She was hired and was granted a raise to $4.25 an hour. The new Village budget was unveiled, showing rent for the Wee Wah Beach Club at $3,850. During this time, Tom had continued to explore a five-year lease extension between the Beach Club and the Village. While Mayor Rodgers was willing to consider it, he told Tom there were not enough votes on the Village Board of Trustees for passage.

The real change in the Beach Club is reflected in the minutes for the Annual Meeting held at the Tuxedo Historical Society in the Hamlet on May 8, 1980. Although there were now over two hundred members, other than the Executive Committee, only five other members were in attendance. Except for the old guard, so to speak, and a few newcomers, the days of volunteers doing the work appeared over. A dedicated few were now responsible for safely maintaining and operating what had become a 200-plus member beachfront and recreation club. Pursuant to changes in New York State law, there was now a need for three lifeguards to cover the waterfront, and numerous reports had to be filed with state and local regulatory agencies on a regular basis. The number of on-duty lifeguards was based on the number of people in the water and the use of the raft. This required a separate guard for the swimming area, one for the diving board, and a separate guard for the baby pool. This fenced section was all of ten feet by eight feet in size in the shallow water beside the dock. The committee decided the beach would now be open on weekends starting in May from 9:00 a.m. to 9:00 p.m., but no swimming was allowed until the lifeguards reported for duty at 11:00 a.m. Marion Hekl was advised that the checkers would be responsible for making certain the beach was clean, and that trash from smaller containers was placed into the new dumpster now located outside the Beach Club area.

As it turned out, 1980 was an excellent year for the Wee Wah Beach Club. The beach was in great condition, the old guard fulfilled their usual responsibilities, and the membership enjoyed the summer. After the beach closed, a wrap-up meeting of the Executive Committee, with spouses, took place at Dan Winfield's house in the Hamlet on September 19. My aunt recalled there was a great feeling of accomplishment. Membership had reached 251, and a balance of over $3,000 remained in the bank to carry forward to the 1981 season. This feeling of satisfaction was well deserved when you consider what this small group had accomplished through a total volunteer effort— combined with their good working relationship with the Village Department of Public Works. The topic turned to plans for the next season. My Uncle Buddy reported that the grounds were in excellent shape except for the wall by the baby pool, which should be fixed while the water level was low. Guest privilege issues continued to be a source of concern as members abused it, didn't understand it, and tested it with unique circumstances. All and all, it had been a great season. Tom and his wife, Terry Salierno, whose family were original members back in 1936, were thought to be working above and beyond the call of duty. As a surprise, the Executive Committee presented them with a card and gift. An igloo cooler for Tom and a magnetic hide-a-way car key that was a popular product at the time for Terry. There was no comment when this author questioned Tom and Terry as to whether these gifts were considered compensation and the value was reported as personal income. Of course, throughout Beach Club history, all service as officers or on the Executive Committee was voluntary.

The Wee Wah Beach Club was no longer a mom-and-pop operation, so it was decided that Executive Committee meetings would be continued on a monthly basis. The next meeting took place October 17, 1980. The main agenda item involved the wall repair mentioned by Buddy at the fall closing meeting. A wide range of bids for the wall repair had come in. The low bid was $12,000, which they could not afford, on up to a staggering $45,000. Tom had visited with Mayor Rodgers, who stated there was no money in the Village budget for the work, and suggested the Wee Wah Beach Club consider taking out a loan. The mayor said he could likely get the other trustees of the Village to contribute $1,000 toward it. Mayor Rodgers would personally co-sign any loan and see what he could do with the new Village budget. Tom also continued to press for a five-year lease, with rent being capped for the first three years. This seemed agreeable to Mayor Rodgers, but convincing the trustees was always the problem. Here they were in 1980, and a majority of the trustees were Tuxedo Club members. They were elected by Park residents, most of whom were members of the Tuxedo Club as well. Their constituents did not include anyone who lived outside the gates. There were also newer residents of the Park who felt Hamlet members of the Beach Club should not have the privilege of entry through the gates, and that the Beach Club property should be exclusively for the benefit of Village residents. This group remained upset that the Wee Wah Beach Club was accepting members from the Hamlet outside the gates of Tuxedo Park. In response to Mayor Rodgers's comments, the Executive Committee of the Wee Wah Beach Club agreed to match the $1,000 from Mayor Rodgers from the Beach Club operating account, to try to securing a loan, and to proceed with the low bidder. Their unclear plan for repaying the loan was tabled for a future meeting, as the repairs had to be made, and it was time for work to begin.

The big change entering the 1981 summer season was the Beach Club now had a loan and interest expense line on its financial statements. A loan had been taken out for $2,500 to go forward with the wall repair. Tom's hard work and constant communication with Mayor Rodgers and other trustees had achieved positive results. The Village trustees could see that the Wee Wah had competent people in charge, was being well run, and provided an attractive facility for Village residents who were not members of the private Tuxedo Club, as well as for Hamlet resident members who were grandfathered in under the geographic boundary determined way back in 1936. Mayor Rodgers came through with a commitment that the Village would try to get the funds from a recreation line in the Village budget to pay off the loan. Alternatively, the Beach Club might be able to deduct the loan payments from its seasonal rent. It also looked like approval would be given for a two-year lease, and possibly the Beach Club's preferred five-year term.

The lawsuit brought by the fireman from outside the Village and the Hamlet who had fallen at the picnic in 1978 had been settled by the insurance company for $25,000. However, this had been a major source of anxiety and irritation for all. Mabel Tansey and Buddy McCarroll were named as individual defendants, which resulted in their having to take time from their regular jobs for depositions, court hearings, and many meetings with lawyers. There was also the outside threat of personal financial exposure, although there was never a doubt that the club's Executive Committee would find a way to cover any judgment in excess of the policy limits, should that occur. Everyone wanted to continue with the fire department picnic on the Fourth of July, but changes needed to be made regarding insurance, crowd control, who would be allowed entry, and limitations on guests. Bill Iannone and Sam Venezia from the Fire Department expressed their personal and the department's regret about the lawsuit, and they presented the fire department's views on how to prevent similar incidents. I'm certain that limiting the picnic to non-alcoholic beverages was not one of the suggestions from the fire department. As to usual agenda items, no one had yet requested the job as checker. How could this be? Although young people were not hard to find, as it typically provided a source of summer jobs for the children of members who requested them, there was a need for a senior checker.

A few weeks later, the call came in from Marion Mottola to my Aunt Marie. Mrs. Hekl had spoken with her and was ready to go to work as the senior checker after all. In fact, she did not even request a raise! Lifeguards now had chairs that were built by Bill Iannone, and they were supplied with umbrellas and bullhorns. Gravel for the parking lots had been delivered and spread. The basketball court had been freshly blacktopped.

There was more good news. President Tom Salierno communicated to the membership that a four-year lease had been drawn up: three years at $3,850, and $4,235 for the fourth year. In view of the growth of the Wee Wah Beach Club, and the increased expenses along with it, a motion was made, seconded, and after much discussion, it passed. Dues would increase to $55, a $5 increase, and guest privileges would be $20, which reflected an increase of $5.

Discussions on use of the one telephone at the beach had gone on for years. Nina Matthews had made numerous attempts to work something out that would allow for a direct line to the police department at the main gate, along with a public phone, but it was prohibitively expensive. Finally, she was able to find a solution: one line would be installed in the shed attached to the bathhouse, and a payphone would be installed on the beachfront. Remember, this was years before mobile phones became mainstream. When you take a moment to think about those times at the Wee Wah, there was peacefulness. This was a stress-free environment, where the focus was on relaxation, fun, and actually talking to your friends and other members. When you told someone that you were "going to the beach," it meant, except for a newspaper, radio, Scrabble game, or deck of cards, you were taking some time off from the problems of the world and your personal everyday life.

In 1981, Mayor Frank S. Bell, a sixteen-year resident (a newcomer by the standards of many Park residents) succeeded Pen Rodgers as the Incorporated Village's mayor. The TPA had continued to own significant property in Tuxedo Park, with larger holdings in the Town of Tuxedo surrounding the Incorporated Village. This property ownership was its major source of income. The TPA was now controlled by general partners George Boynton, Hazzard Reeves, and Christian Sonne, who were all Park residents and interested in development. Boynton's son, George Jr., was a land planner who provided the Village with a twenty-three-page letter outlining the need for new development to offset mounting expenses for antiquated infrastructure such as the water and sewer lines that were nearing one hundred years old. Zoning at the time required a two-acre minimum for single-family homes, but it was thought the TPA was looking to develop "cluster housing." Another developer, Sterling One, had proposed building "no less than 3,900 housing units on a 20-acre parcel" on the west boundary of the Incorporated Village. The project was approved, but it was never built.

In 1981, Village residents, led by Mary Graetzer, formed the Tuxedo Conservation and Taxpayers Association. Among other issues, they were concerned that Park roads would be opened to non-residents. Six years previously, a group proposed listing Tuxedo Park on the National Register of Historic Places, a move opposed by former Mayor Rodgers. The concern was that it would cause the Park to become open to the public. This was not true, as the "public" requirement only applied to places designated as a National Historic Landmark. An application was filed by a group of residents; no vote was required. The request was approved, and a certificate was issued, although Mayor Bell declined to accept the certificate, and many long-time residents felt no need for such a designation as stated by Town historian Albert Winslow. He was further quoted in an article by the *Yonkers Herald Statesman*: "A lot of foolishness, Tuxedo Park ought to be above this sort of thing." While social barriers were no longer as

pronounced as those during the time of Pierre Lorillard—and well into
the 1940s—preservation of the history as a private playground of the
rich remained a concern to many residents of the Incorporated Village
of Tuxedo Park.[81]

The meeting in the spring before the 1982 season started with
some sad news. Marion Mottola announced her resignation as
secretary. Not that it was not expected, but there was a realization that
father time does not stand still. My aunt Marie remained as treasurer,
but Mabel Tansey had retired in 1979, after thirty-four years as
president, and now Marion, after serving for twenty-seven years, was
stepping down. Marion was Buddy McCarroll's sister, making my aunt
Marie her sister-in-law. Marion was a lifelong resident of Tuxedo, born
in the Hamlet on December 11, 1916. Marion was the daughter of
Randall and Hannah McCarroll. As a girl, she worked at the Tuxedo
Library. She was an outstanding athlete at Tuxedo High School and
was a member of the championship basketball team of 1930-31. She
married Joe "Motts" Mottola, and worked at the school for over
twenty-five years. They lived just off the circle of homes originally
owned and rented by the TPA, but theirs was a fine brick home
befitting of the Italian stonemason who had been brought in to build
Pierre Lorillard's vision of Tuxedo Park. She and Motts raised four
children, who all did well and stayed close to home. Her only son,
Joseph "Jay" Mottola, followed the tradition of great Mottola
basketball players at Tuxedo and went on to star at Lafayette
University. For Jay, it was golf that brought him success, and he retired
as the President of the Metropolitan Golf Association after many years.
He continues to enjoy a well-known reputation within the golf world
and the United States Golf Association (USGA). Jay was also one of

the very few who were part of an original family raised outside the gates of Tuxedo Park to be accepted as a member of the Tuxedo Club. Marion was an active member of the Tuxedo Volunteer Ambulance Corps and the Ladies Auxiliary. For the past fifty years, the Mottola family gathering at the Fourth of July far surpassed any other family, and all Beach Club members would come to pay their respects at Marion's passing many years later in 2009.

The leadership of the Wee Wah Beach Club was undergoing rapid change. Marion's youngest daughter, Honey Hall, was now very active in the Beach Club and took over from Bonny Damato as the director of the Town of Tuxedo's Recreation Department Program, which used the beach daily for a good part of the summer. Joe Heater also resigned from the Executive Committee, and Bill Iannone volunteered to fill Joe's slot. There were no nominations for secretary, and the committee decided to take it up at the next meeting. Terry Salierno stepped forward and took responsibility for the secretary's position on an interim basis so that complete minutes could be preserved of all meetings.

Tom announced another vivid sign of the changing times. After such a storied history that had helped bring the Village and the Hamlet together, there would no longer be a Fourth of July parade in Tuxedo Park, and the fire department would no longer hold its annual Fourth of July picnic at the beach. The meeting continued with the usual agenda items regarding preparation for the 1982 season. There would be no senior checker that year, as Marion Hekl was not requesting the position as she wanted more family time.

Honey Hall, now recreation director, requested beach use from June 28 to August 6 for the Town of Tuxedo's longstanding summer program providing the town's children with access to the beach for swimming and other activities. She also wanted approval to sponsor a new senior lifesaving course. This was a win-win for all and was unanimously approved. Sand was delivered for the children's play area and in front of the benches at the waterfront. The bills were sent to the Village for payment. Recreation was now paying $800 for the use of the beach. As the meeting concluded, there was a discussion of the picnic area and the need for more grills. Many of the older stone fireplaces had seen better days. In keeping with the changes taking place in the world of outdoor cooking and the changing of the guard at the beach as well, the suggestion came up that perhaps the club should try some of the "new" Hibachi grills on stands to see how they work. America's fascination with Hibachis dated back to World War II when soldiers saw them in Japan. In the 1950s, as barbecuing gained popularity, the small rectangular grills were perfect for apartment dwellers and first-time homeowners who had limited outdoor space and limited budgets. In the 1970s, larger grills that could be supported on metal posts supplanted the stone fireplaces built by the original Beach Club members. While I have no record of a vote, the minutes reflect that Buddy agreed to buy some Hibachi grills, and the meeting was adjourned.

The Beach Club opened, and everything ran smoothly. There was some sadness on the Fourth of July, given the absence of the firemen's picnic, but family gatherings were increasing in size. The holiday became a time of reunion for many families whose sons and daughters now lived far from Tuxedo and had families of their own. Some groups now contained four generations, as well as longtime friends, and friends of friends of the young adults who were establishing their own enduring connections to the Beach Club. Everyone in those families tried their best to return to Tuxedo for the July Fourth celebration at the Wee Wah. My wife, Jean, and I were living in South Florida at the time. Jean was pregnant with our first child, but Independence Day at the Wee Wah with family and friends was not an event to be missed. The club's Fourth of July was a must-attend event, a time for multiple generations to meet for a few days to relive a traditional sense of family. Those of us who grew up loving the Beach Club now lived all across the country raising families of our own but returned year after year. In my case, we would arrive for a continuous two to three-day party at the beach with family and friends of family. Later all would return to Marie and Buddy's house for celebrations that lasted well into the wee hours of the morning before returning home to Florida a few days later.

On June 12, 1983, the *New York Times* reported, "Tuxedo Park in Orange County resembles a quiet Scottish loch a century ago. That scene has changed little since 1885 when Pierre Lorillard, scion of the wealthy tobacco family decided to fence in 4,000 acres of hilly, wooded land and built an elegant hunting and gaming retreat for his family and friends. Today Tuxedo Park remains quiet, sporty and most of all secure, its famous guarded front gates still barring all but those who live inside or have been invited."[82]

In actuality, in 1983 a number of homes would sell for seven figures or more, but many of the 300 homes were available at prices within the range of young professional families. By 1983, the initial 1886 requirement of Tuxedo Club membership to purchase a lot or a residence was no longer required, and only half of the residents belonged to the Tuxedo Club. The article mentions the "residents of [the Town of] Tuxedo and Tuxedo Park rarely mingle."[83] Many of the Park's converted stables, gardener cottages, potting sheds, and garages purchased in the late 1940s were now owned by families whose ancestors were employed by Lorillard at the time Tuxedo Park was built and marriages over the years created many family relationships that bridged the Park and what is now the Hamlet in the Town of Tuxedo. These bonds were formed long ago and strengthened over time by the memberships in the Wee Wah Beach Club.

By 1983, the Beach Club was nearing its fiftieth anniversary, and it was truly an integral part of the Tuxedo community, complete with its own distinct place in Tuxedo history. My grandparents (both paternal and maternal), parents, aunts, uncles, and cousins were all heavily woven into the fabric of this unique club. The Incorporated Village of Tuxedo Park was a very private municipality. Reflective of that exclusivity, the Wee Wah Beach Club, despite being more welcoming and widely affordable, continued to be limited to those residents within the old boundaries that included the Hamlet outside the Park. It excluded residents of the Town of Tuxedo who did not live within the boundaries of the "Hamlet" inclusive of the old East Village and Slovak Village (long disappeared due to the New York State Thruway) designated by the Incorporated Village of Tuxedo Park. The majority of members from the Hamlet still consisted mainly of families that were in some way related to the original families who served the estates at the turn of the twentieth century. There had been forty-seven years of Annual Meetings and many later included my uncle Jim Barth's recurring request for a tennis court. This year would be no exception. The son of a Beach Club founder, a fixture on the waterfront as a lifeguard and later as an adult member of the Executive

Committee countless times, Jim once again argued strenuously for building not one but two tennis courts. This occurred at the July 14 meeting of the committee, and once again, Jim's request was denied. Members suggested that anyone who wanted to play tennis should apply for membership in the Tuxedo Club. I mention this because the Wee Wah Beach Club had continued to be a major focus of our family, constantly discussed for as long as I can remember. If I wanted to play tennis or golf when we would come up for the summer, my uncle would laugh and tell me to get an application for the "club down the hill."

A season-ending Executive Committee meeting took place in September at the beach with all twelve members present. The Village had sent a check for $1541.82 to reimburse the Beach Club for sand, grills, benches, and several minor items. An $800 check was received from Tuxedo Recreation for use of the beach. Dan Winfield made a suggestion that was endorsed by all to open the 1983 season at the beach on Memorial Day weekend; as usual, regular hours would start later in June. Roddy and Buddy received kudos for the installation of new benches and the first-ever installation of hibachi grills attached to metal poles entrenched in the ground throughout the picnic area.

At the Executive Committee meeting on March 21, finances looked good, with Marie's treasurer's report showing $2,448.08 in the bank. The Annual Meeting was held April 18 at the high school. Honey Hall took over to nominate the election of the present officers. It was seconded by Bonny Takeuchi, the youngest daughter of original members Frank and Florence Damato, and all nominees were unanimously approved. A new program requested by Tuxedo Recreation was approved; it would provide a six-week, two-hour swim program for preschool children on Tuesday mornings.

Years seemed to be passing quickly. In 1984, the May 9 Annual Meeting at the high school ushered in yet another summer season. Jasper Mottola moved to reelect the officers and Executive Committee, and there was unanimous approval from all members. Buddy reported the raft and diving board were in good condition. A few new benches, new picnic tables, additional hibachi grills, as well as trees, and a new slide in the play area would be in place for the opening. Honey Hall requested use of the club for Tuxedo Recreation, and it was agreed a fee of $900 would cover their use of the beach for the swim program, pre-school program, and lifesaving course. The Fourth of July would be a free guest day. Family memberships would now be $60, single memberships would be $30, and guest passes would cost $15 for ten and $25 for twenty. Melanie Forzano served as the checker this season and, as usual, members were reminded of the guest privilege rules. When on duty as the checker, a lonely and mostly boring job, Melanie would take a break a few times a day and walk across the parking lot down to the beachfront to speak with the lifeguards. This walk caused most of the male activity at the beach to come to a standstill. It seemed like a fashion catwalk showing off the latest in bikinis. Card games, horseshoe matches and conversations paused to observe her walk while the women could only look at their husbands and shake their heads. My family well remembers the day my distracted Uncle Buddy drove the riding mower straight into a boulder at the edge of the parking lot as Melanie went by.

Guests must arrive with a member, and guest passes must have been purchased ahead of time. The pattern of member service and "do it yourself" continued. An example was Buddy's request to acquire new planks for picnic tables and benches in need of repair. Any salvageable hardware would be reused, and members would perform all the work.

Everyone is familiar with stories of Benjamin Franklin encountering electricity when flying his kite in a storm early in the eighteenth century, not too far from Tuxedo Park in Philadelphia. Thomas Edison patented the light bulb in 1879 at Menlo Park, New Jersey. And at last, in 1984, electricity was getting closer to the Beach Club, notwithstanding Tuxedo Park was one of the first communities to take advantage of electricity by forming a power company next to the Ramapo River back in 1890. Tom Salierno reported he had negotiated an annual lease with the Village for four years at $4,000, expiring after the 1988 season. Buried in the lease was a provision regarding electricity. Over a hundred years from Edison's commercialization of the light bulb, and ninety-five years since electricity had illuminated Tuxedo Park homes and roads, there would finally be lights in the bathrooms and changing rooms at the beach! Otherwise, it was business as usual with discussion of improvements and necessary repairs.

At the 1985 Annual Meeting, Dan Winfield took over as president and Tom moved back to vice president due to a heavy personal workload with his thriving construction business. All were unanimously elected. Tina Kusion, another of the old group and another sister-in-law of Marion Mottola, like my Aunt Marie, was appointed to supervise the checkers. Danny, who was a friend and elementary school classmate when I first lived in Tuxedo Park, and my uncle Jim Barth would review applications and hire the lifeguards. Dues would remain the same and improvements were to be made to the bath house facilities. Customary approval was again given for the Tuxedo Hospital annual picnic. Additional planting was suggested for the entrance to the club, and the issue of appointing a manager to oversee day-to-day beach operations was discussed. The maintenance of the Wee Wah was now a full-time job. Long gone were the weekdays when Buddy McCarroll would come down to the beach after finishing his job at Union Carbide in Sterling Forest, hit a few golf balls into the lake, hop on the riding mower to cut the grass, and finish up with a swim in the cool water. Jasper Mottola was asked if he would serve as beach manager for the upcoming season, but he declined; Carmine Mottola, on the other hand, accepted the position, thus keeping the job in the family for yet another year. It wouldn't be the same Beach Club if a Mottola wasn't involved.

Another McGregor generation makes the leap at the Wee Wah Beach Club, ca. 1986

Despite Tom Salierno's attempts to step back, at the Annual meeting on April 22, 1986, Tom again answered the call to replace Dan Winfield as president. Dan and his family were moving out of Tuxedo. Bonny Takeuchi, a well-respected and active community resident in the Hamlet, was elected as vice president, and my Aunt Marie continued as treasurer. Although much younger than the others, like Honey Hall, Bonny was the daughter of original Tuxedo Community Club members and was brought up in a spirit of dedication and service. The Board of Health now required all lifeguards to have certified CPR training. My Uncle Jim would write the annual letter, and Bonny would be in charge of the lifeguards. The Executive Committee was comprised of Jim Barth, Tina Kusion, Nina Matthews,

Frank Damato (Bonny's father), Margaret Iannone, and Honey Hall, the youngest daughter of Marion Mottola. Dues were increased by $10, and guest passes increased as well. Melanie Forzano and Robin Salierno, Tom's daughter, would be the checkers for the 1986 season. The summer slipped by uneventfully, and everyone enjoyed the beach. The recreation and swimming programs operated as expected. The laughter and splashing of the children down at the beachfront and up in the play area could be heard over in the picnic area. Afternoons would find Marie McCarroll, Tina Kusion, Marion Mottola, Margaret Iannone, and others playing Scrabble at a picnic table, and they could be overheard recalling the days before the Beach Club was initially founded as the Tuxedo Community Club in 1936. Rose Damato was always there to keep an eye on the checkers to make sure guests were properly logged in and to help out her daughter Bonny, who was assuming more duties as vice president while raising her two very active young boys.

At this time, my wife Jean and I were also spending more of our summers in Tuxedo Park. We now had one young boy and were renting the one-bedroom cottage owned by Mabel and Joe Tansey down the street from my aunt and uncle. My father, my aunt Marie and uncle Buddy, my uncle Jim Barth, and Jean and I met nightly for dinner to discuss the topics of the day, followed by games like Scrabble, Rummikub, and the like. The ability to now see my son learning to swim with his grandfather and spend his days at the beach brought back so many wonderful memories. Indeed, 1986 was a good summer for my family and for the Wee Wah Beach Club.

All in all, 1986 was also a special year for those who lived in Tuxedo. One hundred years ago, Pierre Lorillard IV's vision for a unique respite from the daily business and social life of city living was realized. He had created a different kind of "private club" from those in New York City. This was not a club contained in one building where one could meet and services would be provided inside its exclusive walls. The upper-class society did not have to close up their mansions in the city and move to Newport for the summer season. "Tuxedo," was to be a new experience to enjoy nature, take part in sports, relax, and live secluded from the clamor of life across the Hudson River within a short train or one day coach ride from their home in the city.

I have tried to explore the social changes that have taken place in our country through the microcosm of Tuxedo and Tuxedo Park. During these 100 years, the gates provided the separation between classes. On occasion, allowance was made to include the community outside the gates. That was the Fourth of July celebration at the Tuxedo Club, where all from outside the gates were allowed in to view the parade celebrating the country's independence. That parade ended many years ago.

There is one tradition that continues to exist. At the conclusion of World War I, the entire community came together to pay tribute to those who served with a Memorial Day parade. This parade was held outside the gates and honored all who served whether they be from the Park or the Hamlet. I remember it as a solemn event as a child and, in many ways, although it reminds us all of our common bonds with a parade, I am always moved by the sacrifices made on behalf of our country. Every year, the parade would proceed up State Road 17 from the high school to the entrance to Tuxedo Park. It mattered not that before the Thruway, Route 17 was a major highway. The sides of the road were filled with people from the town and the Park. When the parade was about to start, traffic on Route 17 going north was stopped when entering Tuxedo, as was traffic heading south into Tuxedo. At the entrance to Tuxedo Park, a memorial with the names of those who died in service to our country was created and a wreath was placed at this small triangle of land, now sacred ground.

At the conclusion of this memorial ceremony, led by veterans, the fire truck, ambulances, and floats would leave, but the marchers (military veterans; police officers; volunteer firemen and ambulance corps; Boy Scouts, Girl Scouts, Cub Scouts, and Brownies; community leaders; among others—together with all who had watched the parade) continued through the gates into Tuxedo Park to the lawn in front of St Mary's Episcopal Church. Another ceremony would begin, led by the pastor, followed by the singing of patriotic songs and then a featured speaker. Next, awards were handed out to school children, acknowledging their outstanding essays reflecting on our country. The ceremony would close with the sound of taps and a gun salute from the cemetery behind the church. People would then return to their homes in Tuxedo Park or back through the gates to their homes in the Hamlet.

While the Memorial Day and the old Fourth of July traditions suggest a somewhat blended community as late as the 100-year anniversary of Lorillard's success, the division of society remained. The *New York Times* reported on the anniversary in an article on May 17, 1986 by Elizabeth Kolbert, "The Talk Of Tuxedo Park; A Retreat Marks 100 Discreetly." In the article, many are quoted as to the division between the Park and the Hamlet. Here we are, one hundred years later, and she quotes John McCarthy, the supervisor of the Town of Tuxedo at the time. He remarked, "You have to understand the attitude of a Parkie. … The old serfdom still exists. … A sociologist would be in seventh heaven here," he said.[84]

Chapter 29: Bonny Takeuchi Continues the Wee Wah Beach Club Tradition

Bonny Damato Takeuchi, who assumed the presidency of the Wee Wah
Beach Club in 1987

As much as Tom Salierno wanted to keep the momentum going, he felt it was time to step down due to the pressures of his business, and he recognized that it was time for new and younger leadership. At the Annual Meeting, held at George F. Baker High

School on April 20, 1987, Hamlet resident Bonny Takeuchi was elected president of the Wee Wah Beach Club. One of the younger members, Bonny was very active in the Town of Tuxedo and well-respected as someone who could get things done. New officers Anne Clark and Tish Catenaro were elected. Continuity and the Beach Club history were maintained with the reelection of my Aunt Marie as treasurer. Executive Committee members included Tom and Terry Salierno, Tina Kusion, Margaret and Bill Iannone, Jim Barth, Frank Damato, Madeline Dowling, and Honey Hall. This represented an impressive mix of established and new leaders.

The successful continuation of the Wee Wah Beach Club over the next decade and into the twenty-first century is the result of persistent voluntary efforts by many who remained grounded in the history of the Beach Club. However, one person in particular stands out in keeping the community organization alive. When Bonny agreed to take over as president, she felt a personal obligation to keep the Beach Club active and relevant. Her family lived in the Hamlet, and their family history goes back well before the formation of the original Tuxedo Community Club. Bonny's mother was a Mottola. Her grandfather, Cono Damato, had immigrated from Italy to Tuxedo to be part of Pierre Lorillard's grand plan and worked as a stone mason building walls inside Tuxedo Park. Her father, Frank, born in 1905, had grown up with the first generation of children who benefitted from life in Tuxedo and the accompanying opportunities provided by the bankers and businessmen who lived in the Park. He went to school through the eighth grade, and later, thanks to introductions from Park residents connected to the railroads, he worked as a railway clerk for over forty-seven years with the Erie Railroad at one of its main stations in Rutherford, New Jersey.

Frank married Florence Mottola, the daughter of John Mottola, one of seven Mottola siblings and cousins who settled in Tuxedo in the early 1900s. Frank and Florence would have three children. Bonny, the youngest, was born in 1951. Together with her older siblings, Frances and John, they grew up in the summer at the beach under the watchful eyes of Florence and Frank. Bonny's father and uncle shared a two-family house in the Hamlet just down the street from the high school. The house was initially rented from the Tuxedo Park Association, as was all property in the Hamlet in the early years. The Damato family purchased the house when the TPA divested some of its interest in Hamlet properties in the late 1940s. Throughout this period until 2002, when Bonny's mother passed away, Florence was a daily presence at the beach, helping her daughter and making sure the rules and regulations were being followed. Florence was a teenager when the Beach Club was formed. As a Mottola, a family renowned for high school sports prowess, Florence played on the Tuxedo school basketball team that set a record of 115 games without a defeat. When Bonny was busy at work or caring for her two children, it was Florence who made sure that the checkers were accurately logging in members and guests, that the beach was clean, and that the lifeguards (which eventually included her grandchildren) were fulfilling their important responsibilities.

The Damato family was from the Hamlet, but the family enjoyed a solid middle-class existence and the opportunities that came with it. After high school, Bonny went on to graduate from the College of New Rochelle and received her master's degree in education from Columbia University. Starting out in New York City, Bonny taught for five years before returning to Tuxedo, where she became active in the Hamlet's activities. As her mother before her, Bonny grew up at the beach in the summers and followed in her brother and sister's footsteps as a checker and lifeguard over the years. One of the youngest members of the board of the Wee Wah Beach Club, Bonny was always willing to take on responsibilities for its operation. She was also active, first as a counselor, then as the head of recreation for the Town of Tuxedo, which was tied to the summer recreation activities that had been started by Mabel Tansey at the Beach Club.

Bonny and her husband, Kunio Takeuchi, raised two boys, Matthew and Michael, in the Hamlet. She and Kunio continue to live in the house to this day. As was custom for many lifelong members, when Matthew and Michael were teenagers, they worked summers as recreation counselors and lifeguards. Each of my three sons did the same.

With the torch passed from Tom Salierno to Bonny, the president's role became much more active and demanding. American social life was changing dramatically. Air conditioning in homes was now common, followed by the ubiquity of cable television, personal computers, and by the late 1990s, the internet, all of which were increasingly capturing young people's time and interests. The economy had long created a need for both parents to work, and women were embracing their own identities. They were seeking college educations and pushing for equal recognition in the workplace. It became increasingly challenging for women to balance family time. The days of a young mother packing a picnic basket and taking her children to the beach became a rarity rather than the norm. Children's pleas of "It's too hot outside; why can't we stay in the house where it's cool and play on the computer?" grew as time passed. America was now firmly entrenched in the technology age and there was no turning back; sadly, elaborate holiday picnics and impromptu family dinners at the beach had become the exception rather than the rule.

In the 1990s, yet another factor was affecting membership. Each year, fewer descendants of the "original families" from the Hamlet and Tuxedo Park residents who were not members of the Tuxedo Club joined the Wee Wah Beach Club. This occurred even though the assumption and practice had been that the right to join the Wee Wah Beach Club transferred with the property in the Hamlet within the original geographic boundary (established in 1936) when a house was sold. Many of these new owners had no familial relationship to the development of Tuxedo Park from 1886 to the 1940s. Many original members of the Beach Club were now elderly grandparents or had passed away. Many who had grown up with memories of the beach as children had departed Tuxedo as well. The ability to relocate and find better jobs elsewhere was commonplace. By the 1980s, many families had begun budgeting for summer vacations rather than remain in the Hamlet to enjoy the Beach Club. Typically, they vacationed for one or two weeks at the Jersey shore as better highways, transportation, and affordable summer rental housing at the ocean became available. Other than family reunions on July Fourth, membership and use of the Wee Wah Beach Club was in decline. New members did not have the same sense of the Beach Club's origins, and those living in the Hamlet lacked a family connection to the history of Lorillard's Tuxedo Park. The original concept that membership for those outside the gates was a privilege bestowed by the founders of the Park had slipped away. New residents believed buying a Hamlet home at this time entitled them to purchase membership in the Wee Wah Beach Club, and during this time, they were correct. This shift from privilege to entitlement was not lost on the residents and taxpayers of the Village of Tuxedo Park.

As early as 1993, issues with leaks in the dam at the North end were an excuse used by the Village trustees for low water levels as the beach seasons started. This resulted in the Beach Club no longer being able to use the diving board on the dock. The "baby pool" was now a section of sand with no water. Although membership records indicated more than 200 members, the low water levels and a change in the town Recreation program to go elsewhere for swimming made the Beach Club less desirable. In addition, there were no funds coming from Recreation's use of the Beach Club, as it was now using a pool at St. Mary's Villa outside the Town of Tuxedo and would not return until 1999.

In 1997, after serving over forty-five years, my aunt Marie stepped down as treasurer but remained on the Executive Committee. In the fall, the Village lowered the lake significantly to make repairs to the dam. The Beach Club continued to survive despite other issues dealing with the operation of running a swimming facility. Over the next few years, the Health Department cited the Beach Club for lifeguard inattention. It appears an inspector stopped by one day when the lifeguard on duty was sitting on a bench a few yards behind his chair. He was still facing the water and talking with the checker. The citation failed to mention that the beach was basically empty at the time, and the only bather in the water was an adult. In 1999, the Beach Club was fined $500 for not paying disability premiums for employees going back to 1985. Apparently, no one knew there was a requirement to do so. After appealing, the fine was reduced to $200. As with decades before, there was always a money crunch, but now matters were becoming more complicated. In fact, the members could no longer run their 50/50 raffles due to state compliance requirements.

The lake as well as the land were now owned by the Village. In 1936, the Beach Club had to provide its membership list to the TPA, and since 1952, the Beach Club needed to apply to the Village for a lease of the property and provide a list of the membership for approval by the Board of Trustees. The TPA had long since sold the property to the Incorporated Village. Conflicts and concerns relating to the use of the land and membership, as well as the lease terms, continued every year with the Board of Trustees of the Incorporated Village. Most years, to Bonny's credit, community involvement, and with thanks to the mayor at the time and a majority of the Village's elected trustees, the conflicts were resolved. Throughout most of this period from the late 1980s and throughout the 1990s, Bonny and the Executive Committee maintained a good relationship with the Village's mayors, including Mayor Susan Goodfellow in 1989, and were given a lease from the Village of Tuxedo Park for three years at $10 per year, given the ongoing, often unacceptable fluctuations in the Wee Wah's water level.

Susan and Jim Goodfellow were residents of the Park and members of the Tuxedo Club, as well as members of the Wee Wah Beach Club. After moving to Tuxedo Park in 1979, they took a strong interest in the community. They led major efforts and donated substantial funds to restore the Tuxedo Library (the Tuxedo History Room is named after them), and they led a campaign to restore the Tuxedo train station back to its original design. Both buildings were wonderful examples of historic restoration and benefited the entire Town of Tuxedo. As members of the Beach Club, the Goodfellows easily mixed with all residents of the Tuxedo community.

Readers of the *New York Times* would no longer see daily references to the comings and goings of high society in Tuxedo Park that occurred weekly if not daily from 1886 through the 1930s with pictures of those in attendance at horse shows, dog shows, and balls at the Tuxedo Club. The paper also reported on sporting activities and the ever-interesting gossip columns. In 1924 the *New York Herald Tribune* was established and competed for the morning news market with the *New York Times*. The weekend edition would print an entire section with a page of pictures of the "goings on" in society at Tuxedo Park and other locations frequented by the social set. Beginning in the 1950s, the *New York Times* exhibited a renewed interest in the community with in-depth feature stories every few years that explored living in Tuxedo Park. The articles always began with an attention-grabbing headline. While this one appeared some forty years later, it's worth sharing: On August 11, 1991, the *New York Times* article on Tuxedo Park in the Real Estate section stated, "King Arthur's Camelot, Du Maurier's Manderley, Coleridge's Xanadu—Tuxedo Park in Orange County, N.Y., has one leg up on these lands of myth and romance: It exists."[85]

About half of the newer residents of the Park had applied for membership in the Wee Wah Beach Club. Many also had applied and been accepted as members of the Tuxedo Club. Most sent their children to the private Tuxedo Park School for their primary years. The children then moved on to northeast, old money boarding schools like Andover, Taft, or Choate. Residents who were not members of the

Tuxedo Club typically sent their children to the public school in the Hamlet. According to the aforementioned 1991 *New York Times* article, not much had changed as to the social distinction emphasized by those iron gates. "The relationship between Tuxedo Park and Tuxedo town is virtually nonexistent, except for a few overlapping services like the library and the fire department."

During this era, referenced in the article, a third of the Hamlet population was over sixty-five, and the vast majority of those were descendants of the immigrant and local workers who were hired to fulfill Lorillard's dream. The one connection that remained with the Park was opportunity to access Wee Wah Lake in the summer as members of the Wee Wah Beach Club.

Bonny continued to be a one-woman dynamo with respect to making sure the Wee Wah Beach Club continued to function with help from her Executive Committee. There was no question her heart, soul, and family ties resulted in her doing her best to make sure the Hamlet members would continue to enjoy access to this wonderful beach and park. Years passed quickly, and the tried-and-true formulas for successfully operating the Beach Club continued to work. Elections and annual meetings were held. Lifeguards and checkers were hired, and, of course, the big July Fourth gatherings continued as well. The *New York Times* continued its sporadic reporting on Tuxedo Park in its Real Estate section on Sundays. In April of 2020, the newspaper would once again give extensive front page coverage to Tuxedo Park in an article by Elizabeth Bumiller, who referred to it as "this Bavarian forest-like retreat built for the Astors, the Pells and their friends who made America's great 19th-century mercantile fortunes." She quoted a resident stating: "Living here is like turning back the clock for all the right reasons."[86]

Bonny's efforts looked hopeful, with a new Mayor of Tuxedo Park, Cornelius J. "Neal" Madera Jr. He was starting his second two-year term after a break from the two-year position he had held in the past. He was an attorney and the Senior Vice President and General Counsel of a major food chain, Shoprite Supermarkets in New York. He was also developer of Woodbury Commons, a large, premium outlet mall located just north of Tuxedo. Madera hoped to work with the Town of Tuxedo to improve communications for the betterment of both communities. On July 11, 1999, Middletown's *Times Herald-Record* quoted Town of Tuxedo Supervisor, Ken Magar's observation that Mayor Madera "[is] a great person to have in the Village. We have had an excellent relationship with the Village when Neal has been there in the past."[87]

Chapter 30: The New Millennium

Wee Wah Beach Club, ca. 2000

By 2000, zoning had been increased to a minimum of four acres for undeveloped residential parcels, and an architectural review board and zoning code required strict compliance to maintain the integrity of Lorillard's vision for the enclave ensconced behind the imposing iron gates. The Village of Tuxedo Park contains no condominiums and no commercial properties. The only properties that are not private residences are the members-only Tuxedo Club and the private Tuxedo Park School.

In 2000, there were just 330 homes in Tuxedo Park, with a population of approximately 700 to 800 residents. While a third of the homes served as weekend getaways or vacation homes for those who lived in the New York City area, some two-thirds of the properties were occupied by full-time residents. Within the gates, the idyllic landscape and quiet lifestyle still reflected the early years where one could escape the mass population growth in "the" City as well as New Jersey, and Connecticut towns within a reasonable commuting distance. There were no leash laws for dogs. Gas-powered boats were not allowed on any of the lakes. There were no house numbers. If you were visiting a resident, you were stopped at the gate to confirm what resident you were there to see. If a resident did not want visitors admitted unless announced, they could inform the gate which maintained a list requesting the resident be notified before admittance. As a guest, either you knew how to reach the house, or the guard could provide you with a map at the gatehouse. A *New York Times* article in June of 2000 quoted a resident who said living in Tuxedo Park recalled life in the Lakes District in England; another resident likened it to "Lake Garda in northern Italy."[88]

Each year, Bonny appeared before the Village to request a continuation of the lease for the Beach Club, and each year there would be serious discussion about whether continuation would be granted. While the Village's disinterest was undoubtedly driven by social factors, the trustees often overemphasized external factors that would restrict swimming in the Wee Wah, which would, in effect, serve to shutter the Beach Club. As an example, in 2009 and 2010, the appearance of algae resulted in "no swimming" orders until Bonny could resolve the problem by getting the appropriate New York State department to investigate and clear the lake for swimming. The algae which did not appear in the Wee Wah Beach area was not harmful to health and safety. Addressing the solution never seemed to be a priority for the Village trustees. Throughout it all, Bonny was

committed to preserving the Wee Wah Beach Club, and she was
unanimously elected annually.

Bonny and the Beach Club's Executive Committee had looked
forward to the new millennium with expectations for a pause in the
constant tensions between the Beach club and The Village of Tuxedo
Park. Specifically, they hoped that somehow the new millennium
would put an end to the enduring social distinctions between many of
the residents of the Park and residents of the Hamlet. Early in the
2000s, leaks in the north dam of Wee Wah Lake caused low water
levels. The Village trustees spoke at length about a total repair versus
short-term fixes. Replacing the dam represented a major capital
expenditure, so each year the issue of taxes led to a patchwork of
repairs rather than a full and proper replacement of the dam.
Consequently, low water levels remained an issue for the Beach Club.

Despite these problematic issues with the water level, a
working relationship had developed. New residents of the Village of
Tuxedo Park were less concerned than their predecessors about the use
of the Wee Wah by residents from the Hamlet. After all, for the entire
community to grow and survive, everyone in the Tuxedo community
had to work together. The boards of the school, the library, and the
Tuxedo Historical Society, to name a few, were integrated with Park
and Hamlet residents. So too, the Ambulance Corps and the Fire
Department, now serving the entire Town of Tuxedo and Village of
Tuxedo Park, going back to the days of their founding, had always
been filled with volunteers from both Tuxedo Park and the Hamlet.

In 2000, a local newsletter reported that the Wee Wah Beach
Club was preparing for its sixty-fourth summer season. Susan

Goodfellow, now serving as mayor, and the trustees of the Village had authorized expenditures totaling $5,395 for capital improvements to the Beach Club. This would cover the purchase of ten charcoal grills, three new picnic tables, $1,000 worth of playground equipment, and the renovation of the women's bathroom, including accessibility for the disabled. There were now 100 members from the Hamlet, and 160 members who were voting residents from the Village of Tuxedo Park, some of whom were also members of the Tuxedo Club. Once again, there was talk in the Town of Tuxedo of a plan for a swimming pool outside the gates to service all members of the town, including members from the northern and southern areas who were not permitted to join the Beach Club based on the historical limitation to those who resided in the Hamlet.[89]

However, the election of a new Village mayor, Cornelius Madera in 2001 (he had previously served from 1995 to 1997) appeared to renew the membership qualification issue. The trustees advised Bonny that the Village of Tuxedo Park was no longer willing to fund any capital improvements for the Beach Club. In addition, although historically the Town of Tuxedo would pay the Beach Club for use of the facilities for the summer recreation program, Mayor Madera informed Bonny in 2002 that those payments should now be made directly to the Village. So much for the mayor's talk of improving relations with the Town of Tuxedo, as reported earlier when he took office in the past.

Through her perseverance, Bonny fended off what were now annual attempts by Village trustees to withhold leasing the property to the Wee Wah Beach Club, either outright or by acquiescing to terms the Beach Club could not afford without strict budgeting and without increasing dues to unsustainable levels. Her determination was steeped in family tradition, and she was resolved to preserve the Beach Club so that it could provide summer facilities to the Hamlet where many families had limited funds to budget for recreation. Under Bonny's leadership, the Beach Club continued its tradition of building a stronger community through inclusion. The membership remained over 200, and a beach fund was created to maintain and improve the beach through contributions by members—in addition to memberships. In 2003, over $775 was raised by approximately 50 members.

In 2003, C. Kent Kroeber was elected Mayor of the Village of Tuxedo Park. In 2003 and 2004, pressure was once again aimed at the Beach Club. The Village directed that the beach area be open as an overflow area for those who entered the Village to view fireworks at the Tuxedo Club. July Fourth had been a longstanding tradition when the gates of Tuxedo Park were open to all in the Hamlet to view the fireworks. Village Trustee David Dupont advised Bonny that the Village would be taking more control. He announced that the Village would appoint four of the officers and run the Beach Club as a Village asset. Elections of the Executive Committee now required that there be seven members from the Park and seven from the Hamlet, with the fifteenth member to be the one with the highest vote total who is left. This was quickly changed in 2005 by Mayor Kroeber, who advised there should be only three members from the Park, three members from the Village, and one additional member who would be a Village of Tuxedo Park trustee. As a result of the changes, a demand was made that the Beach Club rewrite its constitution and bylaws. After over fifty years of serving on the Executive Committee, my aunt Marie, now 83 years of age, had enough and resigned. The leaks in the dam had worsened over the summer. The Village stated repairs would be made in the fall of 2006, but nothing had occurred by the 2007 season. Rent was now $5,000 per season with a promise the Village would provide $5,000 for improvements.

From Tuxedo Park's inception in 1886, and through the 1950s, happenings in Tuxedo Park had often been reported in New York's major newspapers, with some stories picked up across the country. Historically Tuxedo Park residents famously shunned publicity. Privacy was an important selling point for residents who called this remote, exclusive gated enclave home. Tuxedo Park did have a remarkable history when one focused on the changing social fabric of our country, which led to articles in major magazines from time to time. In 2002, Simon & Shuster published *Tuxedo Park, A Wall Street Tycoon and the Secret Palace of Science That Changed the Course of World War II* by Jennet Conant.[90] The book focused on Alfred Lee Loomis, an accomplished financier with a passion for scientific research, who lived in Tuxedo Park. The book reached the top ten on the *New York Times* Best Seller list for nonfiction that year. Suddenly there was renewed interest in Tuxedo Park. In August, Ms. Conant again focused on Tuxedo Park, writing an article for the *New York Times* entitled "Tuxedo Park Opens Its Gates, Just a Bit."[91]

Bonny knew that each spring she would have to deal with the Village mayor and trustees in order to lease the beach area of Pigeon Point for the Beach Club. Each spring brought new issues and rumors that had to be dealt with for the Beach Club to prepare for the summer season. Despite tension and rising interest and prices for living in Tuxedo Park, visually, the Beach Club had not changed much over the decades. It was basic, but the beach, sand play area for the children, and picnic areas were jewels. One new resident of the Park responded to a *New York Times* reporter by observing how Tuxedo Park, where ornate mansions on large lots balance atop tall cliffs, reminded him of the most gorgeous resorts in Europe, despite being located fewer than forty miles from midtown Manhattan.[92]

In April 2005, the issue of the Beach Club's existence once again created tension in Tuxedo between the Village and the Hamlet. Mayor Kroeber announced that the Wee Wah Beach Club lease was up for renewal and requested comments from Village residents. A majority of the respondents, many of whom were not members of the Beach Club nor the Tuxedo Club, expressed a desire to renew the lease. However, some respondents felt strongly that residents who lived in the Hamlet, and therefore did not pay taxes in the Park, should not have access to Wee Wah Beach; rather, they believed the beach and the surrounding area should be restricted to Village residents only. An article, "Rift Over Wee Wah," in the *Middletown Times Herald-Record*, published on April 15, 2005, reported comments such as, "Kick out the townies. Disband the Beach Club." Many felt the issue did not deserve such attention and ultimately Mayor Kroeber said, "Under my watch, the village will not be taking over the Beach Club, and it will not be making it exclusive to villagers."[93]

Tom Salierno, Marie McCarroll, Marion Mottola, and James Barth observe

"Marie McCarroll Day," at the Wee Wah on July 4, 2005

In 2005, Bonny's hard work resulted in a new three-year lease for the Beach Club, but issues with the dam and a potential threat from an invasive species of weed called Eurasian water milfoil did not make for carefree summers. The underlying issues of Village control and limiting access to Village residents "only" was never far from the surface. July 4, 2005 was a special day as the Wee Wah Beach Club celebrated my Aunt Marie's association with the Beach Club. My aunt, Marie McGregor McCarroll, was honored by the Beach Club members, and by her family as well as friends, for her continued service for well over fifty years. She continued as the matriarch of the July Fourth family celebration of the McCarroll, McGregor, Billy, Wagner and Trehy families that had been gathering from all over the country for over sixty-five years until her passing in July 2019 at the

371

age of ninety-six. She was the oldest living resident of Tuxedo Park at that time. This combination of families was the result of when Marie and her girlfriends grew up in Tuxedo Park. You could always expect families and friends of the families and children of Alice Boutry Billy, Peggy Dodge Wagner, and her sister Winnifred Dodge Trehy to show up. Alice and Marie worked and shared an apartment in New York City during the mid-1940s. The traditional gathering continued with the children, grandchildren, and great-grandchildren and friends every year.

In June 2005, Mayor David McFadden succeeded Mayor Kroeber but faced a contentious run for reelection in 2007 for a second term, ultimately losing to Houston Stebbins. The election centered on several issues, including ownership of Village and Town property by Tuxedo Park Associates, which was a partnership of approximately ninety members, mostly descendants of former residents. The partnership was formed by several Tuxedo Park residents who had purchased the assets from the Lorillard family in 1925.

In January 2008, Mayor Stebbins addressed the coming summer season by indicating his concern that leaks in the dam had to be addressed and that water-quality studies be undertaken before the Wee Wah Beach Club could open. There was the possibility that the lake would need to be drained to repair the dam. Once again, the age-old issue of membership by those in the Hamlet outside the gates was on the table as the former mayor, David McFadden, led opposition to renewing the Beach Club's lease and called for the Village to take total control over the property leased to the Beach Club.

When the new lease came up at the meeting of trustees before a packed audience, Mayor Stebbins asked for proposals to change the relationship between the Beach Club and the Village. It was a tense meeting, as the underlying concern of social differences remained at issue. Management, access, and tax issues for residents of the Village, along with resident privacy and security, were all among the expressed concerns. There were strong proponents from a number of Village residents to take control over the Beach Club and disenfranchise Hamlet members which would effectively end the Wee Wah Beach Club. Middletown's *Times Herald-Record* reported, "For 70 years, the summertime Beach Club has arguably been the tightest bond between the Village and the town. Membership is open to Tuxedo Park residents and residents who live near it [outside the gates] in an area known as the Hamlet. There are 139 Tuxedo Park memberships, including families, and 118 from the Hamlet. The club has long been managed by the Wee Wah Beach Club, a committee of village and Hamlet residents who pay a nominal [voluntary] fee to operate it."[94]

Mayor Stebbins, while not in favor of excluding the Hamlet resident members, was interested in increasing the rent up to $4000 a year for the June through Labor Day lease. Trustee Charlotte Worthy opposed the takeover. The article reported that Trustee Worthy said she didn't want to promote the stereotype of the elitist Tuxedo Park snob. "I am a member of the [Tuxedo] Club who welcomes a visit and chat with a Hamlet resident." Bonny addressed the trustees and the audience, reminding all of the Beach Club's importance. "It's treasured by people in the community," she said. "There are two institutions people in the Hamlet feel strongly about: the Beach Club and the school."[95]

The Beach Club received its lease, but rising expenses and

nagging issues with the dam presented problems over the next four years. As a result of continual low water levels in the Wee Wah, the diving board was removed from the dock area for good in 2012, and the baby pool, which now consisted of nothing but dry sand, was closed. Revenue-producing recreation was gone. Seesaws and swings, originally donated by the son of the Amory family, earlier mentioned as longtime members of the Tuxedo Club and the owners of one of the great estates, Renamor, were removed due to liability concerns.

As the swimming season approached in 2012, the Village trustees, along with another new mayor, Tom Wilson, closed the Wee Wah for swimming due to a mulch pile operation in the Sterling Forest area west of the Village of Tuxedo Park. The operation was releasing effluent into the forest ponds outside the Park boundaries that fed the streams that emptied into the Park lakes. Apparently, it did not affect the community's drinking water in Tuxedo Lake. However, the discussion went on as to whether this would cause a bathing risk in the Wee Wah. While the details are vague, indeed the beach was closed for swimming and the Mayor and trustees had a chain-link fence installed across the waterfront. There was no factual basis for the Village's decision other than stating that the closing was due to an abundance of caution.

Chain-link fence across the beach installed by the Village of Tuxedo Park,
June 2012

A beach without access to the water is not a beach. With the approach of the annual July Fourth picnic, Bonny decided to determine if the water was safe for swimming. The July Fourth picnic was a tradition from the founding of the Beach Club, and it was now in jeopardy. If the Village wanted to end the Beach Club, this would certainly send a powerful visual message. Bonny brought in water experts from the state and received reports that there was no health hazard associated with swimming. She then had to schedule state inspectors to come down and approve the roping of the waterfront area and compliance with other state requirements. Despite approvals from the state as to the water quality, the trustees refused to lift the swimming ban.

On the day prior to the annual planned picnic, July 3, Bonny called out for volunteers as she had received a guarantee from the state inspector that he would come to Tuxedo Park the day before the Fourth of July holiday to approve swimming if everything was in order. The volunteers, including the author, showed up and set the ropes to the inspector's satisfaction. Together with the water experts' reports and the state approval in hand, Bonny convinced the mayor to remove the "no swimming" order on July 3. The Village DPW removed the fence, and the Fourth of July picnic once again became a wonderful day of celebration at the Wee Wah Beach Club. But the diving board was gone, and there was not much room for the little ones to swim due to the low level of water in the lake. The shoreline for the water was very close to a drop off from the shallow area. The raft was in place. Happy little faces, splashing water, and boisterous laughter were welcome sounds once more. Thanks to Bonny's tireless efforts and last-minute success, a Wee Wah Beach Club tradition continued. Families, extended families, and old friends gathered for their holiday picnic, family histories were retold (no doubt the stories changed a little each time), and new memories were made. While the tension between the Village trustees and the board of the Wee Wah Beach Club was palpable, all was forgotten, at least for a while, as the picnic and the July Fourth tradition had continued.

For Bonny, being president presented ever-increasing time-consuming duties. State and community regulations required meetings with agencies and inspectors, complicated paperwork, and the allocation of the money necessary to comply. As an example of how times had changed, when the lake was full in the earlier years, one lifeguard had been deemed adequate to cover the entire waterfront, the raft, and the diving board. But now the diving board was a memory, the water level was low, and yet the state now required three lifeguards: one on the waterfront, one on the dock, and one on the raft.

The area defined by the square footage and depth of the water enclosed by ropes was now used to determine the maximum number of bathers allowed in the swimming area. A small, fenced baby pool with a depth of one to two feet required a lifeguard—even though no babies were allowed in without an accompanying adult. Of course, after 2012, there was no baby pool and no diving board so expenses for lifeguards could be reduced. However, the state still required two lifeguards when the number of bathers reached a certain threshold that occurred on weekends and July Fourth.

Matters regarding employees and insurance, compliance issues, the hiring of lifeguards and checkers, and oversight of beach maintenance were all left to Bonny. Despite the increased responsibilities, Bonny saw to it that the beach opened for the summer seasons. When the beach entered the twenty-first century, the facilities had needed much improvement. Bonny always attempted to moderate membership dues so as to keep the Beach Club affordable for Hamlet residents. Improvements were made with gifts, and with the sweat and labor of volunteer members. Over the years, the Beach Club received playground equipment and a new large play set as gifts, and Tom Salierno volunteered to build numerous new rafts and picnic tabletops over the years.

When the Wee Wah Beach Club entered this new millennium, the conflicts with Tuxedo Club members (who were also Village of Tuxedo Park residents) were disappearing. The Tuxedo Club itself had changed dramatically and was now accepting new members who had no relationship to Tuxedo Park. The Tuxedo Club was facing a problem that many historic, very exclusive private clubs were facing at this time. In the latter part of the twentieth century, the restrictive nature of these clubs had resulted in smaller memberships that found it fiscally difficult to keep the clubs solvent. It was not so grand to be a club member while watching water leak through the ceilings of dining rooms, and with food service becoming mediocre at best, as the excessive costs to maintain the properties was now spread among fewer members, resulting in increased annual membership fees. In addition, many members had long claimed their dues as business expenses on their income taxes, but the IRS no longer granted these deductions. Up and down the East Coast and across the country, decisions were made to expand memberships, necessary for the very survival of these once ultra-exclusive clubs. The Tuxedo Club was no different. The reputation of the Tuxedo Club's golf course, designed by famed golf course architect Robert Trent Jones, attracted people who lived in New Jersey and elsewhere who wanted the prestigious Tuxedo Club membership that was steeped in the history of social privilege. In addition, many new Village residents had bought their properties as weekend homes, alluring getaways from New York City, but many of these residents did not join the Tuxedo Club.

Now well into the twenty-first century, Tuxedo Park was also more than one hundred years old. The Incorporated Village itself was more than fifty years old and new Village residents, whether or not they were Tuxedo Club members, were suitably concerned with taxes as well as the security, privacy, and panache they sought when buying in the Village of Tuxedo Park. The Village mayors and trustees were elected to two-year terms. Elected officials were focused on budgets, roads, the water and sewer system (also over one hundred years old), and the usual problems of operating a modern municipality.

In the Hamlet, few of the residents now had roots to Tuxedo Park's creation. One constant question on the minds of Village trustees about access for those who lived in the Hamlet, and of course Bonny, regarded the fragile future of the Wee Wah Beach Club on Pigeon Point. Each year, Bonny was reelected as president, but despite her indefatigable efforts and keen leadership style, time had taken its toll on the dam at the north end. As a result, there was little water for a bathing beach, and how can a Beach Club survive without water alongside its beach? Membership in the Beach Club declined. Meanwhile, the Village trustees approved continual "fixes," but kept on delaying the replacement of the north dam. However, there was no intent to allow more water into the Wee Wah for summer months as had been done in the past by temporarily plugging leaks at the northern end of the Wee Wah and allowing water flowing from the Tuxedo Lake through Pond 3 at the south end dam to be released.

Chapter 31: Some Notable Wee Wah Beach Club Members

Actors Richard Kiley and Robert Duvall and composer and conductor Howard Shore

Tuxedo and Tuxedo Park history is a microcosm that parallels changes that have occurred in the social history of our country. The Hamlet and the Park are defined by, and divided by, a magnificent, gated entrance. And so much has changed! In the early days of Tuxedo Park, at the turn of the twentieth century in the so-called Gilded Age, actors and others involved in entertainment were not "acceptable" for membership in the Tuxedo Club and, as a result, they were not welcome within the gates. And while wealth was an obvious barrier to entry, one need not apply without "old wealth" among other attributes, and one's status was subject to change regardless of finances. In the early days, if one was a Tuxedo Club member in good standing but then married a person from the theatrical world, to mention one example, it would present problems. James Brown Potter and Cora Urquhart were one of those couples.

Cora Urquhart married James Brown Potter of New York City in 1877 and became a favorite of society dinner parties for her drawing room recitations. Potter was a coffee broker, a partner in Brown Bros. & Company, and one of the first to join Pierre Lorillard's new recreational Tuxedo Club. Cora went on to appear in amateur performances in the Madison Square Theater, and her rendering of the poem, "Ostler Joe," in a society gathering in Washington, D.C. brought upon her a storm of criticism as the poem described a woman who left her husband and baby for another man. The poem was thought to be not proper for such an audience and the newspaper reporting made her known throughout the United States.[96]

"In 1887, Cora left her husband and her children who disapproved of her decision to enter acting. She went to London where she started her professional acting career and was no less social and popular than she was in New York. She ran with a crowd that included the Prince of Wales, and she later dedicated a book, *My Recitations*, to her friend Robert Browning."[97]

Her husband was one of the original members of the Tuxedo Club. Although she was accepted in the city, her time in Tuxedo caused a stir. Anyone who would consider socializing with them or joining them at the Tuxedo Club would be discouraged from doing so. Associating with "that type of person" risked being ostracized and becoming the subject of conversations regarding questionable morals and conduct. James Brown Potter subsequently divorced Cora in 1903.[98]

Almost one hundred years later, the Tuxedo Club expanded its membership to accept many who were not residents in Tuxedo Park and opened its doors to prospective members by invitation without concern for race, color, or religion.

From its launch in 1936, the Beach Club obviously did not embrace the sort of exclusivity practiced by the Tuxedo Club. The only requirement for membership was residency within the geographical boundaries set by the TPA and later, the Incorporated Village. Starting in the early 1960s, many celebrities were finding Tuxedo Park to be a welcome retreat from the constant attention they received in the busy New York City scene. One of the first to take up residence was Richard Kiley, who purchased Kincraig, the former mansion of George Grant Mason. He also became a member of the Beach Club, where he could enjoy the benefits without harassment or interruption from other members. Everyone was open and friendly but offered personal privacy as well. Kiley was a presence on the Broadway stage in the 1950s and went on to win a Tony Award for Best Actor in a Musical in 1966 for *Man of La Mancha*. The show opened in November of 1965 and became a smash hit on Broadway, winning five Tony Awards. Kiley's singing and recording of the "The Impossible Dream" from the show also became a hit and has remained a classic. My aunt Marie's eldest daughter recalls going to the beach and finding the actor down by the water practicing his lines as Don Quixote and singing the tunes in preparation for the show.

Another Broadway and movie star, Robert Duvall, spent many years in Tuxedo Park and was a member of the Wee Wah Beach Club. He and my uncle Buddy became friends and Duvall fit in as just another member. One looking at membership lists in recent years would find other famous names such as Linda Johnson, better known as Whoopie Goldberg. Whoopie purchased one of the early homes on Tuxedo Lake. Due to her severe fear of flying, which Ms. Goldberg has reportedly overcome to some extent, she traveled across the United States and elsewhere (and perhaps still does) in a large purple bus. The bus was too large to navigate the roads in the Park, and thus it had to be parked by St. Mary's Church just inside the main gate whenever she was in residence. During Whoopie's tenure in Tuxedo Park, if you saw a huge purple bus parked by the church, you could be assured that Whoopie Goldberg was probably in town.

In the 1990s, Greg Anthony also became the owner of Kincraig, the former estate of George Grant Mason and later Richard Kiley. Anthony renovated the top floor that contained rooms for the staff into a gym and moved the kitchen to the main floor from the basement. As you would typically see in restored Gilded Age mansions, the kitchens were in the basement, and food would be delivered to a butler's pantry on the main floor and then served in the dining room. Anthony, who also joined the Wee Wah Beach Club, was a star player for the NBA's New York Knickerbockers from 1991 through 1995, and subsequently became a lead commentator for CBS Sports. It was not unusual during the summer months to see Anthony walking out of the Beach Club with a ball after shooting baskets at the court on the other side of the parking area. Although Anthony and his wife had been accepted as members of the Tuxedo Club, there were no basketball courts on the Tuxedo Club premises.

Another long-time member and supporter of the Beach Club was musical composer and conductor, Howard Shore. Shore's property reached down to the water of the Wee Wah Lake and included a boathouse he beautifully restored that looks out to the Beach Club further north on the point. During his illustrious career, Shore has won three Academy Awards for *The Lord of the Rings* trilogy, three *Golden*

Globe Awards, and four *Grammy Awards*, among dozens of other accolades. Best known for his film scores, Shore has composed scores for more than 80 movies, and served as the musical director for the TV series *Saturday Night Live* from 1975 to 1980.

These folks are but a few of the public noteworthy past members and guests of the Wee Wah Beach Club. Over the years, one could always be surprised at who might be "at the beach." I recall the weekday my wife and I came down to the beach to relax and cool off. The beach was empty but for two people sitting on the far bench talking and looking out over the water. My wife remarked that one of them appeared to be Academy Award-winning actress, Diane Keaton, to which I replied "No way. What would she be doing here?" Arriving back at the house, my Aunt Marie said, "You will never guess who was seen having lunch at the drugstore today." Needless to say, indeed it was Diane Keaton. I have learned not to doubt my wife.

In addition to some of the familiar names above, I would be remiss if I didn't mention the descendants of the original members and those who joined the Wee Wah Beach Club over the first fifty years. As these family members typically returned for the annual July Fourth family picnics, the picnic area and beach were filled each year with doctors, lawyers, engineers, Wall Street executives, teachers, and seemingly members of every profession, evidence of the how the promise of the American Dream was a reality. Observing the look of pride on the faces of the older generations—in a location that started in such humble conditions—was simply priceless!

Chapter 32: Nearing the End

The Annual July 4th picnic in 2019, alongside the empty Wee Wah

On April 3, 2017, Mary Jo Guinchard, Village Mayor at the time, stated in her monthly letter to residents and neighbors, "The Wee Wah dam rehabilitation project is shovel ready." However, for several years, due to complex governmental regulations, budget concerns, and inaction by the Village of Tuxedo Park, the lake remained lowered to the point that swimming was not possible. In 2018, the lake was drained, and major repairs and renovations were finally begun to create an entire new Wee Wah Lake dam. That summer, Wee Wah Beach Club membership plummeted. As a result, the Beach Club could not afford insurance for use of the beach facilities; consequently, the Village would not give approval for opening the Beach Club. None of this came as a surprise. A patch of sand beside an empty lake, once again, and a dam under construction, is not exactly a "beach club."

The Town of Tuxedo's Parks and Recreation department, which provided a revenue stream to offset club expenses, searched out other locations where the children could swim. Throughout this period, Bonny and her Executive Committee continued their efforts to keep the club alive. The beach's picnic grove, the athletic facilities, and the play area were still available, but the gate remained closed. The breeze and abundant shade near the lake, despite the absence of water, still beckoned when you wanted to escape the air-conditioning for some fresh air. Many of the old-time members continued their memberships with the hope that normal water levels would return to the lake. They were cautiously optimistic that the Village trustees, if asked, would agree to a reasonable lease for the Beach Club for whatever remained of the season upon completion of the repairs. There was also tradition to hold on to—specifically the July Fourth family picnic that dated back to the club's creation in 1936. During the period of construction to the dam that would take years to complete due to the numerous governmental agency approvals involved, the Village mayor and trustees allowed the Beach Club to continue with one or two-year leases for $1 annually, so long as the Beach Club complied with several provisions, most notably, insurance.

The future appeared bleak. There was a lease still in effect between the Village and the Beach Club. Bonny asked the Village trustees to allow the Wee Wah Beach Club to open for only one day, July Fourth, so that dues-paying members and their guests could enjoy their traditional family picnics, even though the lake remained empty. Of course, there would be no swimming or beachfront activities. She explained that the Beach Club had secured insurance for that day and that only the picnic area, basketball court, horseshoe pits, volleyball court, and children's play area would be used. However, Bonny also mentioned that the Beach Club could not afford insurance and staffing to open the Pigeon Point beach area for all town residents to view the July Fourth fireworks at the Tuxedo Club. This had become a tradition in recent years, as the location provided a great view of the fireworks after an afternoon and early evening of picnicking. In addition, there would be overflow crowds at the Tuxedo Club, with police directing people to the Beach Club area where they could enjoy the spectacular view. Expecting a quick response to Bonny's request, many residents of the Village who were members of the Beach Club were shocked at the extended debate by the Village trustees. In the end, four trustees voted to approve the one-day request and one voted to deny it. Although the request passed with only one "no" vote, the discussion indicated the future was not looking good. Many worried about the future of the Wee Wah Beach Club's existence. This vote posed ominous implications for the future once the new dam was completed and the lake was properly filled. After all, the present request was for one day only. How would they vote when entire swimming seasons were on the agenda?

January 2020 began with bitter cold weather. The Tuxedo Lake froze, a rare occurrence in recent history. In the early years of Tuxedo Park, a frozen lake was common, inviting ice skating, ice fishing, ice sailing, and curling on the lake in front of the Tuxedo Club. After work on the dam was finally complete, the Wee Wah was filled with water for the 2021 season. Bonny and those who had continued their memberships were excited for the upcoming summer months. She had a new Executive Committee, and all were working to encourage qualified residents to apply for membership, including those who had never joined previously. This was a new decade, and the Wee Wah Beach Club needed new members who were eager to carry on decades of tradition and build new memories.

However, a troubling sign arrived in late spring. Although the new dam was now complete, the water was approximately two feet lower than usual, making it too shallow to install the diving board at the end of the concrete dock. Reminiscent of the emotions felt by Mabel Tansey and other members in the early years, recent members who had continued their memberships were surprised and disheartened by a letter from the mayor to Bonny stating the Wee Wah Beach Club would be closed for swimming at least until August due to a toxic algae bloom and that foreign invader called Eurasian water milfoil, aka EWM. This weed grows in shallow areas until it reaches the surface and essentially strangles a lake. For the Wee Wah, the more serious problem was the possibility that the algae bloom could cause public health concerns. Environmental changes over the years have affected lakes in the Northeast, including the Village lakes. The trustees had previously formed a Lakes Committee to study the problem and had developed a plan to address it, but governments sometimes work slowly to implement plans that cost money. The letter came as a surprise, because these problems were well-known and predated the draining of the Wee Wah. Here it was three years since the algae bloom initially presented itself and nothing had been done to solve these issues. Bonny called a meeting of both Park and Hamlet Beach Club members to prepare a response to the mayor's letter. One of the main points was why the Village trustees needed to address this now.

For the past forty-plus years, the water had been tested continuously by the state to ensure it was safe for swimming. There had been instances of algae blooms in the past, when the state had required the Beach Club to close the waterfront for swimming, but then the beach would reopen once further testing indicated that the water was safe. If the state said it was safe, wasn't this sufficient? Once again, the state testing indicated the water was indeed safe for swimming, and yet swimming was banned. With one year left on the Beach Club's lease, meetings continued. The trustees ultimately relented, and the beach was opened for the season. So right on cue, on July 4, 2021, cars filled the parking lot inside and outside the entrance as well as down the road. One of the successful events held during the summer was the renewal of hosting the family campout and sleepover, comparable to those Mabel Tansey had started years ago for the children when Bonny was a child.

However, recent years had taken their toll on membership. Lack of funds shortened the Beach Club hours from 1:00 p.m. to 8:00 p.m., and the Town of Tuxedo's Parks and Recreation no longer used the beach. With the coming of August, few cars were visible in the parking lot. Except for occasional birthday parties, picnics, and family cookouts, the Beach Club was a shadow of its former self. With the lake filled, although at least two feet below its proper level, Beach Club members returned. There would no longer be a diving board where children for decades experienced, for the first time, the ten-foot leap into the unknown that was a Beach Club rite of passage.

The writing was on the wall. Literally! You could see the writing on the dock protruding out into the lake. There the painted line remained clearly visible, indicating the water level height from years past. Despite assurances from the Village that Wee Wah Lake would be properly refilled upon completion of the new dam, due to insurance costs and concerns about the water depth where the dock ended, the diving board would not return any time soon, if ever. The years of watching youngsters cannonballing, and teenagers and grownups competing on the ten-meter springboard with flips, backflips, "the one and a half" and "two-by-a-few," pikes and tucks, along with jackknifes and handstands, and so many more, were long gone.

In the early 2020s, some eighty-five years of tradition were coming to an end due to the reluctance of the new Village of Tuxedo Park administration and pressure from some Village residents to end the Beach Club. In 2021, and for several years prior, Bonny had to search for young people, mostly college students, to cover the beachfront and the other responsibilities associated with the position that had previously been filled by children of members. Nothing showed the tradition more clearly than looking back at the lifeguards who worked at the Beach Club in summers past. Reviewing the records going back to 1940, the lifeguard names reflected the sons, daughters, grandchildren, and great-grandchildren of the founders. There were too many to list, but I will mention a few whose last names you have seen often in this book. There was my Uncle John Barth in 1940; my Aunt Helen Barth in 1944; My Uncle Jim Barth, who returned from World War II and became a teacher (1946-1950, 1960, and 1963); my father, James McGregor; and my Aunt Marie in 1949 and 1950.

In the 1950s, the next generation assumed most of the lifeguard responsibilities. There was Mabel Tansey's daughter Barbara and son Joe, along with Margaret Henderson, Nancy Albanese, and Jerry Magurno, to name a few. In the 1960s, it was the grandchildren's turn. Ian Henderson; Bonny and her brother John Damato; Danny and Ricky Winfield; and Honey and Jay Mottola. In 1968, my cousin and Marie's oldest daughter, Leith McCarroll, was hired and served through 1971, when her sister Lisa took over for three more years. Of course, Bonny is listed in the 1970s as well. The well-known names continued through the 1990s as the third generation assumed the lifeguard chair. By the start of the new millennium, Honey Mottola's twin sons, Chris and Dave Hall, patrolled the beachfront and taught lifesaving courses to my three sons, James, Andrew, and Michael, who later became lifeguards themselves and then continued the Wee Wah tradition of teaching others. Of course, in these later years when the beach opened, who would you find back in the lifeguard chairs other than Bonny's grown adult sons, Matthew and Michael Takeuchi.

Chapter 33: A New "Wee Wah Park and Beach Club"

Wee Wah Park and Beach Club, 2023

There were times in the history of the Wee Wah Beach Club when discussions took place by Village trustees about the future of the organization. David McFadden, once again elected Mayor in 2019, was never a fan of the Wee Wah Beach Club. He had made his feelings known during a prior term in 2005. The Beach Club had operated under an unwritten agreement with the TPA since its beginning in 1936. Later the agreement evolved into an annual lease, or sometimes a multiple-year lease, that continued with the Incorporated Village since the Village was formed in 1952. Many times, attempts to shut the Beach Club down went no further than discussion at meetings.

In 2020, the Beach Club was not allowed to open due to the COVID-19 pandemic that reached the United States several months earlier. In early 2021, an attempt was made to end the WWBC, but ultimately a new lease was negotiated with the Village with membership limited to Wee Wah Beach Club members from outside the Village of Tuxedo Park who had been members in 2019. As a result of the lost summer of 2020 due to COVID-19, coupled with the lengthy delay in building a new dam at the north end that resulted in an empty lake for a few years, membership had further plummeted. Who joins a beach club if you can't use the beach? In addition, although Village trustees approved a new lease, they also did vote to prohibit the Wee Wah Beach Club from soliciting new members. That prohibition prevented the Beach Club from publicizing that it was back in business and rebuilding its membership base. Many of the existing members, some of whom had been members for decades, continued paying their membership dues during the closure in what would prove to be a doomed effort to keep the Wee Wah Beach Club viable.

At the start of 2021, it was abundantly clear that this time the WWBC was indeed coming to an end. Mayor McFadden, who had been reelected for a second term, expressed his desire at trustee meetings to not renew the Beach Club's lease. Rather than allow the Wee Wah Beach Club to operate autonomously with administration and oversight as to membership (subject to Village review), the mayor expressed his position that the officers of the Wee Wah Beach Club operate the beach only with respect to supervision and hiring of lifeguards. That meant that the Beach Club would essentially serve as an unpaid management company for the Village. All funds would be controlled by the Village, notwithstanding that no officers of the Beach Club had ever taken any compensation for the successful eighty-five years the Beach Club was in operation.

Mayor McFadden also proclaimed a name change. The portion of Pigeon Point that operated as the Wee Wah Beach Club from May to September would now be known as "Wee Wah Park" and would be open to entry by all Village residents from September to May and during off hours when the newly minted Wee Wah Park lakefront was closed to swimming. One should note that the property had always been open to Village of Tuxedo Park residents at all times with the exception of the summer season, during the hours the property was leased to the Wee Wah Beach Club. Of course, a simple solution was for those Village residents who had not joined the Beach Club to easily do so by purchasing a membership. Membership fees were minimal. The policy of the Village for years had always been that no swimming was allowed in the Wee Wah Lake beach area unless a lifeguard was present. During off hours and throughout the off-season, unless you owned property on the Wee Wah Lake, the Wee Wah Beach Club gate had remained closed to avoid attracting swimmers to the water. Village residents were required to park outside the gate and could walk in any time other than the hours when the Beach Club was open during the summer season under its lease with the Village.

The now former Wee Wah Beach Club officers and Executive Committee who had worked voluntarily for years were not interested in what was basically a managerial function overseen by the Village. They realized that they could easily be held liable should there be an accident. They had no interest in being under the direct control of Village trustees who would now be making decisions concerning the operation of the beach. Another old adage was heard often at the Village meetings when the Wee Wah Beach Club was discussed: "If it ain't broke, why fix it?"

In November 2021, a "Village residents" committee formed by the mayor, without any former Wee Wah Beach Club members as appointees, reported back that the Village should take over operating the Beach Club and hire a management company to operate it. Voila!

With a vote by the trustees, the eighty-five-year-old Wee Wah Beach Club was finished.

There is no question that improvements were sorely needed and that such a beautiful location should be enjoyed by the residents of the Village. It appears that little thought was given to how much it would cost to operate the beach other than the plan to solicit contributions from Village residents. Membership costs for 2022 would remain at the levels they had been under the leadership of the Wee Wah Beach Club for the 2021 season. Would Village taxpayers be responsible to cover shortfalls? Bids were sent to three beach management companies and a bid was selected and approved. Details would be worked out later in the spring. There was discussion as to a name change, but that matter was tabled. The newly called "Wee Wah Park" would now be open to all Village residents all year, from morning to nightfall, but somehow swimming at the beach would still require a membership. How would they distinguish between residents of the Park who wanted to swim, and non-member residents who simply wanted to enjoy a picnic or otherwise enjoy the newly dubbed "Wee Wah Park"? Those details were left to be worked out when the 2022 season opened.

In defense of the mayor's decision to end the storied history associated with the founding of the Wee Wah Beach Club and its relationship to the Hamlet outside the gates, times indeed do change. For better or worse, a new approach to this beautiful picturesque recreational facility area was underway. What Mayor Buell had said at a June 12, 1968 Village meeting in response to those who wanted to end the Wee Wah Beach Club was true at the time. "I think I can speak for the trustees also, the people from the Hamlet will not be turned away from an area that they have used for so long they call it their own." Now, nearly fifty-five years after Mayor Buell spoke those words, times had changed, and what had always been "a privilege and not a right" had come to an end.

As to the old Wee Wah Beach Club, new residents of Tuxedo Park, and many old ones as well, did not understand why, as taxpayers to the Village, they did not enjoy access to a beach recreation area during a summer season without joining another "club," especially a club into which they seemed to have no input. Many of these residents were, of course, also members of the Tuxedo Club. Now those present generations of families who built and serviced Tuxedo Park needed a new identity. There were very few residents left outside the gates who still lived within the boundaries of the Hamlet who could trace their families back to the times when all who lived there worked or served those living in the Park. Meanwhile, improvements to the beach area were sorely needed.

The mayor and trustees made two exceptions with respect to Wee Wah Park being a strictly private entity of the Village of Tuxedo Park (and therefore available to Village residents only). One, Hamlet members from outside the gates who were members of the Wee Wah Beach Club in 2019 could continue to apply for membership and be "grandfathered" in. Two, any family in the Hamlet boundary that could "historically prove" their ancestors worked for the Tuxedo Park Association that serviced the Park before its incorporation in 1952 could also apply for membership.

For the first time since 1936, the Wee Wah Beach Club did not open its gates to its members with the arrival of the 2022 season. It was now the Wee Wah Park and Beach Club. Changes to long-standing traditions can be difficult. Looking back, on March 25, 1941, an article in the *Daily News* entitled *"Army of Blue Bloods Seek Tuxedo Cards"* by Nancy Randolf reported, "The 200 new associate members to be admitted to the super-exclusive Tuxedo Club on April 1 can be said to have literally muscled in." Apparently, the Tuxedo Club was looking for new members in order to stay afloat. These new "associate members" would not have the right to vote but would enjoy all other privileges. "Mothers with daughters approaching debutante age have been especially interested in being admitted to club membership. The $50 yearly dues will give mamma the right to give big parties (at extra charge) at the Tuxedo Club. It will also give her the right to present her daughter at the famous Tuxedo Park Autumn Ball as one of the official debutantes."[99]

By 1950, high society was in decline. One of the most widely reported activities of the Tuxedo Club was the Autumn Ball, starting in 1886 where the Tuxedo jacket first made its appearance. This event ushered in the start of the New York social season with the "coming out" of the daughters of the very rich that was annually recorded with special sections in the social pages of the New York editions of the *Herald Tribune* and the *New York Times*. That time honored tradition ended in 1971, the first year without the Autumn Ball. Here were two examples of things actually changing.

What has become of Pigeon Point today? The new Wee Wah Park and Beach Club is operated by the Village of Tuxedo Park, which contracts with a beach management company to provide lifeguard services. Improvements have been made. The gravel parking area separated from the picnic area by large boulders is now gone and is now covered with grass. New trees have been planted. The gate is gone. Although you can still drive in, it is only to drop off your chairs, coolers and the like, and then you must drive out to park as parking inside is no longer allowed but for a few handicapped spaces. Most improvements have resulted in a much more functional and beautiful park area with a pathway along the tip of the point to the old North Beach area. Kayaks and canoes are now available for members. Dogs are allowed. The improvements to the property such as the sand in the play area, the picnic tables, the newly seeded grass area once used for parking, were made by the Department of Public Works and they now continue to maintain the area. It is reported that all expenses for the new Wee Wah Park were paid for by private donations and not Village taxpayer dollars. The flagpole has been moved down to the beach front. Gone are the memorial plaques such as the one on the flagpole base in memory of my uncle, Buddy McCarroll. Also gone is a plaque on one of the large rocks dedicated to the spot where the Zupko family settled on so many July 4ths through 2021. They never claimed a table and preferred to set out blankets and chairs by the rock. Today it is a different beach.

But for now, sitting in a chair, on Buddy's bench, or reclined in a comfy chaise lounge, you can feel the peacefulness and marvel at the beautiful setting of the lake and the hillsides dotted with mansions dating back to the Gilded Age. The Frelinghuysen mansion perched at the top still exists and is just one of the great homes that reflect the glory of Gilded Age architecture.

Close your eyes and open them. It is 1886, and you can still see a swampy area filling with water flowing from the stream and dam at the south end. As the basin rises, you can hear men shouting as trees are felled and teams of horses pull plows along the shoreline to create roads. You can hear the pickaxes and shovels and the languages of Italian and Slavic workers clearing brush, grunting, and cursing as they push huge boulders, abandoned by the ice age millions of years ago, to the side of the newly formed road.

Close and open your eyes again. It is 1900. Grand mansions decorate the hillsides, accessorized with horse-drawn coaches and bicycles. Men and women walk along the roads, resplendent in the changing leaves of fall or in the spring colors with rhododendron in full bloom.

Blink again. Now it is 1907, and while you can't see him, you know Mark Twain is visiting and is likely sipping his second or third drink, sitting on the porch of the Voss house, legs crossed and dapper in his white suit and smoking a cigar, on the hill below the Frelinghuysen estate.

Close your eyes and open them again. It is 1915 and horse-drawn carriages share the road with the era's finest automobiles, mostly convertibles, taking a leisurely fall drive in the Park, everything from Mercedes and Rolls Royce to ultra-luxurious American offerings from Pierce Arrow, Auburn, and Duesenberg.

Fast forward again, and it is 1946. World War II ended the previous year, and the scene is alive with the sights and sounds of fire engine sirens and gleeful people walking across the dam on the south end of Pond 3 toward the beach picnic after the July Fourth parade in front of the Tuxedo Club.

Once the sun has passed behind the mountains to the west, it is time to return home to the hillsides, or back down to the Hamlet below, if you are not lucky enough to stay and use the fireplaces under the birch trees for a picnic supper. And then, at last, it's one more late swim before the beach closes and darkness sets in.

Epilogue

In 1849, French writer Jean-Baptiste Alphonse Karr wrote, *"Plus ça change, plus c'est la même chose."* The translation is a well-known phrase: "The more things change, the more they stay the same." Karr's words rang true at the Wee Wah Beach Club, which had remained largely unchanged for eighty-five years. At the end, the active, tireless president for twenty-four years was Bonny Takeuchi, a Hamlet resident and daughter of an original Tuxedo family. The Beach Club had always been a volunteer organization run on a shoestring budget so as to be affordable to most Hamlet residents. Admittedly, this left the grounds and facilities looking worn and lacking in modern amenities, but the beach and water were as beautiful as the day it was completed following Pierre Lorillard's plan for a strictly private recreational community for the upper class of the Gilded Age. Throughout it all Bonny, through her dedicated service, made every attempt to preserve the Beach Club. She was unanimously elected annually and continued as president through the end of 2021. Today, in late 2023, the Wee Wah Beach Club remains an incorporated entity with Bonnie as its president.

Today, economists and social scientists still address segments of our society by "upper, middle, and lower class" although many believe the "middle class" is fast disappearing. In recent years, one could see attitudes shifting regarding this particular beach club, largely populated and enjoyed by members of the Hamlet. They were residents of the Town of Tuxedo, but did not live within the imposing gates of Tuxedo Park. Here in the twenty-first century, the Hamlet is now mostly populated by families with neither a hereditary family attachment to the history of Tuxedo Park, nor are they employed by Tuxedo Park residents. In fact, when a house in the Hamlet has gone on the market in recent years, real estate agents, many who live inside the gates, would take prospective buyers of houses in the Hamlet through the gates to see the Wee Wah Beach Club and promote the availability of membership as a value-added selling point.

I have given this book a subtitle, *An American Story of Social Change.* The history of Tuxedo Park is a story of how the great division of wealth at the end of the nineteenth century and into the beginning of the twentieth century maintained and furthered the separation of a society comprised of "haves and have-nots." It is not much of a stretch to see this happening again in this country, here in the 2020s, as so many individuals have amassed fortunes that rival the wealth of many of the small countries of the world. Referring to Chapter 3 and the disparity of wealth in 1897, it has returned today. Despite income taxes, "Contemporary global inequities are close to the peak levels observed in the early 20th century, at the end of the prewar era (variously described as the Belle Epoque or the Gilded Age) that saw sharp increases in global inequality."[100]

I grew up in a generation that was taught that the United States of America was the "Great Melting Pot," and we were often reminded how the Statute of Liberty, at the base of New York Harbor, held her torch high to all who entered, echoing the words, "Give me your tired, your poor / Your huddled masses yearning to breathe free," as penned by American author and poet Emma Lazarus in 1883. As a youngster taking the school bus back from the Hamlet through the imposing gates, I entered a vastly different world. It was an idyllic place, more like a step back in time than simply a residential community.

Walking from the Park to the Hamlet as a child, since I would be considered a "Parkie," although my family was certainly not wealthy, it seemed like almost every driver would stop and ask, "Would you like a lift to the drugstore soda fountain?" But as we grew older, we learned there were dark sides to the country's history, many of which the country struggles with even today. Colors in our country are often painted with a broad brush and can have disturbing consequences. Over 140 years ago it was blue and gray as, at times, brothers fought brothers in the Civil War. Over 60 years ago it was black and white as black and white men fought side by side in Viet Nam while our country attempted to deal with race in our country. In recent years it has been red and blue as our country appears to be fracturing once again. Ours is a country referred to as "The Great Experiment." The Gilded Age exemplified the separation of wealth and equality. As we compare the enormous wealth of so few to the country's total population today—and the shrinking of a middle class that helped to keep the ship of state from moving too far right or left— we must wonder if our country will survive. Despite all the immense changes over the years, Karr's quote, "The more things change, the more they stay the same," still rings true.

About the Author

Stuart J. McGregor, born 1944 in Tuxedo Park, has enjoyed a lifelong adoration and love for Tuxedo and Tuxedo Park. His maternal and paternal grandparents lived in Tuxedo Park, where both grandfathers were superintendents and head gardeners of estates from the early 1900s and well into the 1950s. He spent his early years living on the Kincraig estate. He graduated from Boston College and began a career on Wall Street. After military service in the late 1960s, he returned to Wall Street and later graduated from Fordham Law School. Stuart and his wife, Jean Connelly, moved to Miami, Florida in 1976, where they raised a family and he successfully practiced trial law for twenty-two years. In 1998, he left the practice of law and worked in investor relations before developing a sports-related business. Now retired, Stuart is still trying to figure out what he wants to do when he grows up. Stuart and Jean reside in Coral Gables, Florida but keep a summer home in Tuxedo Park. They return to Tuxedo annually to reflect on its history and spend time with relatives and friends who have never left this wonderful place.

Additional Reading

The History of Orange County New York, Edited by Russel Headley, Van Dusen & Elms, Middletown, N.Y., 1908

Tuxedo Park, A Journal of Recollections, Albert Foster Winslow, The Tuxedo Historical Society, Tuxedo Park, N.Y., 1992

Tuxedo Park, A Wall Street Tycoon and the Secret Palace of Science That Changed the Course of World War II, Jennet Conant, Simon & Shuster, New York, N.Y., 2002

Who Killed Society, Cleveland Amory, Harper & Brothers, New York, N.Y., 1960

The World with a Fence Around It, Tuxedo Park—The Early Days, George M. Rushmore, Pageant Press, Inc., New York, N.Y., 1957

Stop at The Red Apple Rest, The Restaurant on Route 17, Elaine Freed Lidenblatt, State University of New York Press, Albany, N.Y., 2014

Tuxedo Park Lives, Legacies, Legends, Chiu Yin Hemple, Tuxedo Park Fire Department, Tuxedo, N.Y., 2010

Tuxedo Park Historic Houses, Christian R. Sonne , Tuxedo Historical Society, Tuxedo Park, N.Y. 2007

Ecole de Beaux Palm Beach, New York Social Diary, October 1, 2009

Louis Auchinclaus, A Writers Life, Carol Gelderman, Crown Publishers, 1993

NYTimes, Teacup Tattles, April 19, 1903

740 Park Avenue, The Story of the World's Richest Apartment Building, Michael Gross, Broadway Books, New York, NY 2005

An Original Social Experiment- Tuxedo, B L R Dane, The Cosmopolitan, a Monthly Illustrated Magazine, October 1899, Pg 547.

"Our System Overview." New York State Thruway Authority. https://www.thruway.ny.gove/oursystem/overview.html

Tuxedo Park Historic Photographs, Tuxedo Park Library. "July 4th Parade, 1952." *New York Heritage Digital Collections.* https://cdm16694/contentdm.oclc.org/digital/collection/tpl/id/3974.

"Paid Notice: Deaths Blagden, Crawford," The New York Times, February 14, 1997. https://nytimes.com/1997/02/14/classified/paid-notice-deaths-blagden-crawford.html

Index

Frelinghuysen, Theodore

Notes

Chapter 1: The Beach

[1] Margaret Terry Chanler, *Roman Spring: Memoirs* (Boston: Little, Brown, and Co., 1935), 260.

Chapter 2: A Perfect Site for a Beach

[2] American Antiquarian Society, Obituaries, 1943, p. 127, https://www.americanantiquarian.org/proceedings/44807085.pdf

Chapter 3: Tuxedo Park

[3] Lily Rothman, "How American Inequality in the Gilded Age Compares to Today," *Time,* February 5, 2018, https://time.com/5122375/american-inequality-gilded-age/.

[4] Frank Kintrea, "Tuxedo Park: An Exclusive Preserve of New York's Social Elite—its rise, its Flourishing Years, and its Slide into Genteel Decline," *American Heritage,* September 1978.

[5] B.L.R. Dane, "Tuxedo: An Original Social Experiment," *The Cosmopolitan, A Monthly Illustrated Magazine,* October 1889.

[6] Elisabeth Bumiller, "A Little New Money Comes to a Moneyed Enclave," the *New York Times*, August 4, 1997.

[7] Emily Post, "Tuxedo Park: An American Rural Community," *Century Illustrated Monthly Magazine,* October 1911.

[8] Post.

[9] Add: Emily Post, Daughter of the Gilded Age, Mistress of American Manners, Laura Claridge, Random Books, New York, NY 2008

[10] Albert Foster Winslow, *Tuxedo Park: A Journal of Recollections* (Tuxedo Park, NY: The Tuxedo Historical Society, 1992), 47.

[11] Winslow, 77.

[12] "Pierre Lorillard Dead; Famous in Society, in Commerce, and in the World of Sport. First American to Win the English Derby -- Other Triumphs on the Turf in Both Hemispheres," The *New York Times*, July 8, 1901.

Chapter 4: The Hamlet and East Village

[13] "A Bloody Italian Holiday," The *New York Times*, March 8, 1892.

[14] Harris Starr, Robert Schuyler, et al, *Dictionary of American Biography*; 11-Volume Set (1935–61), Including Supplements 1 and 2; (New York: Scribner's, 1935-61).

[15] Cleveland Amory, *Who Killed Society?* (New York: Harper & Brothers, 1960), 74.

Chapter 5: Pigeon Point

[16] "Princeton Couldn't Score," *The Boston Globe*, October 11, 1890.

[17] "Work Won The Tuxedo Shoot: He Was in Great Form and Only Missed One Bird Yesterday," the *New York Times*, April 15, 1894 .

[18] Albert Foster Winslow, *Tuxedo Park: A Journal of Recollections* (Tuxedo Park, NY: The Tuxedo Historical Society, 1992), 211.

Chapter 6: The Early Tuxedo Club Beach

[19] Emily Post, "Tuxedo Park: An American Rural Community, the *Century Magazine*, October 1911.

[20] Guy Trebay, "Summer Places: At Bailey's Beach, the Ruling Class Keeps its Guard Up," the *New York Times*, July 20, 2003.

[21] "Swim Events," The *New York Times*, July 4, 1907.

[22] Margaret Terry Chanler, *Roman Spring: Memoirs* (Boston: Little, Brown, and Co., 1935), 262.

[23] "Without Any Foundation," The *New York Times*, November 20, 1887.

Chapter 8: The Social Set

[24] "Death of Robert Goelet," The *New York Times*, April 28, 1899.

[25] "Keech Ends Life By Leap In Subway; 71-Year-Old Broker, Indicted Appeals in Burning of Tuxedo Park Mansion, Dies Under Train," the *New York Times*, March 10, 1937.

[26] Allison Davis, *Class Influences About Learning* (Cambridge: Harvard University Press, 1948), Volume 10.

Chapter 9: Mrs. Theodore Frelinghuysen

[27] "Another Count Captured: A Detroit Beauty to Wed a Wealthy German Nobleman," *Pittsburgh Post*, November 1889.

[28] "Fair Woman's World, The Coming Wedding of Miss Thompson and Mr. Cannon," *Detroit Free Press*, February 8, 1891.

[29] "A Brilliant Affair" *Detroit Free Press*, July 10, 1891.

[30] "Table Gossip," *The Boston Globe*, May 31, 1891.

[31] "McAllister is Still at the Head of the 'Four Hundred,'" The Philadelphia Inquirer, December 14, 1891.

[32] "The Lost Mintern Mansion -- Number 60, 5th Avenue," Daytonian in Manhattan, August 11, 2014. http://daytoninmanhattan.blogspot.com/2014/08/the-lost-minturn-mansion-no-60-5th.html/.

[33] "Private Salon Concert—Boston Symphony Concert at the Old Mintern Mansion," The *New York Times*, January 14, 1893.

[34] "H. Le Grand Cannon Dead," *The Evening World* (New York, NY), May 6, 1895.

[35] "A Brilliant Social Event," Burlington Free Press, (Burlington, Vermont), August 27, 1885.
[36] "Weddings of Early June; Mrs. H. Le Grand Cannon and Theodore Frelinghuysen are married at Grace Chantry. Bishop Potter Officiates ...," The *New York Times*, June 3, 1898.

[37] *The Architectural Review,* Vol. 7, January -June 1907.

[38] "A Brilliant Affair" *Detroit Free Press*, July 10, 1891.
[39] "Teacup Tales," The *New York Times*, April 19, 1903

Chapter 10: The Rumor Leads to North Beach

[40] Albert Foster Winslow, *Tuxedo Park: A Journal of Recollections* (Tuxedo Park, NY: The Tuxedo Historical Society, 1992), 55.

[41] "Drowning Mars A Picnic," The *New York Times,* June 21, 1903.

[42] "Major Garrard Comly, Banker, Drowns While Swimming In Lake At Tuxedo Park," The *New York Times,* June 28, 1927.

Chapter 11: George Grant Mason

[43] "Dead Woman in Brook," *The Wilkes-Barre Record*, April 9, 1915.

[44] Frelinghuysen to Joseph E. Stevens, January 18, 1917.

[45] "James H. Smith Dead. Succumbed to Heaart Disease in Japan While on Honeymoon," New York Tribune, March 28, 1907.

[46] "[George Grant Mason] Gets Valuable Parcel," New York Tribune, July 23, 1908.

[47] "James Henry Smith Gives Dinner Dance," The *New York Times,* February 5, 1901.

[48] "James H. Smith to WED Mrs. R. Stewart of N.Y.," The Brooklyn Daily Eagle, September 10, 1906.

[49] "Smith's Body Reaches Honolulu," The *Waukegan Daily Gazette,* April 24, 1907.

[50] "Left but $25,000,000," *Washington Post*, May 9, 1907.

[51] "Fifth Ave Sales," *New York Tribune*, January 5, 1910.

[52] "Yeaman's Hall," *Aiken Standard* (Aiken, SC), January 23, 1931.

[53] "Mason Rites Held Today in the East," *Green Bay Press-Gazette*, (Green Bay, WI), August 6, 1929.

[54] "High Masons Lay Stone of Tuxedo School,"*Middletown Times Record* (New York), January 7, 1932.

Chapter 12: Duncan McGregor

[55] Colt, Sarah. 2018. "The Gilded Age." In *The American Experience,* Season 30, Episode 3.

[56] "Tuxedo Park Scene of Floral Contest," The *New York Times*, September 15, 1934.

[57] "Flower Display Opens at Tuxedo G. S. Amory with 13 Awards, Leads in Honors on First Day of Show," The *New York Times,* September 16, 1939.

[58] "27,419 in Day See Fall Flower Show," The *New York Times*, November 13, 1939.

Chapter 13: The Tuxedo Community Club is Born

[59] "Mrs. Frederic Spedden," *The New York Times,* The *New York Times*, February 11, 1950.

Chapter 16: The 1940s

[60] Amory, Cleveland, *The Last Resort*, 1st Ed (New York: Harper & Brothers, 1948), p. 9

[61] "Tuxedo Park Association Decides to Sell 100 Tenant Homes and Sites in the Village," The *New York Times*, May 25, 1947.

Chapter 17: The Early 1950s

[62] "Plans New Homes For Tuxedo Park," The *New York Times*, May 14, 1950.

[63] "Elite Tuxedo Park to Become Village," The *New York Times*, August 8, 1952.

Chapter 18: The Lake is Empty

[64] "The Autumn Golf Season," The *Sun*, (New York, NY, August 31, 1896.

[65] Johnathan Croyle, "Throwback Thursday: Gov. Dewey breaks ground for Thruway," accessed November, 2022, https://www.syracuse.com/vintage/2016/07/throwback_thursday_gov_dewey_b.html

[66] "New York Toll Road Bisects Park Golf Course," *Battle Creek Enquirer*, (Battle Creek, MI), November 12, 1952.

[67] "Tuxedo Park 'Outsiders' Fight for Swimmin Hole," *New York World Telegram & Sun*, February 24, 1954.

[68] Elaine Freed Lindenblatt, *Stop at The Red Apple: The Restaurant on Route 17* (Albany, NY.: State University of New York Press, 2014).
[69] "War Road of 1778 Found Under Lake," The *New York Times*, March 10,1954.

Chapter 19: 1955

[70] *The Tuxedo Park Association, Inc. Annual Report, 1945*, p 6, Sec. E.

Chapter 21: The 1960s

[71] "Domestic Staffs Lured By Industry's Benefits," The *New York Times*, March 4, 1957.

[72] "More than 120 Debutantes Attend the 74th Tuxedo Autumn Ball, 12 Young Women are Presented at Annual Event," The *New York Times,* October 21, 1962.

[73] "Three Debutantes Bow at Tuxedo Ball," The *New York Times*, October 19, 1970.

[74] "'Rich' Tuxedo Park Collects U.S. Aid," *The Oneonta Star*, (Oneonta, New York), June 10, 1961.

[75] Berger, Joseph, "For $55 Million, New York Acquires Sterling Forest," The *New York Times,* February 11, 1998.

Chapter 22: 1962, Double-Barrel Shotgun

[76] Tip O'Neill with Gary Hymel, *All Politics Is Local, and other Rules of the Game* (New York: Times Books, 1994).

[77] Joel Selvin, *Summer of Love: The Inside Story of LSD, Rock & Roll, Free Love, and High Times in the Wild West,* (New York: Dutton Books, 1994).

[78] Village of Tuxedo Park, "Board of Trustees, Meeting Minutes," May 1969.

Chapter 24: The Early 1970s

[79] "Col. Blagden Dies; World War Hero; Veteran of the 307th Helped to Rescue Lost Battalion in Argonne Forest in 1918; Football Star of 1901; Harvard Tackle Returned to His Alma Mater in After Years to Coach Line Players." *The New York Times,* January 13, 1937.

Chapter 27: The Salierno Years, 1980 – 1984, & 1986
[80] Rick Hampson, "Tuxedo Park: Everyday Look Is In At Ex-Exclusive Community," *Los Angeles Times*, Nov. 9, 1986.

[81] John Dalmas, "Trouble Brewing in Peery's Paradise," *Yonkers Herald*

Statesman (Yonkers, NY), Oct. 10, 1982.

[82] Anthony Depalma, "If You're Thinking of Living in: Tuxedo," *The New York Times*, June 12, 1983.

[83] Depalma.

Chapter 28: Tuxedo Park Celebrates Its First 100 Years
[84] Kolbert, Elizabeth, "The Talk Of Tuxedo Park; A Retreat Marks 100 Discreetly." The *New York Times*, May 17, 1986.

Chapter 29: Bonny Takeuchi Continues the Wee Wah Beach Club Tradition
[85] Dunleavy, M.P., "If You Are Thinking Of Living In Tuxedo Park," The *New York Times*, August 11, 1991.
[86] Elisabeth Bumiller, "Change (Gulp) in Tuxedo Park: A Little New Money Comes to a Moneyed Enclave," *The New York Times*, August 4.1997.

[87] "Village's Mayor Plans to Improve Ties With Town," *Times Herald Record* (Middletown, NY), July 11, 1999.

Chapter 30: The New Millennium
[88] Julia Lawlor, "If You're Thinking of Living in Tuxedo Park, N.Y., 330 Homes, but Not One House Number," The *New York Times*, June 18, 2000.

[89] "Wee Wah Beach Club Prepares for Summer," *Tuxedo Inside Out*, (Newsletter), p 6.

[90] Jennet Conant, *A Wall Street Tycoon and the Secret Palace of Science That Changed the Course of World War II*, Simon & Shuster (New York, NY), 2002.

[91] Jennet Conant, "Tuxedo Park Opens the Gates, Just a Bit," The *New York Times,* August 16, 2002.

[92] C.J. Hughes, "Big Houses, and an Even Bigger Wilderness," The *New York Times*, December 11, 2005.

[93] Mike Dawson, "Rift over Wee Wah," *Times Herald-Record* (Middletown, NY), April 15, 2005.

[94] Matt King, "Battle for the Beach Club," *Times Herald-Record* (Middletown, NY), January 17, 2008.
[95] Matt King, "Battle for the Beach Club," *Times Herald-Record* (Middletown, NY), January 17, 2008.

Chapter 31: Some Notable Wee Wah Beach Club Members
[96] "Ostler Joe," *Daily Alta California*, Vol. 40, No. 13347, March 13, 1886.

[97] "The Life & Times of Joseph Haworth," *Josephhaworth.com*, accessed Aug. 6, 2022, http://www.josephhaworth.com/mrs_james_brown_potter.htm

[98] Haworth.

Chapter 33: A New "Wee Wah Park and Beach Club"
[99] "Army of Blue Bloods Seek Tuxedo Cards," *New York Daily News,* March 25, 1941.

[100] Qureshi, Zia; Rising Inequality: A major issue of our time. Future Development, Brookings, May 16, 2023

www.ingramcontent.com/pod-product-compliance
Lightning Source LLC
Chambersburg PA
CBHW042102150726

48005CB00033B/1803

COMBO OF IMO AND IGCSE GRADE 5

SURYA PRATAP SINGH

Copyright © Surya Pratap Singh
All Rights Reserved.

This book has been self-published with all reasonable efforts taken to make the material error-free by the author. No part of this book shall be used, reproduced in any manner whatsoever without written permission from the author, except in the case of brief quotations embodied in critical articles and reviews.

The Author of this book is solely responsible and liable for its content including but not limited to the views, representations, descriptions, statements, information, opinions and references ["Content"]. The Content of this book shall not constitute or be construed or deemed to reflect the opinion or expression of the Publisher or Editor. Neither the Publisher nor Editor endorse or approve the Content of this book or guarantee the reliability, accuracy or completeness of the Content published herein and do not make any representations or warranties of any kind, express or implied, including but not limited to the implied warranties of merchantability, fitness for a particular purpose. The Publisher and Editor shall not be liable whatsoever for any errors, omissions, whether such errors or omissions result from negligence, accident, or any other cause or claims for loss or damages of any kind, including without limitation, indirect or consequential loss or damage arising out of use, inability to use, or about the reliability, accuracy or sufficiency of the information contained in this book.

Made with ♥ on the Notion Press Platform
www.notionpress.com

Contents

COUNTING ON BACK IN FRACTIONS AND DECIMALS

Count on or back in the steps given

Count on in steps of 0.2

3.5 -.-,-,4.3,--,---,-- 4.9,----,----

Count back in steps of 0.01

6.22,----,-----,------ , 6.18,-----,----,6.15,----,------

Count back in steps of 1/2

8 1/2 ,------,-----,---- 6 1/2 ,----,-----,5,-----,------

Count on or back in the steps given

a. Count on in steps of 0.4

7.7 ,-----,------,-----

b. Count back in steps of 0.03

5.55 ,------,---------,--------

c. Count on in steps of 0.05

3.114 ,-------,-------,------ 2.214,------,-----

Count forwards in steps of 0.05 from 2.11

2.16 2.19 2.22 2.27 2.3 2.34 2.39

2.43 , 2.48, 2.53

Count forwards in 0.6s from 4.6

2nd term -------- 4th term 5th term

FINDING TERMS OF A SQUARE NUMBER SEQUENCE

1x1 = 1

2x2 = 4

A square number is a result when a number has been multiplied by itself

Position Calculation Value

1

2

3

4

5

6

7

8

9

10

Answer the following questions

Find the area of a rectangle whose length = 15 cm breadth = 16 cm

The children in a assembly arrange themselves in 8 rows of 8 How many children are there

The flowers are arranged in 7 rows of 7 How many flowers are there

The beds are arranged in 13 rows of 13 How many beds are there

NUMBER SENSE

1. Write Eighty million Sixty thousand sixty in numeral form

2.Largest 5 digit number that can be formed by using digits 5,3,0,8 each atleast once

3.Shikha makes a profit of rupees thirty five crofit ore four lakh thirty five thousand fifty nine Write the profit in the Indian System

4. What will we get if we add 1 to the smallest 7 digit number

5.Round off the number 46579 to nearest hundreds

6 How many four digit numbers can be formed by using 8,5,0,8 only once in a number

7. The greatest four digit number that can be formed using digits of Gopal car number 2887 will have at its tens place

8. Identify the number using given clues

I am an odd number

My tens digit is greatest one digit number

My hundreds digit is even number

My thousands digit is the latest odd number

9. The difference between the place value of 9 and 5 in 68905

10. 68234 is 68230 when rounded off to the nearest ----------

ADDING POSITIVE AND NEGATIVE NUMBERS

Add

- 4 + 2 -7 +5

-6 + 1 -7 + 17

-8 + 5 -1 + 8

-7 + 4

-10 + 9

-2 + 8

Use the number line to find the sum

-11 + 8

-14 + 13

- 12 + 5

-17 + 12

-18 + 13

-19 + 15

-22 + 19

- 21 + 12

-25 + 17

Calculate the new bank balance Write the calculation

Starting balance Money in New Balance Calculation

-16 32

-18 62

-11 42

-14 23

-4 53

-2 37

Write two numbers a negative augend and a positive addenda that will give each total

------ + --------- =-5

------ +--------- = -7

-------+ --------- =-1

------- + --------- = -6

ADDING POSITIVE AND NEGATIVE NUMBERS (2)

a. What is 7 degrees more than -14 degree C

b. What is 9 degrees more than - 40 degree C

c. What is 12 degrees more than - 8 degree C

d. What is 15 degrees more than - 6 degree C

e . What is 25 degrees more than -14 degree C

f. What is 8 degrees more than - 17 degree C

g. What is 3 degrees more than -13 degreee C

h What is 4 degrees more than - 16 degree C

i What is 5 degrees more than - 12 degrees C

j What is 3 degrees more than - 11 degrees C

k. What is 4 degrees more than -15 degrees C

IDENTIFYING VALUES FOR SYMBOLS IN SUBTRACTION CALCULATIONS

Work out the unknown values

1. 64-a = 32 a=
2. c-19=43 c=
3. b-27 =24 b =
4. 56-d =17 d =
5, 23-g = 18 g =
6 24 -h = 17 h=
7. 45-j = 95 j=
8 24-k = 46 k=
9 14- l = 55 l=
10 17-m =44 m =
11 22-U = 22 U =
12 23-V = 23 V =
13 34 W = 21 W=
14 23-X = 25 X=
15 24- B = 24 B=
16 27-C = 24 C

COMPUTATION OPERATIONS

1. A factory produced 800732 chips in June month Out of these 5478 chips were found of bad quality.How many chips were of good quality

'**2** A factory produced 486812 Natraj pencils and 551653 pens of another kind All the pencils are mixed thouroughly and packed equally in 296 boxes How many pencils are packed in a box

3 Which of the following number is prime

a. 35

b. 66

c. 17

d. 56

4* twice the difference between the 5 th and 15 th multiple of 8 . Find *

5 What must be subtracted from 2 million to get 999600

6 The number of prime factors of 40 are

7 The product of 214 and a number is Y. Taking 39 away from X gives 1339

Find the number

8 Subtract the sum of 65236535 and 1124364 from 51276343

9 The quotient when 22415 is divided by 5

10 Farmer Shyam packed an equal number of apples into each of the 20 packets If each packet contain

65 apples how many apples did he pack

11 A vegetable seller had 79885 vegetables He has to pack them in boxes with each box containing 425 apples Find the number of boxes required to pack vegetables

12 Machine A can produce 6500 biscuits in a day , which is 240 fewer biscuits than what machine B can produce in a day Now 20 biscuits are placed in a pack if both machines A and B are used how many packs of biscuits will be there after 7 days ?

MISCELLANEOUS

1. Calcul;ate 8x4/2

2 Calculate 2/4 + 1/6

3 Count back in from 45 in 8s

4 Complete the sentence using the correct word

In the number 15.862 the 2 represents two ___

5. Write a decimal number on each answer line to make each statement correct

443 hundredths

84 tenths and 2 thousandths

7 ones 2 hundredths and 5 thousandths

7+0.7+0.03

6 Convert into decimals

a.5/20

b.2/5

c.8/10

d.1/4

e.1/2

f.17/50

g.4/5

h.75/1000

i.5/10

j 16/50

7.Add fractions

3/8 + 4/8

2/4 + 1/4

8. On Monday Eve climbs 40 lengths of the tree

On Tuesday she climbs 5o percent more lengths than on Monday

On Wednesday she climbs 50 percent fewer lengths than on Tuesday
Calculate the **Total** number of lengths she climbs on the three days